1932

1932

FDR, Hoover, and the Dawn of a New America

SCOTT MARTELLE

CITADEL PRESS
Kensington Publishing Corp.
www.kensingtonbooks.com

CITADEL PRESS BOOKS are published by

Kensington Publishing Corp.
119 West 40th Street
New York, NY 10018

All Kensington titles, imprints and distributed lines are available at special quantity discounts for bulk purchases for sales promotion, premiums, fund-raising, educational or institutional use.

Special book excerpts or customized printings can also be created to fit specific needs. For details, write or phone the office of the Kensington Special Sales Manager: Kensington Publishing Corp., 119 West 40th Street, New York, NY, 10018. Attn. Special Sales Department. Phone: 1-800-221-2647.

Library of Congress Control Number: 2023942116

CITADEL PRESS and the Citadel logo are Reg. U.S. Pat. & TM Off.
ISBN: 978-0-8065-4186-0
First Citadel Hardcover Edition: December 2023

ISBN: 978-0-8065-4292-8 (ebook)
10 9 8 7 6 5 4 3 2 1
Printed in the United States of America

As always, for the lovely Margaret

CONTENTS

A TIMELINE OF SOME LINCHPIN EVENTS IN 1932

JANUARY

Father Cox leads several thousand people in a march from Pittsburgh, Pennsylvania, to Washington, D.C., demanding jobs and financial assistance. After his return to Pittsburgh, Cox announces the formation of a new Jobless Party under which he will run for president.

New York governor Franklin Delano Roosevelt enters the race for the 1932 Democratic presidential nomination.

President Herbert Hoover creates the Reconstruction Finance Corporation to try to shore up banks facing depositor runs and failures.

MARCH

In Portland, Oregon, Walter Waters begins urging fellow Great War veterans to march on Washington, D.C., to demand early payment of a promised bonus.

Roosevelt begins organizing his Brain Trust of policy advisors.

Four people are killed and about forty-five others are wounded or injured as police and security guards open fire on a "hunger march" at Ford's River Rouge plant near Detroit.

APRIL

Roosevelt delivers his "Forgotten Man" speech in a radio broadcast from Albany, New York.

The Women's Organization for National Prohibition Reform meets in Washington, D.C. to plan its efforts to persuade both major parties to support Prohibition's repeal.

MAY

Waters's Bonus Expeditionary Force, thousands strong, begins arriving in Washington, D.C. and establishes makeshift camps near the Capitol.

Farmers meet at the Iowa State Fairgrounds in Des Moines and plan a month-long "holiday" – a farmers' strike to try to push commodity prices high enough so they could make a profit.

JUNE

Republicans gather at Chicago Stadium in Chicago to renominate Hoover for a second term. The platform contains a plank supporting a new Prohibition amendment giving states the authority to ban or allow alcohol sales.

Democrats convene eleven days later in the same facility to pick their nominee. They come out for full repeal.

JULY

U.S. Army troops, at Hoover's direction, begin evicting veterans from federal buildings along Pennsylvania Avenue; General Douglas MacArthur exceeds the president's directive and rousts the veterans from their massive encampment on the Anacostia flats in Southeast Washington.

AUGUST

Farmers in Iowa begin their holiday by erecting barriers to keep farm products from reaching markets; sporadic violent showdowns break out.

SEPTEMBER

A federal report on the rousting of the veterans blames the showdown on communists and lawbreakers they allege took over the veterans' movement, drawing angry reactions from veterans' groups and their supporters.

In an ominous turn for Hoover and the Republican Party, voters in Maine, traditionally loyal Republicans, elect Democrats to key offices, including governor.

OCTOBER

The campaign heats up with both Roosevelt and Hoover making lengthy train trips around the country to meet voters and deliver speeches.

The United States Supreme Court hears appeals in the convictions and death sentences of eight young Black men and teens convicted of raping two women on a train near Scottsboro, Alabama.

NOVEMBER

Roosevelt wins in a historic landslide.

Banking conditions, which had seemed to stabilize during the summer, begin to rapidly deteriorate.

The Supreme Court orders new trials for the Scottsboro Boys.

DECEMBER

Just before Christmas, Hoover embarks on a ten-day fishing trip to Florida.

JANUARY–FEBRUARY 1933

Banks in Detroit face a significant run by depositors. Hoover sends emissaries to ask Henry Ford to play a role in the banks' survival; he refuses. Hoover also seeks Roosevelt's help in supporting Hoover's efforts; he also refuses.

Congress votes to repeal Prohibition, sending the new proposed Twenty-first Amendment to the states for ratification.

MARCH 1933

Roosevelt is sworn in as the thirty-second president of the United States. Almost immediately he declares a national bank holiday, closing down the system for a week until the government can stabilize it. Hoover takes a train to New York City for a few days, then joins his wife at their home on the Stanford University campus near Palo Alto, California.

What Came Before

JOHN W. HUNEFELD, A "SMALL man with a huge mustache," was a habitual early riser. He had worked for years as a blacksmith in his native Portsmouth, New Hampshire, then in the Boston area before migrating south to Washington, D.C., in 1908 after stomach cancer killed his wife, Christina. By the time the Great Depression descended, Hunefeld was living alone in a cluttered room—clocks were his thing, collecting broken ones and making them tick again—a few blocks from the U.S. Capitol.[1]

Hunefeld led a low-key and rather anonymous life except for one annual step into the spotlight, aided by his predisposition to get out of bed by 5:30 A.M. Beginning in 1926, Hunefeld arrived outside the White House main gate early every New Year's Day morning to be first in line for a tradition launched by President John Adams and his wife, Abigail, in 1801: inviting the public in to shake the president's hand.

On the first day of 1932, Hunefeld, now a sixty-six-year-old part-time painter, stepped out of his boardinghouse into a driving rain. Protected by an umbrella and wearing a new pair of shoes, he began the twenty-block walk to the White House, arriving shortly after 7 A.M. only to find he had been aced out by four other people, two of whom had come directly from a New Year's Eve party at 1 A.M. Disappointed, Hunefeld took his spot behind the others to wait more than five hours before the public reception line would be admitted.

Luck arrived first. Glancing out a White House window, President Herbert Hoover saw the short line of sopping wet people and sent word down to invite them inside for a breakfast of "awful good coffee, eggs, awful sweet bacon and muffins," as one of the impromptu guests told a reporter. Hunefeld, though, missed the meal. Seeing an opportunity, he declined the invitation, and when the other four people went inside, he moved to the front of the line and held his ground until the White House doors opened to all, keeping alive his personal tradition of being the first to shake the president's hand.

Over the years Hunefeld spoke annually with reporters curious about his obsession, and he often carried slips of paper with printed details of his life to save the interviewers some time. Yet he didn't display any particular interest in politics, or in specific politicians. When the New Year's Day White House tradition ended in 1934, Hunefeld continued to show up for the next decade to wait a few hours in case the president came out—he never did. Hunefeld would chat with security guards and passersby before ambling off for breakfast at a nearby diner. It didn't matter much to him who was president.

It did matter, though, to the nation, and voters in 1932 faced one of the most consequential elections in U.S. history. It would be the first presidential vote since the economic engine of the Roaring Twenties began seizing up, symbolized by the October 1929 stock market crash. Economists still argue over the forces that wrecked the Western industrialized economies nearly a century ago, but some contours are clear and trace back to the all-consuming battles that, beginning in 1914, devastated the heart of Europe physically and economically while upending it politically.

Over the Great War's relatively short four years, Tsarist Russia and the Ottoman, Austro-Hungarian, and German empires all collapsed, leading to the restoration of former nations such as Poland and creating new ones, such as Yugoslavia. It also fueled dangerous levels of aggrieved nationalism, particularly in Germany, which had been stripped of territory and billed for reparations in the Treaty of Versailles. In Russia, the Bolsheviks emerged victorious after a brutal civil war and established the Soviet Union, moving communism from the realm of radicals and dissidents into a real-world alternative system to capitalism. Even the victorious allies England and France emerged battered and with their fortunes and colonial empires sharply weakened. The United States, which entered the war late, was a notable exception, emerging with its economy not only intact but, except for a brief postwar depression, thriving. New mass-production techniques and explosive growth in the automotive sector fed demand by a growing middle class that propelled an economic boom through most of the 1920s.

By 1932, though, the economic boom had turned into the worst bust in the nation's history, and the most pressing concern for millions of Americans was finding enough money to buy food, pay bills, and keep up with rents or mortgages. People who had tapped their life savings and borrowed heavily to join the investment frenzy of the Roaring Twenties found themselves near penniless after share prices had lost 80 percent of their value at the start of the year (and had yet to bottom out). Separately, nervous depositors who felt their money would be safer in a drawer at home withdrew cash from their bank accounts, sparking runs that proved fatal to banks large and small. Over the course of 1931, nearly 2,300 banks shut their doors—most of them permanently—up from 1,345 suspensions in 1930. Hundreds of thousands of unlucky depositors who didn't join the runs lost some or all of their savings.[2]

Nationwide, millions of workers, mostly men, had trouble hanging on to jobs they had or finding new ones, leaving them and their families without steady income. In many areas, particularly cities in the South, white leaders pressured employers to replace Black workers with whites, racism pushing the weight of the Great Depression disproportionately onto the shoulders of the already marginalized. Legions of jobless men—and some women—of all races hit the road in hopes of finding better prospects somewhere else, or to escape responsibilities they could no longer meet.

Farmers felt it, too, and perhaps more keenly. During the Great War, many had invested in new machinery and acreage to increase productivity, but demand and prices faltered once the war ended. By the fall of 1931, crop and livestock prices had dropped so low that many farmers lost less money letting crops rot in the fields than by shipping them to markets. Thousands of farmers faced foreclosure or just gave up; creditors auctioned off what little was left.[3]

ALL THAT PROSPERITY in the 1920s had been good to the Republican Party. Two years after it won majorities in both houses of Congress in 1918, the party focused on maintaining its hold and electing a Republican successor to Democratic president Woodrow Wilson, who was much more incapacitated by a stroke than the nation had been told, and who had lost the support of his own party, evaporating any ambitions he might have had for a third term.

Amid labor strikes, sporadic acts of terrorism by anarchists and leftists, and the rise of the Ku Klux Klan as a political force, neither party had a marquee political leader to rally around. After multiple ballots at each nominating convention, both parties turned to Ohio for their standard-bearers. The Republicans nominated Senator Warren G. Harding, a former newspaper editor, and running mate Calvin Coolidge, the governor of Massachusetts. The Democrats went with James Cox, a newspaper publisher and former governor and congressman, and running mate Franklin D. Roosevelt, a former New York legislator and current assistant secretary of the navy in the Wilson administration, best known as a distant cousin of former president Teddy Roosevelt.

Harding swamped Cox, winning 60 percent of the popular vote and 76 percent of the electoral college. With the exception of Tennessee, Cox won the South, but Harding won everywhere else, campaigning on the simplistic notion of "a return to normalcy" after the upheaval of the Great War. Harding's appointees included a former mine manager and mining financier from eastern Iowa, Herbert Hoover, who seemed to combine all the traits that America esteemed at the time. Born poor and orphaned young, Hoover made himself wealthy and applied a technocrat's dispassionate eye toward solving problems. And he already had crafted a public image as a man who could get things done.[4]

Hoover's profile began rising in London as he organized a food relief program to aid Belgium, whose people were starving under German occupation and subject to a British blockade. Once the United States entered the war, Hoover moved to Washington, D.C., where Wilson appointed him to run the U.S. Food Administration—a wartime food czar. When Harding won the 1920 election, he named Hoover his commerce secretary—and with Harding's death the new president, Coolidge, kept Hoover on.

Hoover would be called on to put his significant logistical and organizational skills to work when, in late 1926, biblical levels of rain began falling in the central United Sates and continued through the spring of 1927, leading the Mississippi River and its tributaries to breach levees and overflow banks. Floodwaters inundated more than twenty-six thousand square miles—one stretch of the Mississippi measured eighty miles across—in one of the nation's worst natural disasters. Damages surpassed $300 million, including 41,487 destroyed buildings, 162,017 flooded homes, tens of thousands of acres of destroyed cropland, and the deaths of at least 246 people and more than 1.5 million farm animals. Coolidge dispatched Hoover to oversee relief efforts. Part of his strategy: commandeering fleets of private boats to save people threatened by rising waters. Hoover's efforts further enhanced his reputation as a can-do administrator.[5]

"Herb Hoover is out here among us. He is just waiting around between calamities," the humorist Will Rogers wrote in his August 19, 1927, syndicated *Daily Telegram* newspaper column. "When we, as individuals, get sick or hurt, we send for a doctor. But when whole States get sick we send for Hoover. He is America's family physician. He is a great guy, is Doc Hoover, and I hope they don't spoil him by putting him into politics."[6]

If getting into politics would spoil Hoover, then it would be self-inflicted. Hoover had long harbored political ambitions, yet all his public roles had been appointments and, except for flirting with a run for the 1920 Republican presidential nomination, he had never put himself forward as a candidate for any elected office.

When Coolidge surprised the nation in August 1927 by declining to run for a second term, Hoover—who had been nervously waiting in the wings for his boss's decision—emerged as the early favorite, despite fierce opposition by ranking party members. Hoover, who disliked the kind of glad-handing that came with building a political base, did not involve himself to much extent in internal Republican politics. As a result he had nurtured few allies among the party's key players. He was a public figure, not a party figure. But an effort to persuade Coolidge to change his mind failed, and at the June convention in Kansas City, Hoover easily won the nomination on the first ballot. Presaging future political battles, his victory came not only despite the opposition of key party figures, but also over fierce objections by delegates from farm states still in the grips of the postwar agricultural recession. While he may have emerged as the Republicans' standard-bearer and de facto leader, his grip on the party was anything but firm.[7]

The Democrats also had their early favorite in four-term New York governor Al Smith, despite some heavy political baggage. Although Smith had never been implicated in corruption, his political career was entwined with Tammany Hall, the kingmaker seat of patronage and graft in New York City. Smith was a Catholic, and Protestant-dominated areas of the nation—which included the electoral vote–heavy South and the Midwest—viewed him with a mix of skepticism and prejudice. And as a Wet, he believed Prohibition should be repealed, an issue that had divided the Democrats' rank and file.

Hoover steamrolled Smith in the general election, riding the perception that his presidency would keep the economic boom going. However, within months of taking the oath of office in March 1929, the economic foundation began to crack, and the first bricks began to fall. In the 1930 midterm election, a year after the stock market crash, the Democrats picked up eight seats in the Senate, leaving the Republicans with a thin majority. They gained fifty-two seats in the House, falling one short of a majority, but special elections to fill vacancies soon put them in control.

Conditions failed to improve, and economic isolationism grew. In 1930, Congress had passed, and Hoover signed into law, the Smoot-Hawley Tariff Act, which increased already-high import tariffs another 20 percent to try to protect American businesses and farmers from foreign competition. It backfired, as more than two dozen trading partners, mostly in Europe, imposed their own retaliatory tariffs on American products, adding yet more impediments to a global economy struggling to find equilibrium. And the economic collapse continued.

SO, ON NEW Year's Eve, the cusp of 1932, Americans had little to celebrate, but much to try to forget, even if only for a few hours. North Adams, a farm-and-textile town in Massachusetts's Berkshire Mountains, offered a typical array of events. The local Atlas Theater scheduled a three-hour program beginning at 11:30 P.M.

of short movies, a vaudeville act, the distribution of "3,000 novelties," followed by the midnight hour, and a "half hour frolic." Nearby, the Mohawk Hotel offered a $2-a-person dinner dance. At Trinity Methodist Episcopal Church, Reverend James M. Cass set "Looking into the New Year" as the topic for his weekly prayer service, scheduled for 7:30 P.M., which let the faithful pray for the future, then go out and celebrate it.[8]

The bigger cities, of course, had bigger parties. In downtown Los Angeles, ten square blocks were sealed off to motor vehicles. City police officials warned that seventy agents from the vice squad would fan out to check restaurants and private clubs for alcohol and charge anyone they found at a table with booze present, as well as the wait staffs and managers. "Technically, anyone found in possession of liquor at a table or at any other place is guilty of a violation of the law and we cannot wink at such violations," Chief of Police Roy Steckel told the Los Angeles Times. Federal agents also planned to keep an eye on suspected bootleggers, while the Salvation Army opened two temples to serve free meals to five thousand people.[9]

In Chicago, where the 1929 St. Valentine's Day Massacre cemented the city's reputation as the heart of America's gangland, the police decided to wink as more than twenty thousand people filled the streets of the Inner Loop for a night of revelry among scores of restaurants, hotels, and clubs charging $20 a head— lower than the going rate just a year before. In New York City, where Times Square and its ceremonial ball drop anchored the nation's festivities, a raid the day before had shuttered the Royal Box, a hot midtown dance club, but hundreds of other clubs and speakeasies were open, and the streets were packed "with a din of tin horns, cowbells and other noisemaking devices."[10]

Farther north, at the Roosevelt family's Hyde Park estate, Governor Franklin D. Roosevelt spent the evening with family and close friends and advisors, many of whom were actively planning his as-yet-unannounced campaign for the Democratic

Party's presidential nomination. The candidacy was an open secret after several of his closest advisors launched the Friends of Roosevelt Committee earlier in the year and spent months wrangling grassroots support from local Democratic activists around the country.[11]

The most famous address in the nation, 1600 Pennsylvania Avenue, stood as an oasis of dry calm amid parties scattered across the District of Columbia, all duly noted in the local papers. The Hoover family may have just been exhausted after a whirlwind holiday season of family dinners and White House receptions, all carefully planned with a frugal eye and an appreciation for the symbolism inherent in the behavior of the first family.

Allan Hoover, the younger son, had arrived from Los Angeles on December 21, followed a day later by Herbert Jr., his wife, Peggy, and their two oldest children. First Lady Lou Hoover spent $80 for forty pairs of copper candlesticks as part of the seasonal decorations and table settings, an extravagance, one suspects, in the eyes of many who were out of work, and out on the street. Even a candle would be a luxury in "Hooverville," the sarcastic nickname for tent cities and other settlements of the destitute. The purchase carried other layers of symbolism, too. Wounded military veterans, mostly from World War I, had crafted the candlesticks during occupational therapy sessions at Walter Reed General Hospital and the copper came from stills seized in Prohibition raids. It was a double message acknowledging the hardships endured by former soldiers and the continuing, yet losing, battle against bootleggers, gangsters, and Wets flouting the Eighteenth Amendment.[12]

Lou Hoover also made a show of halving her usual budget for decorations and donating the savings to charities, an act that society hostesses emulated. Similarly, the Hoover grandchildren "hosted" a party two days before Christmas at which the little guests were told not to expect a gift and urged to bring one to donate to needy children. All three generations of Hoovers emerged from the White House on Christmas Eve for the lighting of the national Christmas tree, a short walk away at Sherman Square, south of the Treasury Building; and then a second children's party came Christmas afternoon, followed by a dinner for family and close friends. A special ball feting Allan followed a couple of nights later, bringing together much of Washington society.

By New Year's Eve, though, the Hoover children and grand-children had drifted back to their own homes. The first couple planned no celebrations at the White House and were fast abed well before the clamorous change of the year as the nation buried the past and celebrated an uncertain future.

DIARIES I

Friday, January 1[1]

NELLIE COWLEY, GLENDORA, CALIFORNIA
I have a vague recollection of waking sometime during the night and hearing whistles, but otherwise the New Year came in unattended by me. No rain, but a good many clouds and quite cool. I stayed out in the yard first of the morning. Everything is so green, the Chinese lilies are budding, and the raindrops in the grass sparkle like jewels. I left [the house] a while after dinner to go up the trail but it was too cold and cloudy. I straightened up some of Mamma's papers and tax receipts.

What this year holds in store is hard telling, but it is not beginning auspiciously. Japan has taken Manchuria in the face of protests by the League of Nations and the United States. India is on the brink of rebellion. Unemployment has increased. Europe seems drifting toward financial chaos. Germany is ready to revolt. I wonder if there has ever before been such worldwide distress and misery. It needs co-operation between the nations if it is to be remedied, and no nation trusts any other.

Saturday, January 2

FAY WEBB GARDNER, SHELBY, NORTH CAROLINA
Beautiful clear, cold day. Many bills coming in! Max (her husband, the governor), Mama, Madge and I talked over business. Busy all

*morning getting [suitcases] packed and things together to leave tomor-
row for Raleigh. Dr. Beam is here to fix James' teeth...Mama had a
degree of fever with her cold so to bed with a mustard plaster. Ralph
went to the Dellinger dinner party. Bev Gold ate with Max Jr. and both
went to the pictures. Max went to Charlotte, was back at 11:30 p.m. all
distressed about forty-one banks in South Carolina failing to open.*

Wednesday, January 6

FAY WEBB GARDNER, SHELBY, NORTH CAROLINA

*Rained most of the night and part of the day. Dark and gloomy...
Read a lot, catching up with magazines. Madge is up in her room,
Mama downstairs. Dr. Gold came in the afternoon and advised her
to "lie around" more and watch her diet. She has pus in her kidney
and is running a degree of fever occasionally. He sent Madge some
medicine. Neither are fully well yet. I talked to George and James late
after both came home from the Key Club. The newspapers say the
Democrats were warned by National Chairman John Jakob Raskob
to find common ground on Prohibition or the party will be split!*

Sunday, January 17

EMILY A. C. RICH, OGDEN, UTAH

*Have not been out of the house today. Cooked chicken dinner.
Thair and Cloteel (son and daughter-in-law) were here to enjoy it
with us. Dr. (Edward Rich, her husband) has done very little today.
Junior called late this evening. All business seems to be getting worse.
The Paine & Hurst Store building went into the hands of a receiver.
Banks are loaning no money and are pressing those who owe them
to pay. No sales for real estate of any kind, and stocks and bonds are
very low. Dr. is having the hardest time to meet his obligations since
we were married. He has always been able to meet what he needed to,
but business is bad, also collections, and office expenses are high. He
has never seemed to worry much until now.*

Tuesday, January 19

WILLIAM E. WARFIELD, FORT WAYNE, INDIANA

Elena Alsop called to talk to my wife. She had just been down to see about paying her delinquent taxes. Many people have been unable to pay their taxes and their properties are up for sale and they are hustling to save their properties. Times for the last two years are harder than ever known in this country.

CHAPTER 1

Father Cox for President

AS THE HOOVER FAMILY PREPARED for the holidays in the White House, Father James R. Cox seethed in his Pittsburgh parish.

For more than a year local Unemployed Councils had been organizing demonstrations and "hunger marches" around the country to demand the government provide the poor with food, shelter, and a job, and to fight evictions of unemployed tenants from their homes. Cox, pastor of Old Saint Patrick Church in the city's Strip District, had no issue with the intent of the protests. A Pittsburgh native and Great War veteran, Cox had spent a large part of his two decades in the priesthood agitating on behalf of thousands of his working-class parishioners and neighbors, operating a basement soup kitchen, and regularly speaking against the often-inhumane conditions in which the impoverished lived.

As much as Cox sympathized with the hunger marches, he despised the political radicals and communists who were behind the Unemployed Councils, an offshoot of the Communist Party USA's Trade Union Unity League. Cox and many mainstream political figures feared communists were using the economic crisis to foment unrest by blaming the depression on the failures of

1

capitalism. But Cox had too much work with his parish and soup kitchen to take on the communists, too.[1]

Then came a December 7 hunger march on Washington, timed to coincide with the reconvening of Congress. The event interested the media more than the masses. Only a couple thousand people took part, and congressional leaders to whom they had hoped to present their demands easily ignored them. Right message, Cox thought, but the wrong messengers. He began to think he might just be the right one.

Cox came by his affinity for the working class as a birthright. Raised among laborers in the industrialized Lawrenceville section of Pittsburgh, a couple of miles up the Allegheny River from the heart of the city, Cox held a series of jobs—paperboy, retail clerk, railroad worker, mill hand, taxi company supervisor—before entering the priesthood in 1911 at age twenty-five. When the United States entered the war in Europe, Cox enlisted in a Pittsburgh-organized medical unit and served as chaplain in a military hospital housed in a converted seminary in Angers, France.[2]

After the armistice Cox returned to Pittsburgh and in 1923 took charge of Old St. Patrick's. A former dispatcher, Cox became an advocate for cabdrivers, in 1930, during a violent four-month strike the cabbies directed from the church basement. His alliances with workers earned him the label "Pittsburgh's labor priest," and his profile grew further through semi-weekly programs, including his Sunday-morning sermon, broadcast over radio station WJAS. So when Cox preached, he reached a far wider audience than just the folks settled into St. Patrick's pews.[3]

By the time the depression hit, St. Patrick's already served about one hundred meals a day to the hungry; a year after the stock market crash, the number had grown to more than one thousand. Cox, working publicly through the radio, and privately through personal entreaties to businesses and the wealthy, raised cash for his Father Cox Relief Fund and persuaded Pennsylvania Railroad, which owned land adjacent to the church, to let him establish a shantytown for about two hundred people. In the winter he made room for another three hundred men by converting the church basement into a dormitory—yet thousands needed help.[4]

The magnitude of the need overwhelmed the existing relief system, and the inability of agencies—many of them private charities—to meet the demand gnawed at Cox. In a region of mass unemployment, the generosity of the relatively few who could afford it was woefully inadequate. People needed jobs, not just cash and food to help them through. However, dreadfully little work could be found while Pittsburgh's main industry—producing steel—remained a shell of its former self.

It would take a new approach, Cox believed, and federal help. A few days after the failed march on Washington, Cox told a radio interviewer in Pittsburgh that he "condemned all Red demonstrations" and believed "that a body of real American citizens should go to Washington and protest against unemployment conditions which existed without any reason in the United States today." Cox added that "if sufficient interest in this suggestion were shown, I personally would lead an army of unemployed to Washington." As he no doubt anticipated, phone calls and letters came pouring in, and Cox heeded the public call he had invited.[5]

The first organizational meeting Cox convened in the church basement drew so many people that for the second gathering he had loudspeakers placed outside the church. Cox emphasized that his marchers would not demand changes to the economic system itself. It was the unfairness of the gap between the wealthy and the rest of the nation that needed addressing, a disparity that he believed could be fixed without tossing over capitalism itself. But, he believed, neither President Hoover nor current congressional leaders cared about the plight of the jobless.

"The ears of our president seem to be open only to the bankers and the very wealthy and are not open to the cries of the poor and the distressed," Cox said. "The only thing we are demanding is work. We are not going to try to change the economic order or dabble in politics, but there is enough wealth and law that, with the proper administration of both, there would be a job for everybody."[6]

Cox reached out to contacts across Pennsylvania, Maryland, and Washington, D.C., as he plotted out a route. The timing was uncertain; Cox didn't want to set a start date until he knew he had a large enough body of demonstrators to draw national attention, and to send a message to the power structure in Washington. And while it would be called a march, "parade" served as a more accurate term, since Cox planned to move east primarily by car and truck. Cox and his fellow organizers thought 2,500 participants ought to be a sufficient, manageable crowd. After Christmas, as the ranks of the committed grew, Cox set the start for 8 A.M. on Tuesday, January 5.

That morning, Cox's expected parade quadrupled to ten thousand people, all men at Cox's order, with even more supporters clogging some sixty square blocks around Old St. Patrick's. At least four thousand people were left behind for lack of transportation, despite having nearly one thousand vehicles lined up in the caravan. In a nod to a similar jobless march led by Jacob Coxey in 1894, the Pittsburgh throng picked up the nickname of Cox's Army. It set out amid raucous cheers and a state police escort, its every move chronicled by news reporters.

The demonstrators traveled slowly, picking up fresh additions and cheers from crowds along the way. After a brief stop for speeches in Johnstown, they began arriving in Huntingdon, one hundred miles east of Pittsburgh, around dusk and amid a pelting January rain. Local officials opened a fairground for the caravan to park, share a late meal of sandwiches, and sleep. It took four hours for the last of the parade to arrive, more than doubling the population of Huntingdon.[7]

The next day, the caravan continued east to Harrisburg for food and more speeches, then south past Gettysburg and through Maryland, entering the District of Columbia in the dark, before carrying on down Wisconsin Avenue to the heart of Washington. The U.S. Army had set up field kitchens along sidewalks to feed the throng, now some twenty thousand strong, and local police had established campgrounds and designated empty buildings in which people could sleep. The next morning, the caravan reassembled on Maryland Avenue backing up from First Street NE and paraded counterclockwise around the Capitol before assembling on the eastern lawn, where Cox climbed the steps to present the marchers' demands to Senator James J. Davis and Representative Clyde Kelly, both Republicans from Pittsburgh, who a short time later had them read into the records of each house.

Cox had not intended to meet with President Hoover. For that matter, Hoover had no intention of meeting with Cox, either. But meet they did, with Senator Davis making the arrangements. Cox, accompanied by a dozen fellow marchers and Pennsylvania politicians, arrived at the White House at 12:25 P.M. and, after a short wait, was ushered into the executive offices to meet the president. Cox again condemned the conditions in which the poor were forced to live and presented Hoover with a list of demands, including aid to local governments and farmers, a $5-billion jobs program, public takeover of utilities and free medical care, all to be funded by selling bonds and raising taxes on large estates, intergenerational gifts, and incomes of the wealthy (which included Hoover).

After telling Cox he sympathized with the plight of the jobless and that the government had already invested $500 million a year to try to create jobs, Hoover sidestepped the demands. "The real victory is to restore men to employment through their regular jobs," Hoover said. "That is our object. We are giving this question our undivided attention."[8]

Cox was polite immediately after leaving the meeting, but deeply dissatisfied. Hoover had been "courteous," Cox said in an interview that evening over Pittsburgh radio station WCAE. The government managed to raise billions to wage war in Europe, he

said, but Hoover, who had done such good things to alleviate starvation in Belgium, couldn't be moved to raise taxes to help his
own impoverished fellow Americans.[9]

By the time Cox arrived back in Pittsburgh the next day (apparently traveling by train), he already had plans in mind for a
bigger move. He believed Hoover had no idea how bad conditions were for average Americans, and no idea of what to do
about it. Both major political parties were failing the nation's
needy. The solution: He would form a new political organization,
the Jobless Party. And he would be its presidential candidate.

The people of Pittsburgh, at least, were receptive. On January
16, just nine days after he met with Hoover, Cox led a rally of fifty-
five thousand people at Pitt Stadium, the open-air home of the
University of Pittsburgh Panthers, that brought together the hungry and the ragged with "finely gloved...women in furs." A
series of speakers railed against Washington policies and extolled
the leadership of Cox, who in a theatrical moment strode to an
honor guard standing before the speakers' podium, grabbed an
American flag from the hands of a man in uniform, and began
waving it back and forth in an exaggerated motion, eliciting thunderous applause from the stands.[10]

When Cox finally stepped to the microphone, he delivered
his now-familiar demand for federal relief for the jobless and a
government that saw to the needs of the people before the interests of the wealthy. To a fresh round of cheers, he announced that
the first national convention of the new Jobless Party would be
held in St. Louis on Labor Day.

"We have begun a movement which shall grow and expand
through the nation," Cox said, his voice echoing through the stadium's loudspeakers, "a movement which shall determine whether
our government shall be the voice of Wall Street or the voice of
Main Street."

It was a populist's plea for a recalibration of American democracy.

ON THE OTHER side of the country, Walter Waters had similar thoughts.

Waters was born on January 8, 1898, in the small ranching town of Burns, Oregon, and moved as a child with his family to Weiser, Idaho, along the Snake River border with Oregon. At age eighteen, "restless, with no further 'West' to conquer," he joined the Idaho National Guard in May 1916. Two months later, he found himself and the rest of his regiment patrolling the Mexican border at Nogales, Arizona, under the Wilson administration's Punitive Expedition to Mexico. The target: Francisco "Pancho" Villa, the Mexican revolutionary who led violent raids against an American-owned mine in Chihuahua and, north of the border, at a military garrison in Columbus in the American New Mexico Territory, killing ten American troops and eight civilians. Villa's troops were trying to seize weapons and draw the United States into the ongoing struggle for power within Mexico. Wilson, with an eye on the war in Europe, had tried to stay out, but the deaths of American soldiers and civilians demanded a U.S. response.

In announcing the expedition, Wilson pledged the troops would have "the single object of capturing [Villa] and putting a stop to his forays," a decision his administration had reached without bothering to let the Mexican government know. The American incursion ended eleven months later in ignominious failure. "We . . . are now sneaking home under cover like a whipped cur with his tail between his legs," expedition leader General John J. Pershing wrote to his father-in-law as he led his forces back home across the border.[11]

That experience did not sour Waters on further service. Two months after mustering out, and as U.S. involvement in the war in Europe seemed ever more likely, Waters enlisted in the Oregon National Guard. Less than a week later, Wilson stood before a joint session of Congress and, citing Germany's declaration that all ships approaching Europe were subject to attack, asked for a declaration of war. He got it. On Christmas Eve, Waters, now assigned to a medical unit attached to the 146ᵗʰ Field Artillery of the 41ˢᵗ Infantry Division, joined 1,900 American soldiers aboard the Red Star Line's SS *Lapland* in New York City and headed for Europe. Over the span of one year, Waters had gone from idleness, to being part of a failed excursion into Mexico, to joining the largest war the world had yet known.[12]

Waters eventually served in the First Corps Depot Division, which operated training and health inspection sites for fresh arrivals; manned field hospitals and behind-the-lines convalescent facilities for the wounded and the sick; and oversaw sanitation—a critical task in a war zone in which pneumonia, typhoid, trench foot, and other illnesses were just as deadly and debilitating as enemy fire.[13]

After the war ended on November 11, 1918, Waters's division remained behind to support the Allies' occupation force in Germany, so Waters missed out on the emotional celebrations that greeted most of the soldiers when they returned home. But eight months later, Waters, too, got his orders. He boarded the USS *Peerless* at Saint-Nazaire, France, on June 3, 1919, and arrived in Brooklyn, New York, on June 15. Eleven days later, he mustered out at Camp Merritt, New Jersey, with an honorable discharge and headed west to Weiser and his family.[14]

After his release Waters "tried to take up the threads of my life where I dropped them," but "I had no occupation or profession to resume." He tried working as a mechanic, a car salesman, on a farm, and in a bakery, but "each one ended as an equally dismal failure." He did find love, though. On March 29, 1920, Waters married Lena Olson, whose name shows up in the January 1920 Census as living down the street from Waters and his parents in Weiser.

The war had "unsettling effects" on Waters. He later wrote that he suffered from an unspecified illness and "spent several months in a hospital under the care of various physicians," apparently in the Eastern State Hospital in Medical Lake, Washington, a psychiatric facility. The couple had two daughters, Betty Jo, born in 1921, and Elizabeth "Billie" Louise, born in 1924. The girls' mother died in 1927 of an infection after surgery, and the family sent Betty Jo to live with Waters's parents and Billie to live with Lena's parents.[15]

The children were parceled out because Waters, overwhelmed by what he saw as his personal failures, had disappeared; Lena's death certificate described her as divorced. Waters eventually popped up in the harvest fields of eastern Washington, using the name Bill Kincaid, and spent the next few years moving from job to job around the country, including a stint selling cars in Hebron, Indiana, where he met Wilma Albertson. They married and moved to Oregon, where Waters hired on at a Starr Foods cannery near Portland. But just months into the depression, the cannery shut down. The couple moved into the city, looking for work, though none was to be found. Waters returned to Weiser and remarried Wilma, on June 16, 1931, under his real name now. But finding no job prospects there, the couple returned to Portland, where, after burning through their savings, they began selling off belongings for food and rent money.[16]

Waters, like hundreds of thousands of Great War veterans, believed the government owed him a debt. Some, including Waters, had volunteered for service, but three out of five of the American soldiers had been drafted. Few contemplated that they would lose significant financial ground to those who stayed home. New army privates received about a dollar a day with food, lodging, and transportation covered by the government. Divided into an eight-hour shift (which was not yet the norm), that meant soldiers averaged 12.5 cents an hour. Meanwhile, folks holding manufacturing jobs back home were making an average of thirty-four cents an hour when the United States entered the war. Even farmhands, at an average of 14.6 cents an hour plus board, made more than soldiers.[17]

As the war progressed, military wages increased incrementally, while back home wages in the manufacturing sector rose two-thirds by the war's end. When they mustered out, the lowest-paid privates were making twelve to fourteen cents an hour; factory workers averaged fifty-two cents an hour. And once they were home, many of the veterans found they had been replaced at their old worksites, so they had no job to which to return. The brothers-in-arms found, too, that they were now competing with each other for work.

Sympathetic politicians, supported by the American Legion and the Veterans of Foreign Wars, began pushing dozens of measures to put extra cash in veterans' pockets, but faced significant headwinds over the cost—up to $2 billion under one plan. None of the measures gained much traction until the World War Adjusted Compensation Act finally passed in 1924 with a veto-proof majority in both houses—crucial because of President Coolidge's opposition over its cost.[18]

The Bonus Act, as it became known, promised $1 to veterans for each day of statewide military service during the war, and $1.25 per day for overseas service. After immediate payments to those with limited service (those eligible for less than $50), the measure would send just over $3.4 billion to just under 3.4 million vets, an average of about $1,000 per soldier. But to get enough support in Congress for the Bonus Bill, its backers agreed to a compromise: The money would not be paid until 1945. Veterans began referring to it as the "tombstone bonus," because the money would likely be collected by their heirs. Shortly after it passed, well before the depression began, veterans and their supporters began calling for immediate payment of the bonus. The argument: The veterans had already suffered financially in going off to war, and a pay differential delivered a quarter-century later would not help them catch up.[19]

The pressure built as the depression deepened. Waters, and countless of his fellow veterans, desperately needed the money now and didn't care about the politics. Congress voted in early 1931 to move the calendar up and issue the bonuses immediately. Again, however, the cost drew significant opposition—now from President Hoover and other fiscal conservatives, who believed the government, faced with declining tax revenues, could not afford the payments. Hoover vetoed the measure arguing in part that local communities were already taking care of the needy vets, an easily refuted declaration, and that "the number of veterans in need of such relief is a minor percentage of the whole . . . The breach of fundamental principle in this proposal is the requirement of the Federal Government to provide an enormous sum of money to a vast majority who are able to care for themselves and who are caring for themselves."[20]

Waters's financial predicament put the lie to Hoover's assessment. Waters was more than capable, and quite eager, to work, but could not find a job. Waters and his wife remained in their two-room apartment "in one of the poorer sections of the city" because of the generosity of the landlord, a fellow veteran. Meals came from food kitchens. "My interest in all of this was not inspired through pure curiosity or altruistic benevolence," Waters wrote later. "I was broke."

Waters had read about Father Cox's march of the unemployed, and the earlier communist-organized hunger marches. He began to think that the veterans ought to organize their own march, too, and demand the bonus payments now when their pockets and stomachs were empty. Politically, the veterans were unarmed. The only pressure they could bring to bear was their presence. "We had no money, but perhaps as a group, whose only support was in its numbers, [we] might go to Congress to gain an impression."[21]

Waters began talking up the idea with other veterans and was allowed to raise the issue at the March 15, 1932, meeting of the Portland chapter of the National Veterans' Association. He spent several days preparing by first writing out, then memorizing his speech, while "pacing around the block at night, sometimes until dawn."

The delegates gave him their polite attention, but little more. In Waters's view, the "speech fell flat." He resumed his fruitless search for work, but a few days later saw a notice about an unrelated gathering of unemployed veterans to discuss a march on Washington. He spoke at that rally, too, and at another rally the next day. Slowly his message took root, and it would add to the grassroots political pressures growing around the nation.

NEWSREEL I

January to March, 1932

In the first day of trading in the new year, the Dow Jones Industrial Average closes at 74.6 points, down three points from the previous close and more than three hundred points below the peak of 381.5 reached in early September 1929 ... The federal Department of Agriculture reports farm incomes dropped again last year to 42 percent below 1929 levels, pulled down by collapsing prices as the grinding economic slump keeps millions of people out of work ... Hattie Caraway, the Arkansas Democrat appointed temporarily to her husband's seat in the U.S. Senate after his sudden death last year, is the surprise winner of a special election, becoming the first woman elected to the Senate ... Huey Long finally takes his seat in the U.S. Senate after nearly a year of wrangling over who would succeed him in the Louisiana governor's mansion ... Harlem Renaissance poet Countee Cullen publishes his only novel, One Way to Heaven, depicting Harlem life ... The two-week-long III Olympic Winter Games, drawing athletes from seventeen nations, opens in Lake Placid, New York, with a ceremony led by New York Governor Franklin D. Roosevelt ... Clyde Barrow gets released from a Texas prison farm and reunites with Bonnie Parker; together they lead a gang that robs and murders its way across the South and Midwest ... Shortly after a dinner in his honor in Reading, Pennsylvania, composer John Philip Sousa dies in his hotel room of a heart attack at age *seventy-seven . . . George Eastman, wealthy founder of Eastman Kodak Company, kills himself at age seventy-seven in his Rochester, New York, mansion; he had been suffering from a painful spinal disorder. His suicide note: "To my friends, my work is done—why wait? GE". . . Aldous Huxley publishes* Brave New World, *a dystopic novel of a futuristic society of technology-driven conformity . . . Erskine Caldwell publishes* Tobacco Road, *a dissection of the crumbled lives of a Georgia sharecropping family . . . Suspected anti-fascists mail a dozen bombs to American supporters and representatives of the Italian and Argentinian governments, including Generoso Pope, owner of the Progresso Italo-Americano newspaper in Manhattan, and his top editor, Italo C. Falbo. The bombs are discovered when a suspicious postal worker in Easton, Pennsylvania, accidentally detonates one. A second package later explodes as a bomb expert examines it. Three people are killed in all, none of them the intended recipients . . . More than three dozen tornadoes sweep through the Deep South over the span of a week, killing at least three hundred people and injuring two thousand others . . . American adventurer and writer Richard Halliburton and pilot Moyes Stephens, circumnavigating the globe in an open-top airplane, fail in their effort to fly over Mt. Everest, but take the first-ever aerial photo of the top of the world's tallest mountain . . . In India, Mahatma Gandhi is arrested yet again in his struggle against British rule . . . Nearly two years after invading Manchuria, Japan cements control in northeast China by establishing the puppet state Manchukuo to secure access to natural resources to fuel its ambitions of becoming a global power.*

CHAPTER 2

Roosevelt Runs

UST TWO DAYS BEFORE FATHER Cox addressed his fifty-five
thousand supporters in Pitt Stadium, F. W. McLean, an attorney and secretary of the North Dakota Democratic Party's
Central Committee, sent a letter from Grand Forks to Governor
Franklin Roosevelt in Albany, New York, informing him that the
party's state convention had unanimously endorsed him as candidate for the president of the United States. As required by a
North Dakota election law, McLean asked for Governor Roosevelt's permission to circulate petitions that would put his name
on the March 15 primary ballot.

"If it is the desire of our party leaders in your state that my
name be presented," Roosevelt wrote back, "I willingly give my
consent, with full appreciation of the honor that has been done
me. It is the simple duty of any American to serve in public position if called upon."[1]

Newspapers framed Roosevelt's correspondence as a declaration of his candidacy, but it did not come as a surprise. *The New
York Times* reported that Roosevelt's letter, which his staff also
distributed to the press corps in Albany, "follows two years of ret-
icence on the subject of his candidacy, during which his friends

have worked intensively to build up an organization" to win him the nomination. In fact, Roosevelt's plans for the White House had been gestating for much longer than two years.

The Roosevelt name already had cachet in American politics by the time young Franklin entered Harvard College in 1900. In November, his distant cousin Theodore Roosevelt, a Republican, was elected vice president under President William McKinley. Theodore had spent years in New York politics as a populist re-former, including as governor, and did a star turn in the Spanish-American War, leading the Rough Riders. Shortly after Franklin began his sophomore year at Harvard, a gun-wielding assassin shot McKinley at a public reception during the Pan-American Exposition in Buffalo, New York. Eight days later, McKinley died of gangrene caused by the bullet wounds, thus el-evating Theodore to the White House. Franklin graduated in spring 1904; Theodore won the presidency on his own that fall.

Although Franklin Roosevelt studied law at Columbia Univer-sity after leaving Harvard, he found its actual practice boring. He told friends his future lay in politics, and in 1910, the Democratic newcomer surprised political watchers by winning the election for New York State Senate in a Republican district in the Hudson Val-ley, which included his family's Hyde Park estate and farmlands. His last name and his wealth helped enormously, but Franklin's lasting strength lay in an innate grasp—and enjoyment—of retail politics, regularly venturing out in public to meet voters. He spent weeks driving around the district in a car, a luxury possession at the time, talking with voters and giving impromptu speeches, an unusually intimate campaign strategy for the era.[2]

Two years later, as Roosevelt faced a tough reelection fight, a bout of typhoid left him largely bedridden in his Manhattan home and incapable of traveling the district. He summoned a po-litical journalist, Louis McHenry Howe, who worked the capital part-time during legislative sessions, to see if he could help with the campaign.

Howe cut an odd figure in politics. He had an utter disregard for how his clothes fit or whether they were washed, and cigar ash dusted him as though in a perpetual snowstorm. He was barely five feet tall, and his face bore the scars of a childhood bicycle accident. His outsized nose and ears led a fellow reporter to nickname him "the medieval gnome," a description Howe embraced. Howe also had both a tremendous grasp of how politics worked and, despite chronic illnesses, including congenital heart problems and bronchitis from asthma, he possessed an enviable capacity for work. Howe had been looking for a way to get more directly involved in politics and saw a bright future for Franklin D. Roosevelt, so he gladly signed on.[3]

Howe immediately proved his worth. He moved to Poughkeepsie, the small Hudson River city at the heart of the three-county state senate district, and began making day trips in a car emblazoned with Roosevelt campaign signs and flags. Where Roosevelt had followed a wide-net approach when he first ran, appealing to all voters across the region, Howe targeted specific constituencies. He told farmers that a reelected Franklin Roosevelt would chair the New York Senate Agriculture Committee and would push for laws to reduce the role of the middlemen between farmers and retailers. He promised a law to standardize the size of apple barrels, a pet peeve of growers beholden to often-shifting standards set by the wholesale buyers. He told Hudson River commercial fishers to expect a drop in license fees if Roosevelt won reelection. Full-page newspaper ads pledged Roosevelt's support for women's suffrage. As Roosevelt biographer Jean Edward Smith pointed out, with Howe traveling the district as Roosevelt's surrogate, "voters for the most part remained unaware that Roosevelt was ill."[4]

Roosevelt won reelection handily (aided by Teddy's presence at the top of the ballot running for president on his Bull Moose Party line), but he didn't stay in Albany for long. Roosevelt had played a significant role in pushing the New York Democratic delegation to support Woodrow Wilson for the 1912 presidential nomination, and shortly after the inauguration Roosevelt accepted an appointment as assistant secretary of the navy—the job his cousin Theodore once held under President McKinley. Howe went, too, as Roosevelt's chief of staff.

Roosevelt spent most of Wilson's two terms learning how the federal government operated, building a national network of political supporters, and expanding his Washington contacts. He often golfed with Republican Ohio senator Warren G. Harding and became friends with Herbert Hoover, a fellow Wilson appointee. The Roosevelts and Hoovers occasionally dined together in a relationship that fell somewhere between professional colleagues and personal friends. The two men shared an admiration for Wilson, but also for each other; letters between them opened with "my dear Hoover" and "my dear Roosevelt," and they did occasional bureaucratic favors for each other.[5]

As Wilson's second term was winding down, Roosevelt's longtime friend Louis B. Wehle suggested Democrats approach Hoover, whose party affiliation was generally unknown, about running for president in 1920 as a Democrat, with Roosevelt as his running mate. Just a few days before Wehle raised his idea, Roosevelt had written to Hugh Gibson, a mutual friend with Hoover: "I had some nice talks with Herbert Hoover before he went west for Christmas. He is certainly a wonder, and I wish we could make him President of the United States. There could not be a better one."[6]

Roosevelt gave his blessing to Wehle about approaching Hoover—a mission that included trying to find out whether Hoover, who historically stayed away from electoral politics, was a Democrat or a Republican. Hoover demurred, telling Wehle, "I don't believe I want to get into a situation where I have to deal with a lot of political bosses," and didn't reveal his party affiliation. (Though in his memoirs Hoover wrote that his "Democratic colleagues in Washington" knew that he was a Republican.) Roosevelt even took a shot at wooing Hoover himself, inviting Herbert and Lou to join him and his wife, Eleanor, for dinner. While "Mr. Hoover talked a great deal" and "has an extraordinary knowledge and grasp of present-day problems," he wouldn't reveal where he aligned politically.[7]

Hoover eventually declared himself a progressive Republican. He had enrolled in the party in California in 1898 and he said he supported Theodore Roosevelt in 1912. An attempt, with Hoover's permission, by Republican supporters to make Hoover the party's 1920 nominee failed. Top Republicans who controlled much of the nomination process were suspicious of his work in the Democratic Wilson administration, and it didn't help that Hoover had written a letter in 1918 urging voters to return incumbent Democrats to Congress during the midterm elections to avoid disrupting the war effort.

Roosevelt, on the other hand, worked behind the scenes for a losing contender for the Democratic nomination, then found himself drafted for the vice presidential spot behind Ohio governor James Cox. Hoover sent a congratulatory telegram to his former colleague: "The fact that I do not belong to your political tribe does not deter me from offering my personal congratulations to an old friend. I . . . consider it a contribution to the good of the country that you have been nominated and it will bring the merit of a great public servant to the front."

Despite Roosevelt's extensive campaign trips and retail politicking, the ticket stood little chance against Republicans Warren G. Harding and Calvin Coolidge, who won by a nearly two-to-one margin and took thirty-seven of the forty-eight states in the electoral college. But the campaign gave Roosevelt invaluable experience traipsing the country and establishing personal connections with state and local Democratic leaders that would serve him well twelve years later.[8]

Personal crisis, though, threatened not only Roosevelt's political future, but his very life. In August 1921, high fever and paralysis overwhelmed him while he was vacationing at the family's Campobello Island compound in New Brunswick, Canada, just over the border from eastern Maine. Doctors eventually diagnosed polio. The disease left Roosevelt effectively paralyzed from the waist down, and he spent months in quiet rehabilitation overseen by Eleanor and Louis Howe. In October 1924, Roosevelt and entourage traveled to Warm Springs, Georgia, a resort built around natural pools of warm mineral waters that Roosevelt found soothing and buoyant, making it easier for him to exercise. Two years later, Roosevelt bought the resort and more than one thousand acres of surrounding farmland, where he developed the Warm Springs Foundation, converting the summer getaway for Georgians into a restorative center for people recovering from the ravages of polio.[9]

By then, Roosevelt had already resumed his public life. He co-founded a Wall Street law firm (for which he did little actual work) and began injecting himself into state and national politics. New York governor Al Smith tapped him to manage his 1924 campaign for the Democratic presidential nomination, a mostly symbolic role that gave Roosevelt an active profile. He introduced Smith at the Democratic National Convention, where, using a phrase forced on him by Smith aides, he described Smith as "the happy warrior," a reference to the 1806 William Wordsworth poem "Character of the Happy Warrior." It remains one of the more famous speeches in American politics.[10]

The nomination fight revealed a growing split within the Democratic Party between the primarily anti-Prohibition urban northeastern part of the country, embodied by Smith, and Southern and Midwestern rural conservatives, who coalesced around former Wilson treasury secretary William Gibbs McAdoo, an active proponent of Prohibition, who was also Wilson's son-in-law. Smith's Catholicism made him unpopular with anti-Catholic Protestants, and the Ku Klux Klan, which resurfaced in the aftermath of the Great War, also worked against Smith at the convention.

The acrimonious and uncompromising nomination fight stretched over two weeks and one hundred separate votes, with neither Smith nor McAdoo coming close to the two-thirds majority required by party rules. As the standoff became an embarrassing spectacle for the party, Smith and McAdoo agreed to suspend their efforts. It took the delegates only three more ballots—for a total of 103, a record for either party—to settle on John W. Davis, a Wilson intimate and ambassador to England. Davis and running mate Charles W. Bryan, a former Nebraska governor (and William Jennings Bryan's younger brother), went on to lose badly in the general election to the popular incumbent Coolidge and his running mate, Charles Dawes, a banker and financial expert.[11]

Heading into the 1928 election season, Smith, the sitting governor of New York, had a firm grip on the Democratic presidential nomination. He and other top state Democrats hashed out during a couple of meetings whom to support in the election to succeed him in Albany. The attendees included James A. Farley, a key Smith operative who grew up in the Hudson River village of Grassy Point and had emerged as an influential figure in state party politics by successfully organizing Democrats in predominantly Republican upstate areas. The politicos discussed several names, all immediately torpedoed for different reasons, including dismissing Catholics because they wanted a Protestant as a counter to Smith at the top of the ticket.

When Farley brought up Roosevelt's name, "Smith threw it out on the theory that it was a mistake to nominate a man in his physical condition. He stressed the great amount of work attached to the governorship and said Roosevelt could not be expected to do it." But in a subsequent meeting on the eve of the state convention in Rochester, Roosevelt emerged as the consensus favorite, and easily won the support of the party delegates. It would prove to be a critical juncture for the nation's future. As Farley noted in his memoir, if Smith had stuck to his opposition and the party had nominated someone else, Roosevelt may well have faded into the political background.[12]

Roosevelt and his political advisors also recognized the significance of the moment. They thought that whoever won the 1928 presidential election—they were banking on Smith—would likely win reelection in 1932, and if the winner held to tradition and didn't seek a third term, then 1936 would be Roosevelt's opening. So Roosevelt accepted the nomination out of an interest in doing the job, and also to position himself better for the future.[13]

Hoover, though, overwhelmed Smith that November in what proved to be yet another national landslide for the Republicans. Remarkably, Roosevelt won his governor's seat, even outpolling Smith among New York voters. Then the stock market crashed, and the general economic depression destroyed the Republicans' aura of invincibility. An electorate that credited Republicans for the prosperity of the 1920s quickly came to blame them for the collapse. That created an opening in 1932 for the Democrats, and Roosevelt planned to take advantage of it, even as Smith maneuvered for his own second bite at the apple.

But first, Roosevelt faced a 1930 reelection campaign in New York, where governors at the time served two-year terms. The Republicans nominated Charles H. Tuttle, former U.S. Attorney who was an anti-corruption crusader and Tammany Hall antagonist. While Republicans (and some Democratic reformers) routinely targeted the corrupt Democratic political machine, promises to root out graft, kickbacks, and patronage didn't resonate with voters worried about the continuing economic crisis, and who were increasingly dissatisfied with Prohibition.

Roosevelt focused on national issues and the economic crisis as much as he did on specific matters confronting New York State, often criticizing lack of federal action in relieving the suffering of so many Americans. Like many others, Roosevelt initially dismissed the stock market crash as a routine correction, but quickly recognized the depth and breadth of the crisis and began questioning the nation's wealth gap. In spring 1930, he pushed for the state and local governments to play stronger roles in reducing unemployment through public-works projects. He also began discussing state-run unemployment programs paid for by workers, employers, and taxpayers, making him among the first governors to endorse the concept of a government role in helping people who lost private-sector jobs.[14]

Roosevelt's campaign strategy worked. He didn't just beat Tuttle, he trounced him. Roosevelt predictably ran up wide margins in urban Democratic strongholds from New York City to Buffalo, but he also prevailed among traditionally Republican rural counties stretching from the far northern Adirondacks to the dairy and crop farms in the central and western parts of the state. Roosevelt's 725,000-vote margin out of 3 million ballots cast surprised even his advisors, who expected he would win by six hundred thousand votes, and the traveling corps of campaign reporters. Roosevelt and the journalists took part in a pool predicting the final count, and one of the reporters came closest to picking the margin—though even he was far short at three hundred thousand votes. "This will introduce Mr. James Kieran of *The New York Times*, to whom I lost an Election bet," Roosevelt wrote a close friend, who had been an usher in his wedding twenty-five years earlier. "Will you please see that your tailor does a very good job on a very good suit for him?"[15]

Roosevelt's proven popularity in the nation's most populous state—one in ten Americans were New Yorkers—now made him a main contender for the Democratic Party's nomination in 1932. And history supported him: New Yorkers had been the Democrats' presidential nominee in eight of the sixteen presidential elections since the end of the Civil War. Speculation spread about his ambitions, but just days after his gubernatorial reelection, Roosevelt stuck to the tradition of downplaying political chatter about his potential candidacy, not wanting to seem too eager for a job the entire nation knew he wanted. He released a statement that he was focusing solely on his duties as governor and hewed to the same line in his private correspondence.[16]

But the governor was pretending to play hard to get. Roosevelt wanted his candidacy to be an answer to a summons—a public servant driven not by ambition, but acceding to the pleas of his fellow citizens. It would fall to a small group of advisors and aides to create that invitation. Foremost among them: Howe, whom many viewed as the Machiavelli to Roosevelt's prince. Roosevelt and Howe, who spoke with each other daily, formed a powerful partnership with an impressive pooled political instinct—and decisions often hammered out through invective. Lela Mae Stiles, Howe's secretary and aide, often heard Howe shouting into the phone at Roosevelt, calling him "pighead" and "a damned idiotic fool." Howe once told Roosevelt, then at Warm Springs preparing to enter the baths, "I hope to God you drown!"[17]

The day after the election, as Roosevelt took the noon train from New York City to Albany, Farley, who had moved to Roosevelt's circle after Smith's presidential defeat, and Howe planted a flag on Roosevelt's behalf in a statement summarizing the New York results.

"I fully expect that the call will come to Governor Roosevelt when the first Presidential primary is held," Farley and Howe wrote in a statement attributed to Farley, who also chaired the state Democratic Party. "The Democrats in the nation naturally will want as their next candidate for President the man who has shown himself capable of carrying the most important state in the country by a record-breaking majority. I do not see how Mr. Roosevelt can escape becoming the next Presidential nominee for President of his party, even if no one should raise a finger to bring it about."[18]

Farley and Howe later insisted that Roosevelt didn't know about the statement beforehand, a claim that invites skepticism. But even if true, Roosevelt deeply involved himself in strategizing for the nomination. Many hands, including those of Howe and Farley, were already active "to bring it about," including sending two mass mailings to Democratic party officials across the nation, one a simple introductory booklet about the leadership of the New York Democratic Party intended "to start a conversation with the key men and women of the Democratic Party in other states," and a second that compared Roosevelt's 1930 vote results in New York's rural counties with those of prior Democratic candidates. Combined, they were the seedlings of Howe and Farley's effort to build on Roosevelt's nationwide network of party contacts and supporters ahead of the nominating convention scheduled for June 1932.[19]

By early 1931, the two operatives had opened a six-room "Friends of Roosevelt" office on the seventh floor of 331 Madison Avenue, across the street from the Biltmore Hotel, where the Roosevelt campaign had waited out the 1930 reelection count. Led by Farley's efforts, they amassed an impressive list of names and addresses for nearly every one of the 140,000 Democratic precinct leaders around the country, to whom Roosevelt then sent letters (followed by many more from Farley and Howe). Roosevelt also put together a list of "key men" in each state to tap as his campaign point people, leaving to them such chores as wrangling local party members and submitting letters and articles to local newspapers touting Roosevelt. And they burned up the phone lines, Farley often making several calls to individual precinct captains and supporters in far-flung states. It had the twin benefit of keeping the Roosevelt camp on top of potential problems and challenges and leaving the local recipients of the calls feeling as though they were vital parts of a large movement. Which, in fact, they became.[20]

In June 1931, Farley, a large and garrulous man with a knack for remembering names and faces, traveled the West by train ostensibly to attend the annual Benevolent and Protective Order of Elks convention in Seattle. In reality, though, it was a political mission. Farley made stops in eighteen states over nineteen days to visit with local political figures and measure support for Roosevelt. Meanwhile, the governor himself worked the traditional base in the Deep South, including meeting with regional political figures during visits to Warm Springs to discuss the effects of the depression on farming and other issues—pointedly not as a candidate, but as a fellow farmer from the Hudson Valley.[21]

Roosevelt wasn't the only Democrat interested in the nomination, of course. Despite his statements that he had left politics, Al Smith remained the informal head of the party as its most recent presidential nominee, and his supporters felt he had another shot in him. John Nance "Cactus Jack" Garner, the Texas-born Speaker of the House, had his backers, too, as did a handful of other "favorite son" Democrats in different states.

None of them would step aside willingly.

CHAPTER 3

The Dust Stirs

O N THE MORNING OF JANUARY II, 1932, residents of Havre, Montana, awakened to a surreal environment. A windstorm had whipped up during the night, and as dawn broke, it seemed like a fog enveloped the town . . . at least until people ventured outdoors to discover the fog was "a very fine dust" that permeated everything. "One ate it and felt it in the irritation of the eye." It was, in the melodramatic view of the local newspaper, "a gloom which in ancient times would have been considered the work of dark spirits." The gloom didn't lift until around noon, when the winds died down and the dust began slowly settling out of the air.[1]

Dusty winds were neither new nor unexpected in the Great Plains, a region of semiarid flatness shaped over millennia by wind, seasonal rains, and winter runoff that stretched from central Alberta and Saskatchewan, southward through Montana and the Dakotas, and deep into Texas. The environment responded to the onslaught by developing a natural defense from roots of low plants—bluestem, wheatgrass, purple coneflower, and others—that knitted together into a delicate buffer between moving air and water and vulnerable soil.

Before the arrival of the Europeans, the Great Plains had been home to nomadic indigenous societies and the massive herds of bison upon which they depended for food, clothing, and shelter. European diseases decimated the tribespeople, and European rifles—wielded by natives, European settlers, and tourists—decimated the bison. Cattle ranchers moved in after the Civil War, and over the next two decades, they raised and slaughtered millions of head of cattle primarily to feed growing urban demand. Historian Donald Worster wrote that the livestock "had never really counted for very much in their own right; they were merely the impersonal, massed mechanism for turning grass into money." Massive herds led to severe overgrazing, and when a deep drought hit in 1885 through 1886, the land was too stressed to provide feed. Hundreds of thousands of the animals perished, their desiccated remains dotting the landscape as the ranch boom went bust. Many of the cattle barons simply walked away; some went out of business while holding on to the often-gouged and denuded land.[2]

Crop farmers followed the ranchers. Those lucky enough to grow surpluses traded or sold crops to obtain what they couldn't grow or make themselves. As railroads stitched the nation together and urban centers grew, so did the market for those surpluses. Some of the old cattle ranchers divided their vast sweeps of prairie into smaller crop farms and sold them off. Cheap land, even if the rains were unreliable, enticed more crop farmers and investment speculators to buy up acreage and break up even more of the prairie's protective skin to plant corn, cotton, wheat, and other crops. The advent of farm machinery reduced the amount of labor needed to farm and increased the amount of land that could be plowed up. But machines also increased the farmers' investments, so farmer after farmer trekked to the local bank or insurance company to secure loans, investing in themselves and their families, but also gambling with nature. Sporadic droughts continued to push many out of business, and foreclosures pushed them off the land.

Drought wasn't the only challenge. A farm built on loans and investments needs a market to sell crops. With Europe at war production there collapsed, pushing up demand and prices for American exports, which, in turn, spurred yet more investment by farmers hoping to take advantage of the growing overseas markets.[3]

The end of the war caught farmers flat-footed with excessive debt. The Roaring Twenties' orgy of speakeasies and jazz clubs, gangster bootleggers and silent movies, and dizzying amounts of wealth, didn't reach the rural heart of the nation. Steep declines in demand, and thus prices, for wheat, corn, and hogs ruined thousands of overextended small farmers, which, in turn, imperiled the local banks that issued mortgages and loans to buy more land and machinery, as well as the businesses that sold farm equipment, seed, and fertilizer. Foreclosures exploded, growing from 3.2 percent of farms in 1913 through 1920, to 10.7 percent in the first half of the next decade, to 17.7 percent by 1929. The average value of all farm properties dropped from $12,084 in 1920 to only $8,949 just five years later. Then the depression hit: By the end of 1931, total farm income had dropped 42 percent below 1929 levels.[4]

Drought, broken prairie sod, and fallow farmland made for a disastrous combination, and the winds that kicked up in Havre on that day in January 1932 presaged a dire future for the High Plains, especially in the Texas and Oklahoma Panhandles, eastern Colorado, and western Kansas, a region that became known as the Dust Bowl. The storms were more than a dusty annoyance; they whipped away critical topsoil and rendered croplands barren while silting over pasturelands, leading to the deaths of thousands of head of cattle.

And they killed people. In March 1932, a dust storm reduced visibility in Dodge City, Kansas, so much that motorist Ed Tarbet, of nearby Minneola, lost sight of a roadway and crashed into a ditch, where he died. "Dust pneumonia" from fine dust particles invading the lungs took more than seven thousand lives. Hospital admissions for lung infections increased substantially in the region, with death rates in the counties most affected by airborne soil rising from forty-one to ninety-nine per one hundred thousand from 1932 to 1935. The infant mortality rate similarly increased from 51.6 to 81.5 per one hundred thousand. While an accurate count of total deaths from inhaling dust is elusive, it "was a definite contributory factor in the development of untold numbers of acute infections and materially increased the number of deaths from pneumonia and other complications."[5]

The storm that swept across Havre in the early days of 1932 was a harbinger. The year would record at least fourteen such storms; the next year would see at least thirty-eight major dust storms, twenty-two the year after that, and then an average of sixty a year until 1938. The storms ranged in severity and scope, and some reached epic scale. One that evolved on May 9, 1934, measured 1,500 miles from north to south, nine hundred miles from east to west, and two miles high, ironically hitting the U.S. Capitol as Congress debated a soil conservation program. Overall, the winds would whip away some 850 million tons of topsoil in 1934 alone, and, conspiring with drought, displace some 3.5 million people.[6]

That was the future, though. In January 1932, a single dust storm in the High Plains of north-central Montana rated little more than brief mentions in the local newspapers. The country focused its attention elsewhere: on the economy, on the government, on the stirrings of a presidential campaign, on trying to find enough to eat, and on a brother who might be able to spare a dime.

FAST-MOVING WALLS of dust weren't the only storms brewing on the Great Plains. The drought, coming on the heels of the 1920s collapse of crop prices and land values, had left farmers struggling—and seething in many cases.

In economic terms farmers had long been something of a hybrid. The job was labor-intensive, and farmers, often with their families, worked from before dawn until deep in the night. And while they worked for themselves, owning and managing their own small businesses, they did not set the prices for their crops, as might a baker or other independent producer of goods. Perversely, their success in growing worked against them when it came time to sell; the larger the harvests, the more likely prices would be driven lower. And whether they succeeded often depended on factors beyond human control, such as the weather. A drought could mean disaster. Heavy storms and hail could lay waste to otherwise-verdant and promising fields. At a time when chemical pesticides were yet to be in common use, swarms of Rocky Mountain locusts (one insect cloud in 1875 measured 110 miles wide and 1,800 miles long) could devour an entire field of crops in a matter of hours.[7]

Like prospectors staking a claim and trying to glean profits from the soil, farmers tended to be independent and self-isolating. Yet, over the years, farmers often came together to work for their common good through such avenues as co-ops, political organizations (like the Nonpartisan League and the Farm-Labor Party), and granges.[8]

The American Farm Bureau Federation emerged in the 1920s as an agent for the interests of farmers, though it tended to reflect the largest and most successful outfits—a chamber of commerce for farm businesses—while the agricultural crisis hit deepest among the small and more marginal farms. The Democratic and Republican Parties occasionally took steps to help farmers, such as passing the Packers and Stockyards Act in 1921 to regulate the livestock and the meatpacking industry, shore up the Federal Farm Loan System, and carve out an anti-trust exemption for co-ops. They followed that up with the Grain Futures Act in 1922 that regulated grain futures exchanges.

But such measures were woefully insufficient to protect farmers from the existential threat posed by the depression, which had driven the price of corn from ninety cents a bushel in

1929 to twelve cents in early 1932. And with so many crop farmers borrowing cash to operate and expand their businesses, prices that fell below the cost of production moved farms into bankruptcy territory. In response some farmers began agitating for a new economic model, one in which they would determine a floor price for their crops to ensure a profit rather than placing themselves at the mercy of an open market.[9]

Of course, organizations require organizers, and Milo Reno became one of the most recognized names among Midwestern farmers. Born in 1866, on a farm in Pleasant Township near Ottumwa, in southeastern Iowa, Reno attended classes at a log schoolhouse, because his mother insisted he attend school to "know more than to raise white beans," before he moved at age thirteen with his parents to the small farm village of Batavia. Through her influence he eventually became an ordained minister, but the pulpit was more his mother's ambition for him than his own. Though he often delivered guest sermons, Reno never pastored his own church and turned instead to running the family farm (one can imagine his mother's disappointment) and, ultimately, to organizing other farmers.[10]

Reno pushed a more radical agenda than most. His key issue: who sets the price for farm products. The free market had failed farmers, he argued, setting prices below their cost of production. He believed farmers should be able to set a minimum price for their goods, and seizing that power required farmers to organize and work together. Reno eventually won election as head of the Iowa Farmers Union, a branch of a national group based in Texas, though his rise led some eight thousand more conservative members, about a third of the group, to leave for the rival Iowa Farm Bureau.[11]

Reno began rebuilding the Iowa Farmers Union, which expanded to include the Farmers Union Livestock Commission in Chicago and the Farmers Union Life Insurance, where Reno held executive positions. Working with like-minded farmers, he

pushed for a government-declared moratorium on mortgage foreclosures and a cost-of-production plan under which a committee
of experts would set a price that would lock in a profit for the
farmers, but also limit how much each could produce for domestic consumption (excess could be exported overseas at foreign
market rates).[12]

But those were political solutions, and Reno had given up on
the notion that the government could be relied on to help
farmers. In a 1927 meeting of a loose coalition of farm groups
called the Corn Belt Committee, Reno pushed through a resolution that threw down a marker. "If we cannot obtain justice by
legislation, the time will have arrived when no other course remains than organized refusal to deliver the products of the farm
at less than production costs."[13]

They needed to take direct action themselves, and in unison.
Some were already doing so, and it's murky whether organizers
like Reno were leading the farmers or whether they recognized
the power of self-organizing farmers and merged with them. The
reality is likely a little bit of both. With leaders like Reno openly
espousing relatively radical tactics, farmers in regions with a history of populism were primed for direct action.

Tuberculosis, of all things, displayed what the farmers were
capable of when motivated. In 1929, Iowa legislators mandated
testing all dairy cows for bovine TB, which involved an injection
near the tail, then a follow-up visit a few days later to check for a
reaction. Cows testing positive were slaughtered and the farmers
reimbursed, though the rate often fell below the market value of
the cow. A legal challenge failed, and while most Iowa dairy
farmers eventually went along with the regimen, some refused
and pockets of resistance came together, the largest centered in
the area around Cedar County—birthplace of Herbert Hoover—
in the southeastern part of the state.

Initial resistance to the testing regimen was passive, a page
taken from the nonviolent protest playbook Mahatma Gandhi

followed fighting British rule of India. Whenever state-sanctioned veterinarians arrived at a dairy farm in Cedar County, word went out over the rural phone system and farmers converged—often in the hundreds—on the targeted property to block access to the herd. In April 1931, farmer E. C. Mitchell had acquiesced in letting a veterinarian inject the test serum into a dozen of his cows. However, when the vet returned a few days later, accompanied by several high-level officials, including Iowa Assistant Attorney General Oral Swift, they found a boisterous throng that at one point tried to stampede the cows to avoid the inspection. The standoff ended with the protesters physically ejecting the state officials from the property.

Subsequent TB testing efforts faced similar opposition, and Reno became involved as an intermediary. But the talks achieved little, and by fall 1931, the passive resistance turned into violence, with farmers smashing windows in government buildings and cars in Tipton during a confrontation aimed at keeping inspectors from leaving the village for a nearby farm. The deployment of 1,800 national guardsmen tipped the balance and the testing resumed. But battle lines were drawn.[14]

A few days before Thanksgiving 1931 and well after harvest season, delegates of the National Farmers Union met in Des Moines for the organization's annual convention. Beyond the expected business discussions, more militant members of the group—including Reno, head of the Iowa delegation—pushed resolutions demanding more action and support from the federal government. Reno and a Minnesota activist, John Bosch, proposed that the organization demand congressional relief for mortgages and prices, and set January 1 as the start of a national farm strike if Congress failed to act. Such a bold political move was a step too far for the conservative body and it failed in a vote of sixty-eight to nineteen.[15]

The idea, though, took root. In February 1932, just a few weeks after Roosevelt announced his candidacy for the Democratic presidential nomination, Reno and a contingent of National Farmers Union leaders traveled to Washington, D.C., to testify before two Senate committees to support bills setting low mortgage and loan rates for farmers and establishing minimum crop prices based on cost of production. The measures eventually failed, but the delegation had a broader aim in making the trip: to drive home to Congress that frustration among farmers was growing and their patience fading.

In testimony before the Senate Committee on Agriculture and Forestry, Thomas E. Howard, secretary of the Colorado Farmers Union, warned of the consequences of the farmers' desperation and their belief that the government had no interest in helping their industry and their way of life.

"We are broke and we know it," Howard said. "The farmers of this nation are still a conservative people. I emphasize the 'still.' All over this nation, however, conditions prevail which enable a busted farmer to gather the idea that if the government is against him, and for every other kind of industry, he is possibly not going to be so conservative." Howard said he was "trying to interpret for you the mental condition of the farmers of the nation."

"Threats are being made, are they not?" asked Senator Elmer Thomas, a Democrat from Oklahoma.

"They are being made, Senator."[16]

CHAPTER 4

Hoover

FEW DOUBTED THAT HERBERT HOOVER would be the Republican nominee for a second term, even if many of his fellow Republicans feared an uphill fight, given the broke, scared, and hungry state of the nation. And Hoover's personality didn't help their confidence in his chances.

The president generally took an engineer's approach to political and policy issues, amassing facts and then charting out a course that made the most sense to him. But politics is more art than science. It requires personal persuasion skills to mediate conflicting interests and draw together support for political initiatives. Hoover, who had little experience with politics until the 1928 election, was still a novice at it. He had an outsized faith in himself, yet was thin-skinned, and criticism made him defensive. He lacked the charisma, let alone the personal inclination, to move people. He knew the answer to the problem—why couldn't people see that and do it his way?

Hoover's public persona before the election had been largely crafted by the media, which lionized him as he first rose to public stature while in London during the early war years leading the Commission for Relief in Belgium, where 7.5 million people faced starvation. Working on behalf of the CRB, with the permission of the Wilson administration, Hoover navigated the logistical and political minefield between nations at war to raise millions of dollars (much of the money eventually provided by the American government) to buy food in the United States, Australia, and Argentina, arrange for ships to transport it with the blessings of the British and German governments, then hand it over to a Belgian relief organization with an existing distribution network. When the United States entered the war in 1917, Hoover lost his veneer of neutrality, turned control over to organizations based in Spain and the Netherlands, and returned home. Over the two and a half years that Hoover ran the CRB, it raised and spent $200 million and delivered 2.5 million tons of food.[1]

Newspapers back home widely praised Hoover's performance in Europe. American journalist Mollie Best, working in London at the time, wrote one of the first fawning articles about Hoover in December 1915, a two-page *Evening Star* Sunday magazine profile of Hoover and his wife, Lou. The piece centered on their work helping stranded Americans leave Europe in the early days of the war, and as Hoover took charge of "the greatest relief work ever undertaken—the feeding of seven million starving Belgians." Other lionizing articles about his logistical prowess and unflagging energy during and after the war painted Hoover as the personification of the American success story. A real-life Horatio Alger–style hero, Hoover had risen from poverty to wealth through grit, perseverance, and a heavy dose of personal initiative. Then, out of a spirit of social debt and personal generosity, Hoover began a second career in public service.[2]

Even before his repatriation, Hoover had been preparing for his next role by ingratiating himself with the Wilson administration. As the nation turned to war footing, Wilson appointed Hoover to direct the U.S. Food Administration. It was a similar but much broader mission than what he faced in Belgium: ensuring that the nation continued to produce enough food for its own needs and to bolster those of war-torn European allies. And he was helped by a coterie of aides, some of whom followed him from Belgium. They referred to themselves as "the Firm" and to Hoover as "the Chief," a nickname they would use for decades to come. They proved to be an effective team. Hoover again won accolades in the newspapers for his performance, and after the armistice Wilson put Hoover in charge of the American Relief Administration to send humanitarian supplies to Europe.[3]

Hoover, notably, was a Republican working in a Democratic administration, though he also was an outsider to the GOP itself. He embraced policies generally favorable to business and shared the reflexive Republican belief that the smaller the government, the better, but he also believed government could involve itself in the economy by adopting tariffs and protections for American business. Still, he held to the notion that in a capitalist system bankruptcies and business failures served a Darwinian role weeding out the weak and unsustainable, while rewarding the strong and profitable, no matter the impact on the lives of workers and communities.

Hoover also saw a role for government investments in infrastructure and in areas of public good where private enterprise would be insufficient—such as an aggressive, six-year, $120-million plan he floated to improve the Mississippi River Valley. He sought to stake out turf that respected individual action and self-reliance, but that also relied on an "associative state" of nongovernment trade associations and farm organizations to propel economic growth and opportunity. He believed the government's role should be limited to getting out of the way while investing in public infrastructure for the public—and economic—good.[4]

Hoover, as commerce secretary, spent a lot of time with journalists. He opened the first publicity bureau within the department and made himself a willing source for a wide range of issues that intersected within his domain, leading pundits to

call him "secretary of Commerce and assistant secretary of everything else." He struck up a personal friendship with Mark
Sullivan, a syndicated columnist who happened to live next door
to the Hoovers, and he became one of Hoover's close advisors.
Yet, Hoover shrewdly recognized that the same media that
helped propel him could easily derail him. Once he began running for president, he became less available to reporters and after
the election antagonized the White House press corps by refus-
ing to let them quote him by name. If questions arose outside
press conferences, he required reporters to submit them in writing, then routinely sidestepped the questions and handed out
statements and background briefs on topics in which the reporters had little interest.[5]

Unsurprisingly, the beast turned. Hoover became a piñata for
pundits, and an easy target for the Democrats' new, and not-so-
secret, weapon, Charles "Charley" Michelson, a former journalist
who, by early 1932, had spent more than three years chipping away
at Hoover's reputation for probity and unrivaled competence.

Traditionally, at the end of a presidential election, the major
political parties would send their national organizations into hi-
bernation, shutting down offices, discharging staff, and waiting
until the next cycle, usually at some point before the national nominating conventions, to revive the operation. After the shellacking
the Democratic Party suffered in 1928, party chair John Jakob Raskob decided it made little sense for the party to sit idle for three
years. (Raskob was a wealthy business executive who simultaneously served in top financial positions for DuPont and General
Motors, in which the du Ponts held a controlling interest.) A
major supporter of Al Smith, Raskob believed that if the party
maintained a permanent national staff and office, it would be able
to mount a better organized and effective campaign come 1932,
when, he presumed, Smith would once again take on Hoover.[6]

Raskob financed the operation himself at a cost of about $1 mil-
lion and committed to it through the 1932 election. Among the

early hires was Michelson, then the Washington bureau chief of the *New York World,* who would run the publicity bureau, making him the first permanent publicity director for a major party in American politics. Michelson recognized that were he to just crank out press releases extolling Democrats and criticizing Hoover, few journalists would pay them any heed and only the partisan outlets would run them. So he devised a strategy of crafting letters to the editor, speeches, and other items that he doled out to Democratic members of Congress, who would obligingly make the statements their own, and harder for newspapers to ignore.[7]

Michelson signed on in June 1929, and over the next twenty-two months launched 504 press releases and reports; of those, 344 releases were attached to the names of seventy-six top Democrats, including fifty-three representatives and senators. About one-fifth of the releases focused on a tariff debate that eventually gave rise to the protectionist Smoot-Hawley Tariff Act, which was hugely unpopular among voters and that Hoover signed into law over his own misgivings. The plight of farmers received a lot of attention, too, along with the Democrats' take that Hoover and the Republicans were doing little to help them.[8]

Michelson pummeled Hoover and his administration mercilessly, especially after the depression began. The underlying theme pointed out that Hoover and the Republicans won election in 1928 in a landslide primarily by promising to steward the nation's booming economy, for which the Republicans took credit. Michelson made sure the nation blamed Hoover and the Republicans when things reversed. Mockery was a ready tool. Michelson is widely credited with coining the derogatory phrase "Hoovervilles" to refer to shantytowns erected by the jobless, a throwback to the Great War term "Hooverize," referring to doing things on the cheap. But Hooverville seems to have more organic roots. *The New York Times* mentioned a self-named Hooverville in Chicago in November 1930 (it had a mayor and street names); another sprang up in St. Louis. There is little doubt, though, that Michelson helped spread the term far and wide as just one of many zingers aimed at nettling the president. Cartoons depicted men with their pockets turned out in "Hoover flags," and rabbits and other small game hunted by the hungry were "Hoover hogs." Newspapers under which the homeless slept were "Hoover blankets." The depression itself, in a phrase that Michelson apparently did coin, was the "Hoover panic."[9]

Michelson's relentlessness had an impact. "It hampered the President's work," according to his press secretary, Theodore G. Joslin. "It made him resentful." The Republican Party leadership failed to respond in any meaningful way. In January 1930, it finally hired James West, an Associated Press writer, as Michelson's counterpart, but he lacked the fire, and the easy target, that propelled Michelson. In January 1932, Hoover's longtime close advisor James H. MacLafferty privately described West as "incompetent" and "a total loss," but failed to get him replaced. That effectively left Michelson and the Democrats free to define Hoover's presidency to an electorate already blaming Hoover for the depression.[10]

Then there were the books. At least six titles appeared, beginning in 1930, with the last published in 1932, that amounted to little more than a smear campaign against Hoover. Varying in tone and intensity, they delved into Hoover's mining history, and spun out conspiracy theories related to a lawsuit Hoover and his colleagues lost in England to Chinese officials, who complained they were swindled in a mining deal. These books generally worked to paint Hoover as an unscrupulous capitalist driven by greed—going so far in one book as to claim that the Belgian relief effort was a get-rich scheme. The books did poorly commercially (although one made it to a few depression-dampened bestseller lists), and only one drew scattered reviews in newspapers and magazines that mostly dismissed it as unseemly libel.[11]

But the books sparked "deep concern" in the easily offended Hoover. He blamed Raskob, believing the wealthy Democrat had underwritten the publications on behalf of the Democratic National Committee (no evidence exists that he did). Yet, Hoover felt impotent to respond. "He could blow any and all of them out of the water, but in doing so, would give their publication the [widest] possible notice," Joslin wrote in his diary. There were regular meetings among Hoover's top advisors in the White House to discuss a strategy, and Hoover contemplated different approaches, including a series of magazine articles refuting details in the books. The Republicans hired researchers to scour campaign finance reports filed by the Democratic Party seeking a financial connection with one of the authors, James J. O'Brien, whose *Hoover's Millions and How He Made Them* particularly rankled Hoover. But the money trail didn't exist.[12]

Ultimately, the Firm, Hoover's cadre of loyal supporters, took control. They amassed affidavits refuting one of the books' allegations of malfeasance by Hoover and others and then arranged for writer and lawyer Arthur Train to summarize the reports in a February 1932 issue of *Collier's*. Then they mailed fifty-five thousand copies of the article to newspapers and Hoover supporters around the country, followed in June by a book, *The Truth About Hoover,* by former war correspondent Herbert Corey. This undertaking was so poorly done, it could have provoked ridicule of the president (it praised Hoover for reading in bed "in defiance of the rules of optometrics"), but in the end didn't make any more of a public splash than had the smear books.[13]

Still, the attacks took an emotional toll on a man already overloaded with the national crisis. And they found one troubling audience. Some of Hoover's fellow Republicans, cool to him in the first place, wondered if the books' contents made him vulnerable in the November election. Hoover was indeed vulnerable, but no one could blame the books.

As the depression dragged on, and the 1932 campaign loomed into view, Hoover began complaining of fatigue, and often didn't sleep well, despite beginning each day with a half hour of exercise.

He devised with White House physician Joel T. Boone (a decorated Great War naval doctor) a morning regimen in which Hoover, Boone, and a shifting cast of fellow participants (including cabinet secretaries and Supreme Court justices) would meet at seven o'clock in nearly any kind of weather. The men would spend a half hour throwing a medicine ball back and forth over an eight-foot net on the White House lawn, akin to volleyball. The players were dubbed the "medicine ball cabinet," and the game "Hooverball." It helped Hoover lose fifteen pounds, and it was the only exercise he managed to get.[14]

The president's only other diversion was a weekend retreat that he and his wife had paid for and built on 164 acres of land along the headwaters of the Rapidan River in the foothills of the Blue Ridge Mountains, about one hundred miles from the White House. Called simply Rapidan Camp, or Rapidan, Hoover visited often to go fishing, and regularly entertained diplomatic representatives and political leaders there for the privacy it afforded. Rapidan's remote location made it hard to get to, and journalists, who were rarely allowed on the property, were unable to stake it out.

By May 1932, though, there were fewer trips to the camp, partly because Hoover feared public perceptions: *While the nation stumbles through the crisis, the president takes time out to catch some fish.* He believed that for the sake of national morale, he had to work ceaselessly, and it took a physical toll. His hair had grayed, he stooped a bit, and the skin on his face had softened and sagged under his eyes. He complained to Boone, who saw him almost daily, that "he was so tired now he could not sleep properly" and that "he couldn't see why anyone wanted this 'damnable job.'" MacLafferty noted in his journal that Hoover told him "that his bones ache and that he is getting very poor sleep." He worried that Hoover might be nearing a physical breakdown.[15]

The public noticed. A supporter wrote to Boone that Hoover ought to sign up for a large health insurance policy to counter rumors that his health was flagging. No insurance company, the writer suggested, would issue a policy for up to $150,000 if there were doubts about the health of the insured. Rather than dismissing the suggestion, Boone circulated the proposal among some of the president's aides, though it seems nothing ever came of it.[16]

IF THE POLITICAL pressure on Hoover was relentless, so, too, was the depression, fueled in part by Hoover's dogmatic belief that the banks and other private enterprises bore responsibility for fixing their own miseries. In 1931, he persuaded leading banks to band together in a mutual-aid coalition to help each other in the face of bank runs or liquidity problems, but the coalition, the National Credit Corporation, worked better in theory than reality. After it opened in November 1931, it quickly became clear, through demands for onerous collateral for the bank-saving loans, that its leaders had little interest in bailing each other out.

So, early in 1932, Hoover compromised his position and with Congress created the Reconstruction Finance Corporation as a government-operated backstop to the private banks. Congress appropriated $500 million and gave the RFC the authority to borrow up to $1.5 billion as needed. In a desire for openness and to shore up public faith in the system, Congress eventually required monthly reports identifying which banks had applied for loans, a forced confession of financial troubles that banks feared would add to their problems by undercutting depositors' faith in their viability—the main catalyst of bank runs.

Still, the RFC helped. In January, before it came into being, 342 banks with deposits totaling $219 million suspended operations. In February, it dropped to 121 banks with $57.3 million in deposits, and by March, only 46 banks with $14.8 million in deposits suspended operations. But the stability didn't last. In keeping with Hoover's intractable position, the RFC shored up banks and other lending institutions to stabilize the availability of credit to businesses that, the reasoning went, would then re-hire the jobless. It didn't work out.

By summertime, suspensions were creeping back up in differ-ent regions of the country, where lack of economic activity led more businesses to slash jobs or close completely. By June 1932, farm income, which supported a quarter of the country, fell to half of what it had been in 1929. Nationwide, one in four workers were jobless, and many of those who managed to keep jobs had been moved to part-time or scheduled for short weeks, with re-duced income to match. Total income paid out across all sectors of the economy dropped to about 60 percent of what it had been four years earlier. Nevada cattle ranchers and mine operators were especially hard-hit as the price of beef and ore fell to half pre-depression levels; unemployment in some mining towns reached 75 percent. Notably, the RFC wasn't designed to offer di-rect help to the people most affected by the depression.[17]

Hoover believed that the way out of the depression—a term he preferred to the traditional "panic" applied to previous periods of economic turmoil—would be found by maintaining faith in capitalism and free markets, and a federal budget kept in balance by not issuing bonds for "public works of remote useful-ness." Yet, he also urged governments at all levels to provide jobs through income-producing infrastructure projects, such as wa-terworks, toll roads, and other investments that brought in user fees. And he sped up the calendar on planned federal construc-tion projects to increase the flow of money into the economy in the near term.[18]

To Hoover, responsibility for helping to house and feed mil-lions of unemployed and their dependents did not fall to federal taxpayers. He saw a limited role for the federal government in providing cash to states and local governments, even though they were staggering to offer aid to suffering members of their com-munities. He held firm on the notion that using federal tax dollars to provide relief for the unemployed would just exacerbate the economic troubles by siphoning off capital that otherwise might be used to support job-creating and profitable businesses. He saw government as a facilitator of economic solutions, not the creator of them.

In fact, less than a month after the stock market crash, and as it became clear that the crisis was more than just a market correction, Hoover announced that he would convene a series of meetings in Washington, D.C., drawing together, in separate sessions, leaders of business and industry (including, among others, Henry Ford and the heads of General Motors, US Steel, DuPont, R. H. Macy and Co., Sears and Roebuck, and the chamber of commerce), organized labor, railroads, building and construction firms, farmers' organizations, and public utilities. Hoover wanted them to work together to preserve jobs until the economy settled down. "Any lack of confidence in the economic future and the basic strength of business in the United States is simply foolish," Hoover told news reporters. "Our national capacity for hard work and intelligent cooperation is ample guaranty of the future of the United States."[19]

That approach proved to be woefully inadequate to deal with the crisis, but Hoover clung to it as the nation fell deeper and deeper into the economic abyss.

CHAPTER 5

Marches, Violence, and Deportations

THE SCOPE OF THE ECONOMIC depression spared no section of the country, but it had a particularly devastating impact on Detroit, which over the previous few decades had transformed from a regional market hub and small diverse manufacturing center—metal stoves, railroad cars, and pharmaceuticals leading the way—into a massive boomtown at the heart of the nation's rapidly growing automotive industry. Between 1910 and 1930, the city's population more than tripled from 466,000 people to 1.6 million, making it the fourth largest city in the country and dominated by the auto industry and businesses that relied on them.

Of course, when people are thrown out of work, they tend not to plunk down cash for new cars, so as the nation's economy collapsed, Detroit's massive manufacturing engine all but froze. By one estimate, auto factory production dropped by two-thirds between 1929 and 1932, idling more than half of the workforce and pushing the state's unemployment rate to 40 percent, and as high as 70 percent in some communities. By early March 1932, about a third of Detroit's families had no income whatsoever.[1]

Much like in Father Cox's Pittsburgh, the need in Detroit overwhelmed the capacity to help. Desperation drove increases in petty crimes and suicides; scavengers by the scores hung around the Eastern Market, a produce wholesale hub, to scoop up whatever rotting fruits and vegetables the vendors might toss out. As the unemployment rate in the city surpassed 60 percent, evictions mounted, and homelessness grew.

Such economic pain provided fertile ground for debates over how to fix an economic system that had provided so much for so few, and so little for so many. Communist and socialist organizers competed for ears and supporters, often climbing atop short stepladders to draw attention in places like Hastings Street, in the heart of the city's main Black neighborhood, and Woodward Avenue, the commercial artery running from the Detroit River to the northern suburbs. Neighborhoods began coming together in communist-spawned Unemployed Councils. "Landlords used to send people to evict people and move their furniture out onto the street," recalled David Moore, a member of the Leland Street Unemployed Council, "but wherever there was an Unemployed Council, we would go and move the furniture back in . . . Out of the desperation and trials that we all had to go through—and when I say all of us, I am talking about white people as well—a rebellious attitude began to develop."[2]

Members of the local councils decided that they could be more effective if they worked together, which would also give them higher visibility. Leaders of the local councils met at Yemans Hall in Hamtramck, a predominantly Polish-American city surrounded by Detroit. "We were meeting to raise hell about the conditions we had to live under," Moore recalled. "But what were we going to do about it other than to complain among ourselves about how our government was doing nothing for us?"

John Schmies, a communist activist and onetime Detroit mayoral candidate, and Albert Goetz, a communist organizer of Unemployed Councils, led the discussion among representatives and members of various groups, including organizers for the communist-linked Auto Workers' Union (not to be confused with the later United Auto Workers). The activists agreed to hold a march. Some argued that the demonstrators should go to the homes of leading auto industry executives, a poignant juxtaposition of the suffering of the former employees with the relative comfort of the people who threw them out of work. But so many homes made for too diffuse a target, so they decided to go directly to where the jobs were supposed to be—a factory. But which one? GM and Chrysler each owned several plants scattered around the Detroit area, which created the same challenge as targeting executives' homes. Henry Ford, though, had placed most of his operations in a single site, the River Rouge plant, just over the city's southwestern border in Dearborn.

With ninety-three buildings encompassing 15.8 million square feet, it was the largest industrial facility in the world that, when humming at full capacity, could roll a new car off the assembly line faster than one per minute. It also epitomized the scope and the often-inhumane nature of assembly line factories. At the time the Rouge plant was grotesquely underused. Less than a third of the plant's ninety-eight thousand hourly workers still had jobs, though many had seen their wages decreased by 10 percent or more, depending on classification, and most often worked reduced hours. Henry Ford also was the face of the Detroit automotive industry, so it was to his Rouge plant that the hungry would march.[3]

Early March in Detroit felt closer to winter than to spring. A late-season blizzard had swept from Canada south into the Great Plains, and then pushed eastward, dropping temperatures in Detroit into the teens, with winds measuring twenty-five miles per hour. Scattered snow squalls added to the misery. But hunger, and anger, can be powerful motivators. On Sunday, March 6, 1932, some four thousand people made their way to the Danceland Arena on Woodward Avenue, near Forest Avenue, and paid fifteen cents each to hear speeches urging them to march the next day against the economic system that had left them in such dire straits.[4]

The headliner that afternoon was William Z. Foster, a onetime railway inspector and current Stalinist general secretary of the Communist Party USA. He believed communism's future in the United States would come through syndicalism—radicalizing existing trade unions and using general strikes, sabotage, and other tactics to destabilize and ultimately end capitalism. Slightly built, with a soft voice and a chronically bad heart, Foster was given to unusually harsh rhetoric and advocated violence and mass action to effect change, believing that elections did little more than affirm the status quo and shore up existing power structures.[5]

The march on the Ford plant fit right in with that vision—a mass action by jobless workers demanding their former bosses rehire them. But the march organizers had other demands, too, finalized during the Danceland meeting. They included a slowdown of assembly line speeds, regular fifteen-minute rest breaks, free health care, a fifty-dollar winter relief grant, mortgage assistance, and the right to organize a union. Few expected Ford to grant any of those demands, but just coming together in a united front to make the demands would send an unmistakable message about the potential power of mass action.[6]

The neighborhood Unemployed Councils agreed to gather in different locations on the morning of March 7 before merging for the main march. The Detroit groups met at Russell and Ferry Streets near the Poletown neighborhood, while the Hamtramck groups gathered at Yemans Hall, with both groups marching westward to Woodward Avenue, where a contingent from Highland Park, another city completely encircled by Detroit, planned to join them. Other people interested in the cause joined in, some hopping off streetcars without paying (fares were collected upon departure).

When the different contingents converged at Woodward Avenue in midtown Detroit, the parade quickly grew into a raucous crowd following a phalanx of guitars, trumpets and saxophones, a noisy mass that picked up fresh recruits as it moved along.[7]

The makeshift parade moved southward to City Hall at Michigan Avenue, where Mayor Frank Murphy, a pro-labor Democrat, "came out and waved at us and said, 'I'm with you all the way' . . . That sent up a big yell." Murphy also arranged for two motorcycle cops to escort the marchers westward on Michigan Avenue to Vernor Highway, where they veered southwest to the city line near Dix Avenue, within sight of the Rouge plant. Running out of jurisdiction, Murphy's deployed motorcycle escort turned around. The marchers continued for a few hundred yards and, around 12:30 P.M., reached the intersection of Dix and Miller Road, where separate contingents of Unemployed Councils from Lincoln Park, Inkster, River Rouge, and Romulus (known collectively as downriver cities) had arrived.[8]

So, too, had Dearborn police and members of Ford's private security force under the direction of Harry Bennett, second only to Ford himself in wielding power within the plants. (Bennett's reliance on a network of workforce spies was a special point of tension and bitterness for workers.) A delegation of cops and guards approached the marchers and spoke with leaders Al Goetz and Bill McKie, asking whether they had a permit for the march. They did not—their application to Dearborn City Hall had been denied. The police advised them to abandon the march until they obtained a permit.

Goetz, McKie, and a couple of other organizers took turns speaking to the crowd from the back of a pickup truck, passing on the police directive, which drew jeers from the crowd. Run-ins with police during protests was nothing new. Schmies, Goetz, and many other activists had already been arrested during other demonstrations. In fact, Schmies at the moment was fighting a ninety-day sentence for disturbing the peace the previous November after a violent clash in Grand Circus Park, in the heart of downtown Detroit. A leader of the downriver Lincoln Park Unemployed Council, William Reynolds, received a similar sentence from a separate confrontation; he and several other communists and other leftists also had been savagely beaten by an unidentified gang of hooded men.[9]

The leaders climbed down from the back of the truck as the crowd began moving forward to Miller Road, which ran along the east side of the Rouge plant. As they neared, a line of some fifty Dearborn police and Ford security men blocking their path launched tear gas canisters, then moved forward, swinging batons. Instead of retreating, the marchers spread out widely, some climbing to a railroad trestle, and began pelting the police and guards with rocks. The security forces fell back to another line of defense centered on two fire trucks whose crews intended to hose down the crowd. But they failed to attach their equipment to hydrants before the marchers reached them, and the retreat continued.[10]

The security forces regrouped outside Gate 3, near a pedestrian bridge over Miller Road, where another contingent of firefighters waited with hoses already charged. They let loose, soaking the marchers on the frigid afternoon. Police, including some Michigan State troopers, blocked the roadway and began firing more tear gas into the crowd. The marchers responded with even more rocks. The outnumbered security force turned to their firearms, unleashing a withering attack. At least twenty-two marchers fell to the ground, three of them dead or dying, as the rest of the crowd turned and fled. Organizers began ordering the marchers to leave to avoid more violence, but Harry Bennett was not finished. A car carrying him sped out of Gate 3 and he opened fire with a handgun. The car stopped and he jumped out; a rock struck him in the head, knocking him to the ground. The forces opened fire again, this time including a tommy gun, wounding yet more marchers and killing a fourth victim.

The march ended. A grievously wounded demonstrator would die of his wounds three months later, pushing the total dead to five. At least twenty-nine others were shot, including a *Detroit Free Press* photographer, and another fifteen or so marchers suffered non-firearm injuries. A summary reported in the next day's *Detroit Free Press* listed nine members of the security force treated at Ford Hospital for bruises and lacerations. None, notably, had been shot, despite official, and unsupported, claims that one of the marchers had started the gunfight.

Within hours of the melee's end, many of the injured protesters would be chained to their hospital beds as the authorities, rather than going after the police and security guards who did the shooting, rounded up the people who had done the protesting. More than sixty protesters or suspected communists were arrested, and prosecutors sought murder charges against Foster, Schmies, Goetz, Reynolds, and other organizers, even though they acknowledged the activists had been a small part of an otherwise-homegrown grassroots march.[11]

In the end the intended message by the hunger marchers—the need for food, for jobs, for help in just surviving—had been countered by a more powerful message about the price of protest.

THE VIOLENCE AT Ford's Rouge plant was the deadliest such showdown of the year, but it was not the only one. Just a few days into January, a hunger march that started in Los Angeles's Skid Row deteriorated into a riot when a speaker called for "force in the overthrow of the United States government." This rhetoric proved to be too incendiary for Captain William Hynes, of the Los Angeles police, who sent his officers to arrest the speaker. The crowd resisted, the speaker escaped, and "beset upon by the Reds and their sympathizers, the police were forced to use their sticks in restoring order" in a "riot" that lasted about fifteen minutes. Ambulances carried off two women for treatment of head wounds, but the march continued, eventually ending two miles away at San Pedro and East Twenty-Second Streets.[12]

A few days later and across the country, about one thousand people gathered outside Manhattan's City Hall to demand jobs. Police again waded in with their batons, one of several such showdowns in the city that winter and spring. In early February, around five thousand people took part in a demonstration in McKeesport, Pennsylvania, about fifteen miles southeast of Pittsburgh. This time police used tear gas to break up the crowd, arresting and beating several people who tried to make speeches, including one young man hauled down from a telegraph pole. Around the same time a smaller crowd formed in Pittsburgh's Hill District—near Father Cox's Old Saint Patrick Church—but they, too, were quickly shut down by police, who made fifty arrests. In mid-April, more than thirty people were arrested and dozens injured when Philadelphia police broke up an unpermitted parade in that city.[13]

The newspapers covering the demonstrations generally sided with police and dismissed the gatherings as communist-inspired, the implication being that were it not for the Reds, the protests would not be happening. What seems more likely is that experienced, if often unsuccessful, organizers from leftist groups merely galvanized some of the self-organizing that arose from the deep poverty and frustration among those most battered by the depression. In fact, organizers from the Communist Party USA, the Socialist Party of America, as well as from the Conference for Progressive Labor Action—commonly referred to as Musteites, after leader A. J. Muste—all struggled to tap that discontent for their own political movements.

Their efforts encountered similar and long-running tensions between advocating for a new social and economic order—under a noncapitalist system unemployment would not be an issue, they promised—with the more practical need to score some wins in the here and now. Hungry masses might well respond to leadership and direction, but not usually to political abstraction. Arguments among Stalinists, Trotskyists, and Musteites didn't matter much to people simply trying to hang on to their homes and feed their children.

Ultimately, direct action became an effective organizing point, such as the neighbors in Detroit who banded together under the loose lead of communist organizers to stop evictions. In Seattle, a citywide Unemployed Citizens League emerged under the direction of Musteite Carl Branin and began agitating for public-works jobs to absorb some of the idled labor. It eventually established a bartering system for some six thousand families that by early 1932 "had obtained 120,000 pounds of fish, 10,000 cords of firewood, and eight carloads of potatoes, pears, and apples." Musteite activists similarly worked in small Ohio towns and cities to help the unemployed lobby for better work relief programs.[14]

Such efforts often were successful because they involved local people, even if some of them were Reds, agitating for help from local political structures. Yet none of the leftist political organizations were able to translate those Main Street successes into broader political success. For instance, the Communist Party doubled its number of dues-paying members between 1929 and 1932, but that amounted to an expansion of a very small pond, reaching just under fourteen thousand dues-payers nationwide in the spring of 1932. And more than half of the dues-payers lived in New York City, Chicago, and Minneapolis, even though Unemployed Councils sprang up across the country and engaged in more than seven hundred protests or other actions from 1930 through 1932.[15]

Ultimately, theoretical arguments to raise class consciousness were insufficient to overcome family and ethnic ties, racism, workers who self-identified around the type of labor they performed, and other personal connections in a broader society that valued concepts of individualism and lauded the self-made millionaire. Also, people drawn into political action by their employment status tend to drift away once they land jobs, making it even more difficult to convert the one-off Unemployed Councils into sustained political organizations. People living without paychecks and facing hunger and homelessness often are overwhelmed by their circumstances. These conditions tend to lead to "despair, apathy, and listlessness, rather than rebellion. Because of the persistence of the work ethic throughout the Depression, many of those without work began to see themselves as worthless. Such men and women were more likely to withdraw from society than to actively protest against it."[16]

It is true that political radicals sought to seize the moment, viewing the Great Depression as irrefutable evidence that capitalism was a failed economic model built on exploiting the labor of the less powerful, an industrial-era version of the lord-serf relationship of medieval Europe. But for all the weaknesses exposed by the economic crisis, American capitalism's foundation survived. It didn't help that whenever leftists organized demonstrations, local police—enforcers of the status quo—readily beat them down with truncheons and hauled participants off to jail, while separating out the foreign-born participants for deportation, with newspapers cheering on the repression of the Reds.

IN LATE APRIL, two contrasting scenes unfolded at railroad stations about two thousand miles apart. In Detroit, celebrated Mexican muralist Diego Rivera and his wife, fellow artist Frida Kahlo, stepped down from a train at the Michigan Central Station to be greeted by Wilhelm "William" Valentiner, director of the Detroit Institute of the Arts, and Clyde Burroughs, the museum's curator, as well as a small crowd of Mexican Americans led by the local Mexican consul. Rivera had been commissioned by Valentiner, using a $25,000 donation from Edsel Ford, Henry's son, to paint a twenty-seven-panel mural on the walls of an interior courtyard of the city's five-year-old art museum. The subject: Detroit's industries.[17]

It was an unusual commission. Rivera openly embraced communism and had spent part of 1927 through 1928 in the Soviet Union, though the party had recently expelled him for suspected Trotskyite beliefs, which Rivera found "wryly amusing. For the Trotskyites had always reviled me as a Stalinist." But while Rivera supported communism, he already had been paid to paint the *Allegory of California* fresco on a wall of the Pacific Stock Exchange in San Francisco. Before he arrived in Detroit, he had been in New York City for a retrospective of his work sponsored by the Rockefellers in the three-year-old Museum of Modern Art. And now he would undertake a job paid for by one of the best-known capitalist families in the nation. Apparently, Rivera's dedication to communism did not deter him from taking commissions from some of the wealthiest of American capitalists. He accepted the job for the Fords just two weeks after Ford security officials and local police had opened fire on workers and fellow communists at the Rouge plant, which Rivera would soon depict in the murals.[18]

Rivera didn't mention the Rouge deaths when he arrived in Detroit. One of his first steps, he said, would be to meet with Edsel Ford and the museum leaders and then spend a few days visiting the plant and other industrial sites. "I will drive about the city and think about what I see before I go to work," Rivera said before leaving the train station for the couple's hotel rooms near the museum. "It may take many days—even weeks—before I begin to paint." The work itself could take months, he said.

Not commented upon was Rivera's status as a Mexican working in the United States. An artist's vision is singular, but there was little public discussion about whether museum executives and Ford should have hired an American muralist. But that's the exact line that many people, including top members of the Hoover administration, took when it came to other kinds of work. In fact, deporting workers had become part of the administration's response to high unemployment rates: kick out the foreigners to preserve jobs for Americans. And most of those affected by the policy were Mexicans, like Rivera.

Around the time Rivera arrived at the train depot in Detroit, three trains loaded with about 1,600 Mexicans and native-born American citizens of Mexican descent left Los Angeles's Union

Station headed south into Mexico, where the passengers would be dropped off at scattered locations between the border and Mexico City. It was not a one-off event; the April 29 trip marked the seventh time since early 1931 that large groups of Mexicans and Mexican Americans had been escorted from Los Angeles into Mexico. The trips, which were arranged by local authorities working with the Mexican consulate, were ostensibly meant to reduce the number of out-of-work families that needed local welfare assistance. Many of those boarding trains—and a few ships in the ports of Los Angeles and Long Beach—were doing so willingly, but many also had been pressured.[19]

Los Angeles's efforts began as part of a national campaign endorsed by Hoover and implemented by Labor Secretary William N. Doak, whose department oversaw immigration enforcement. Doak, a West Virginia native, had worked on railroads before rising to the vice presidency of the Brotherhood of Railroad Trainmen union, yet he was no radical labor advocate. Rail executives described him as "a conservative businessman in the labor movement." Foster, the head of the Communist Party USA, described Doak as "the infamous labor traitor," who as labor secretary had deported hundreds of foreign-born activists in the communist-backed Trade Union Unity League.[20]

Even before the Great Depression, nativist conservatives fretted about the "Mexicanization" of the southwest United States, never mind that Spanish-speaking people had been living in the area for nearly four hundred years. But in the aftermath of the 1910 Mexican Revolution, and subsequent efforts by the pre-Bolshevik socialist government to undermine the considerable power of the Roman Catholic Church, more Mexicans began arriving. By 1930, there were more than 1.4 million Mexicans living in the United States, many of indeterminable legal status, given the porousness of the border and a long-standing reliance by operators of large farms and ranches on seasonal Mexican laborers to do the backbreaking—and low-paying—

field work. But Mexican laborers also worked on the railroads and in mines, making them and their labor important to significant American industries.[21]

Names of some of the deportees were gleaned from local welfare rolls, but many people, even those with jobs, were harassed until they decided they'd had enough or decided to flee before they were pushed. Blatant racism propelled the expulsions, with news reports often describing Mexicans as undesirable and living in squalor. Authorities also regularly swept through immigrant neighborhoods detaining anyone who couldn't show paperwork attesting to the legal right to be in the country—including native-born Americans.

Despite claims by government officials that the expulsions were humane, conditions were harsh with limited food and water and people overpacked into coach cars for days without space to sleep. People in poor health died on the journey on a nearly daily basis: One train, a Mexican newspaper reported, suffered the deaths of twenty-five children and adults as illness, exacerbated by malnutrition, spread among the travelers. In many cases local welfare officials who shooed people out of their jurisdiction failed to coordinate with the Mexican consulates, which meant countless people arrived at the border without paperwork, leading to long delays as officials tried to sort out citizenship status, and where to resettle the new arrivals. There are no reliable statistics on the number of Mexicans and Mexican Americans who traveled south across the border during the Great Depression, but a reasonable estimate is about 1 million people.[22]

While the U.S. and Mexican governments sought to coordinate the repatriations, sentiment against the American policy ran deep in Mexico. Economic conditions remained worse in Mexico than in the United States, and many of those arriving had no place to stay, so they were often added to relatives' already-overcrowded homes in rural areas. Children, who knew only life in the United States, had to adjust to a new reality of no running water, a hole in the ground for a bathroom, and in many cases a language they did not speak.

Mexicans weren't the only targets. Authorities sought to eject Japanese and Chinese immigrants as well. In one darkly ironic twist the prejudice south of the border against Chinese farmworkers and laborers had led countless Chinese to flee northward to the United States. Those apprehended at the border were deported—back to their home countries, not Mexico. But the brunt of the impact fell on Mexicans and Mexican Americans.[23]

Among those helping to repatriate Mexicans was Rivera. While he worked on his Detroit mural, Rivera helped found a cultural organization, a Spanish-language newspaper, and La Liga de Obreros y Campesinos—the League of Workers and Farm Laborers—modeled after one in Mexico City and designed to protect Mexican workers. But it also became instrumental in Detroit's efforts to repatriate Mexicans, working with local welfare authorities and the Mexican consul to arrange transportation.

To Rivera, he was helping his fellow countrymen return home, where he assured many that space would be found for them in workers cooperatives. But word began filtering back to Detroit from those who had left that the workers cooperatives were undersupplied and assigned land too rocky and poor to farm. Many of the returnees had been stranded in Nuevo Laredo, on the Mexican side of the border with Texas, and forced into begging for scraps to survive. Rivera soon gave up his efforts, but for hundreds the damage was already done.[24]

DIARIES II

Wednesday, March 2

FAY WEBB GARDNER, RALEIGH, NORTH CAROLINA
Col. Charles Lindbergh's twenty months old baby kidnapped! Papers full of the news. What a tragedy! Everybody interested and anxiously waiting.

Friday, March 4

FAY WEBB GARDNER, RALEIGH, NORTH CAROLINA
The whole world, tense, emotional, despondent and hopeful, also waits with the Lindberghs for the return of their kidnapped baby. Many clues still, but baby not returned yet. What an awful time for his parents! Every baby in every household now has its parents thinking of how to avoid a like experience.... A big ransom has been asked and the Lindberghs are anxious to pay any amount to get their child. We all sit around and talk of it.

Wednesday, March 16

EMILY A.C. RICH, OGDEN, UTAH
Spent today at Community Service building giving out clothing to the different charity organizations of the city and tired tonight. Orr cleaned the kitchen & breakfast room. Went to Relief Society

Board meeting. Dr. and I sat up late to read. Dr.'s business has dropped off a very great deal the past year and he has a lot to meet financially. Have never known him to worry much before.

Thursday, March 17

EMILY A.C. RICH, OGDEN, UTAH

Have spent the day cleaning cupboards and Orr has been cleaning up stairs. He has had very little work this winter. Has taken care of the Avon Apartments for Dr. and had his rent. This has been a hard winter, hundreds out of work and none to be had. Collections are poor and all dividends stopped except rent from Avon Apartments. Dr. has to pay seven hundred dollars taxes this month and wonders how he will do it. He paid five hundred last month.

Monday, March 28

WILLIAM E. WARFIELD, FORT WAYNE, INDIANA

This afternoon I went down and paid a light and gas bill. Called at the Peoples Trust Co. and at the Old National Bank to see if either is making any real estate loans and found they are not. You can't get a cent on real estate unless you take a small loan and agree to pay it back in a year's time or less. This condition has existed for nearly three years and the end is not in sight.

Friday, April 8

WILLIAM E. WARFIELD, FORT WAYNE, INDIANA

I loaned my lawn roller to Mr. John Hess today and he let William Mills have it. Mills let two other neighbors use it before using it himself and when he sent it home by his son neither he nor his son thanked me for it. Neither Mills nor Shaeffer have ever spoken to me. Mills asked for the roller yesterday. I don't think either will ever get it again. They are white, one Irish and one German. Both are Negro haters.

Thursday, May 12

FAY WEBB GARDNER, RALEIGH, NORTH CAROLINA

"Extras" out about finding Lindbergh baby dead near the Hopewell, N.J., home. A terrible thing after 72 days of hunting, anxiety, money faked from them, etc. We talked and read until 10.

Friday, May 13

FAY WEBB GARDNER, RALEIGH, NORTH CAROLINA

Another very cold and rainy day. Paper filled with the finding of Lindbergh baby near their home with skull fractured. All took time to read.

Saturday, May 21

NELLIE COWLEY, IN TUCSON, ARIZONA, WITH HARRY, HER HUSBAND

Things are getting intolerable with Harry. He doesn't seem to consider that I have any rights about the place. He pays not the slightest attention to anything I say but goes straight ahead and does as he pleases. He expects to come to Glendora to live as soon as I have things in shape, but he tells me frankly that he won't work. I don't see why I should nearly kill myself to pull things through, and then do the work around the yard and house, cook and clean for him, have no chance to read or study because of his talking, and then have him run things as he sees fit ... Harry got some beer and has the icebox full of it; he signed the beer and wine petition and says he is going to vote for the wettest man he could find. He seems to want to sink down to the level of the bums and drag me with him.

Friday, May 27

WILLIAM E. WARFIELD, FORT WAYNE, INDIANA

I went out and cut my front lawn. As usual I was stopped in my work by passersby. First came a man by name of Green, then Jesse

Gaines and then a white fellow with communistic ideas. He is forming an organization that intends to prevent any tenant from being put out for failure to pay rent. If any person (poor) is put out they intend to put the furniture back in the house. I am not in favor of any such action. If a man cannot pay rent let him go in the country and give the landlord a chance to collect his rent which he is entitled to.

CHAPTER 6

Roosevelt Rises

AL SMITH'S APPETITE FOR THE presidency was not easily quieted. Despite the shellacking Hoover gave him in 1928, Smith had come too close to the prize to fade away. And as the nation's economic crisis worsened, it became apparent that President Hoover faced, at best, a rough road to reelection, which meant that whoever won the Democratic nomination stood a very good chance of winning the presidency.

Smith remained popular among Democrats in the Northeast, but Protestants in the Midwest and South still rejected him out of religious bigotry and as a prominent Wet. Roosevelt's back-to-back elections as New York governor made him the party's rising star. Charley Michelson, the Democrats' publicity wizard, encountered Louis Howe, Roosevelt's political advisor, on a Manhattan sidewalk shortly after the 1928 election. "Al Smith isn't going to like this," Howe told Michelson, at the time Washington bureau chief for the *New York World*. "He has lost the state and Franklin has carried it, and the country is not going to forget that when 1932 comes around."[1]

Smith and Roosevelt's relationship began to sour after that election. The former governor seemed to feel that Roosevelt owed him

some fealty, and repeatedly tried to influence his successor's gubernatorial decisions, including keeping on Smith appointees Robert
Moses, as New York secretary of state, and social reformer Belle
Moskowitz, who had been Smith's close advisor and publicist. But
Roosevelt couldn't stand Moses—"He rubs me the wrong way,"
Roosevelt once said—and he saw nothing but risk in adding such
a close Smith ally as Moskowitz to his inner circle. To have acceded
would have given critics cause to dismiss Roosevelt as a Smith puppet. Smith took Roosevelt's rejections personally, and the
once-close relationship began to fray, especially after Roosevelt
stopped inviting Smith to Albany to confer on state issues.[2]

Smith had emerged from the 1928 presidential election in a
petulant mood, and initially stated he was done with politics. As
time passed, Smith's sense of public rejection morphed into bitterness. Even in his speeches on Roosevelt's behalf in the 1930
governor's race, fulfilling a sense of party loyalty more than support for Roosevelt, Smith focused on his own grievances, getting
around to talking up Roosevelt near the end. As the depression
deepened and Hoover's vulnerability grew inversely with Roosevelt's increasing stature, Smith began sending mixed signals
about whether he had really given up his own political ambitions.
And he began aligning himself with a nascent Stop Roosevelt
movement among the party's pro-business leaders.

In March 1931, Smith joined with John Jakob Raskob, the conservative chair of the Democratic National Committee, to try to
commit the party to supporting the Smoot-Hawley Tariff Act
and repealing Prohibition, positions intended to cause problems
for Roosevelt, who opposed the tariffs and wanted to downplay
Prohibition. Roosevelt's political allies, including Senator Cordell Hull, Democrat of Tennessee, got wind of the maneuver and
deftly flanked Smith and Raskob. They lined up committee votes
against the measures on the argument that the Democratic National Committee should not dictate policy; the platform should
be hammered out at the nominating convention.[3]

Besides, from the Roosevelt camp's perspective, Prohibition was the wrong issue to focus on in the coming election. "Basically, I wanted the Democratic fight in 1932 to be waged on economic issues, including low tariffs and commercial policy, and I did not want to see the party splitting on any extraneous issues such as Prohibition," Hull, a Roosevelt advisor who also had chaired the national committee in the early 1920s, later wrote.[4]

If Smith wasn't interested in running, he hardly would be interested in such intraparty jockeying. As late as the fall of 1931, he explained to party insiders that he had too many family bills to pay (a result of stock market losses incurred by two sons and a nephew for whom he felt responsible) to focus on another run for the presidency. Yet, he clearly had a plan.

Just two weeks after the newspapers carried Roosevelt's letter to the North Dakota Democrats that he would be a candidate, Smith announced that he would rise to the occasion if the party wanted him, a coy declaration of a nondeclaration. Claiming that "so many inquiries have come to me from friends throughout the country" about whether he would run again, Smith wrote: "If the Democratic National Convention, after careful consideration, should decide it wants me to lead I will make the fight; but I will not make a pre-convention campaign to secure the support of delegates."[5]

So Smith would not run, but he would accept the nomination. Then he noted that as the most recent Democratic presidential nominee, he remained the titular head of the Democratic Party and "with a full sense of the responsibility thereby imposed I shall not in advance of the convention either support or oppose the candidacy of any aspirant to the nomination." That, of course, meant that he would not be tainted by support for another candidate, should the convention come calling in need of a compromise, and he could inoculate himself against accusations that he was stirring the pot for his own eventual benefit.[6]

Most observers saw through Smith's sly maneuver. Political journalists framed it as a declaration by Smith that he was running and wondered whether it would lead to an intraparty split. Smith supporters began immediately moving to get his name placed on various primary and caucus ballots, while Roosevelt backers reinforced that they remained loyal to him. Southern Democrats voiced their outrage that the party might once again nominate a candidate so aligned with the anti-Prohibition cause. And a Smith-Roosevelt rivalry buoyed "favorite son" candidates from different states who hoped that a contested convention might result in one of them winning as a compromise nominee, should Roosevelt not win two-thirds of the delegates as required under party rules.[7]

The ace up Smith's sleeve was Raskob, the formerly Republican-voting corporate executive who had chaired Smith's 1928 campaign. As the head of the Democratic National Committee, Raskob held considerable sway within the party, and along with Smith and Jouett Shouse, a former member of Congress and assistant secretary of the treasury in the Wilson administration, led the party's conservative, pro-business wing. They also were adamantly against Prohibition and believed it should be repealed.

Raskob came to politics relatively late in life. He was born in 1879 and grew up in Lockport, near Buffalo, New York. He went to work in 1900 as secretary to Pierre S. du Pont at the Johnson Street Rail Company in Lorain, Ohio, which produced steel rails for streetcar systems, then followed him to top financial jobs at the du Pont family's eponymous chemical company, and at General Motors, in which Raskob and the du Ponts had become major shareholders. Beginning in the mid-1920s, Raskob's post with General Motors led him to spend most of his time in New York City, where he immersed himself in the theater scene. He also fell in among fellow Catholic entrepreneurs, through whom he soon got to know and then became close friends with Governor Smith.[8]

The previously apolitical Raskob became interested in politics and the potential for affecting government policy toward business, which he believed ought to be distant and rare. Raskob persuaded Smith to let him manage the 1928 campaign, for which he raised more than $4 million. After Smith's defeat Raskob continued in his party leadership role. As Roosevelt's popularity grew, Raskob worked with Shouse, a former Kentucky congressman and now wealthy lawyer who raised thoroughbred horses, on the Stop Roosevelt campaign in hopes that Raskob and his allies would eventually win an outsized role in picking the 1932 nominee.[9]

Shouse hit the road to deliver speeches on Smith's behalf before large groups of Democrats, while James A. Farley continued his quiet visits with small groups and individuals making the case for Roosevelt. The irony of a Kentucky gentleman stumping for a candidate from the Lower East Side tenements, while the low-born Farley stumped for the scion of an old-money New York family, didn't escape Michelson. "It was a curious anomaly that the aristocrat should be presenting the cause of the man from the sidewalks of New York and the commoner should be promoting the candidacy of the upstate Groton and Harvard graduate."[10]

With his ally Raskob in control of the Democratic National Committee, and support firm among Wets and urban immigrant communities, Smith thought he could see a road to the nomination. His confidence stemmed partly from his disregard for Roosevelt, whom, despite their earlier symbiotic relationship, he thought of as a political lightweight. But Smith grossly underestimated Roosevelt's political instincts and didn't realize how much work his campaign wizards, Howe and Farley, had already done building a national network.

THE PATH TO the 1932 Democratic presidential nomination hardly exemplified the democratic process. Only seventeen of the forty-eight states scheduled primaries to let party members vote on who should be the presidential candidate. And many of those were neither binding nor seriously contested, especially since Smith was not actively seeking the nomination. Most states left the nomination decision in the hands of party leaders and delegates meeting at local and state nominating conventions, which meant that party bosses and political machines, such as Tammany Hall in New York and Tom Pendergast's organization in Kansas City, did a lot of the anointing.

But their control was not absolute, and Farley and Howe had spent nearly two years corresponding and meeting with local contacts across the country, as well as sending out reams of reports and pamphlets extolling Roosevelt, while criticizing Hoover and the Republicans' response to the economic crisis. Farley and Howe's outreach served a secondary purpose: intelligence gathering. They were hearing good things. Farley's summer of 1931 tour of the heart of the country found broad support for Roosevelt primarily, Farley reported, because Democrats were tired of losing.

"There are a lot of Democratic candidates for governor and state offices who believe there is a real chance of winning with you as the nominee, and they feel there is absolutely no hope if anyone else is named," Farley wrote Roosevelt from Seattle. "So these potential candidates are your strongest boosters because they believe that with you as the nominee, they can win. This group of men in every section will be very helpful in getting solid Roosevelt delegations" sent to the national convention.[11]

In February 1932, Connecticut lawyer Homer Cummings, a former Stamford mayor and chair of the Democratic National Committee during the last year of the Wilson administration, wrote to Howe from the Mayflower Hotel in Washington, D.C., that he had "conferred with forty or fifty key men with most glorifying results." Despite scattered support for other candidates, Roosevelt stood in a good place. "Everyone is looking forward to the New Hampshire primaries," he wrote in longhand on hotel stationery. "A smashing victory there will mark the beginning of the end . . . [and] interpreted here as proof positive that the fight is over."[12]

Cummings's analysis of the mood of the "forty or fifty key men" was overly optimistic. Roosevelt undeniably sat at the head of the list of potential Democratic nominees, but there were other viable names, too, reflecting the party's deep divisions. At the end of the Wilson administration, conservatives and progressives had begun jockeying with each other for control of a party struggling to adapt to significant social changes under way across the nation. Northeast urban centers were becoming more and more crowded with new arrivals. Black Americans headed north to flee poverty, Jim Crow laws, and lynching. They were joined by immigrants primarily from Europe, which aroused Nativists in Congress to enact the Immigration Act of 1924, limiting immigration based on national origin. Prohibition also remained a wedge.

The divisions manifested themselves in backroom maneuvering. A January meeting provided the first internal skirmish of the year. Raskob had announced in the fall that he would poll some ninety thousand rank-and-file Democrats on the Prohibition issue. Fearing that the survey presaged another effort by Raskob to get the national committee to declare that the party was formally in favor of repeal, Farley scoured Roosevelt supporters for proxies he could use to counter Raskob during the meeting. Raskob, reading the tea leaves, backed off and the committee voted to send the issue to the convention without a recommendation, a win for Roosevelt and a signal of his growing power within the party, reinforced with the selection of a Roosevelt loyalist, Robert Jackson, of New Hampshire, to fill an open position as party secretary.[13]

The biggest decision facing the committee, though, was where to hold the nominating convention. The main contenders were San Francisco, Atlantic City, Kansas City, and Chicago. Travel was a concern. San Francisco and Atlantic City (or any other city on the coasts) might deter some delegates from attending, especially the Southern and Midwestern delegates Roosevelt had spent so much effort courting. Plus, in Roosevelt's eyes, San Francisco was Garner territory because of the support of powerful newspaper publisher William Randolph Hearst; New Jersey party officials were staunch Smith supporters.

Roosevelt preferred Kansas City, where the Pendergast machine could be counted on to pack in supporters, but the state party couldn't raise enough money to stage the event. In the end the committee voted to hold the convention in Chicago just a few days after the Republicans, and in the same venue: the three-year-old Chicago Stadium where, fittingly enough, the rough-and-tumble Chicago Blackhawks played their home hockey games.

ROOSEVELT HAD ONE key problem, the same mountain that routinely confronts politicians. It's one thing to identify a political issue and something else entirely to come up with solutions for it. The most pressing issue facing the nation was the Great Depression. Roosevelt, as New York's governor, had launched some initiatives to help the worst off, including making New York the first state government to provide work for the unemployed through the new Temporary Emergency Relief Administration. Roosevelt also advocated for the rights of workers to unionize, became the first governor to push for pensions funded by the government and contributions from workers and employers (the template for the future Social Security system). He also sought to take production and distribution of electricity from private hands—consolidated at the time under corporations heavily controlled by John D. Rockefeller Jr., J. P. Morgan Jr., and electrical grid innovator Samuel Insull—and put it under the domain of public utilities.[14]

Roosevelt rooted his policies in the belief that helping the downtrodden was a responsibility of the local communities and governments (as did Hoover), but that the scope of the need birthed in the economic crisis had overwhelmed local aid systems and made it clear that state and federal governments needed to step in. While Roosevelt opposed a dole system—direct payments to the indigent—he did see a role for government in underwriting work relief programs and getting basic supplies to the impoverished. His vision of the responsibility of government would grow in the coming years, but as it was, his call for governmental intervention was already a stark departure from conservative Democrats and Republicans.

But addressing problems in New York was not the same as addressing the nation's ills, and a campaign criticizing Hoover and the Republicans over their response to the economic crisis would ring hollow without proposals for what Roosevelt and the Democrats would do better. He needed some plans.

Roosevelt's advisors knew it. Samuel I. Rosenman, a former state legislator and expert on drafting legislative bills, had moved into Roosevelt's inner circle before the 1928 election as a combination researcher and speechwriter, then joined the administration as the governor's legal counsel. One evening in March 1932, as Rosenman and Roosevelt were finishing up a long day's work, Rosenman shifted their discussion to the presidential campaign. He urged Roosevelt to draw together a circle of advisors to draft reports on the key issues confronting the nation, such as farm crises that predated the depression, tariffs, the health of the railroads, and monetary and government debt policies. But Roosevelt shouldn't rely on industrialists and Wall Street bankers, the usual suspects rounded up as policy advisors, he said.

"They all seem to have failed to produce anything constructive to solve the mess we're in today," Rosenman argued. Instead, he suggested Roosevelt tap academia. "I think they wouldn't be afraid to strike out on new paths just because the paths are new," he said. "They would get away from all the old fuzzy thinking on many subjects, and that seems to me to be the most important thing."[15]

Roosevelt agreed, and approved asking Columbia University law professor Raymond A. Moley, one of his state advisors on criminal justice reform, to seek out politically sympathetic colleagues across academic departments to become what later would be dubbed Roosevelt's "Brain Trust." The group, anchored by Moley, included, among others, corporate law professor Adolf Berle on economic and industrial policy, economics professor Rexford Tugwell on economic planning and agricultural policy, law professor Lindsay Rogers on tariffs, instructor Joseph D. McGoldrick on government finance, and public law department chair Howard L. McBain on constitutional and administrative law.[16]

They quickly got to work.

EVER SINCE ROOSEVELT moved into the governor's office, New Yorkers had grown accustomed to hearing his voice over the radio. The governor recognized early on that live broadcasts let him speak directly to voters, circumventing the reporters and gatekeeper editors at the state's daily newspapers. The radio gave him a powerful tool for building political pressure on the Republican-dominated legislature. And he was a natural at it, with a smooth, engaging voice that gave him an edge on the national stage over President Hoover, who came across on the radio as wooden and tedious, a reciter of facts more than a persuasive or comforting speaker.

Late in the evening of April 7, 1932, the nation heard Roosevelt at his best. *The Lucky Strike Program* began airing that night at ten o'clock from its studios at 711 Fifth Avenue, and after a couple of musical numbers from the Ted Weems Orchestra, host Walter Winchell came on to announce the next segment, a live speech from the Executive Mansion in Albany, some 250 miles to the north.

"We do not know the subject of Governor Roosevelt's speech, but we are sure that it will be of the utmost interest to every American, Democrat or Republican," Winchell told his listeners, adding that the program had broadcast speeches from a Republican rally in Washington, D.C., just two days earlier. The program "takes no sides, but it gives you both sides," Winchell said before introducing Roosevelt, about whom "there are many legends."[17]

After a few seconds of dead air, presumably as the technicians switched to the live microphone on the desk in the governor's study, Roosevelt's voice cut through the static. Where Winchell sounded pinched and rushed, Roosevelt came across as friendly, welcoming, and slower paced. For the next ten minutes Roosevelt spoke to the country not "merely as a Democrat" and not about politics, but about the "present condition of our national affairs," which was "too serious to be viewed through partisan eyes for partisan purposes."

Yet, he was partisan, nonetheless. In direct and flowing terms Roosevelt eviscerated the federal government and its Republican overseers for putting the interests of corporations and financiers ahead of the lives of millions of suffering Americans. In a phrase that would come to define not only the speech, but the focus of his administration, Roosevelt championed the plight of the "forgotten man at the bottom of the economic pyramid," a description that would echo over the ensuing years. While he supported federal and state programs that put people to work building public-works projects, "even all that money would not give employment to the seven million or ten million people who are out of work. Let us admit frankly that it would be only a stopgap. A real economic cure must go to the killing of the bacteria in the system rather than to the treatment of external symptoms."

Roosevelt, even as his Brain Trust worked out specific policies and proposals, spotlighted farmers, whose inability to make a fair return on their investments and labor undermined the nation's economy. He cited the dangers rural and regional banks faced when farmers and related businesses couldn't repay loans. Elsewhere, reduced demand from broke and worried consumers idled factories; Roosevelt denounced tariffs he believed closed off foreign markets for goods that could be made in those underused factories.

"Such objectives as these ... are only a part of ten or a dozen vital factors" to restoring the economy, Roosevelt concluded. "But they seem to be beyond the concern of a national administration which can think in terms only of the top of the social and economic structure."

Roosevelt had begun his speech invoking the time a dozen years earlier in which "a whole nation mobilized for war. Economic, industrial, social, and military resources gathered into a vast unit" that sent millions of soldiers to fight, supported by the efforts and sacrifices of tens of millions of Americans back home. "It is said that Napoleon lost the battle of Waterloo because he forgot his infantry" in favor of the flashier cavalry. "The present administration in Washington provides a close parallel. It has either forgotten or it does not want to remember the infantry of our economic army."

The governor ended his speech by calling the nation to work together to confront what so far had proven to be an insurmountable challenge. "It is high time to admit with courage that we are in the midst of an emergency at least equal to that of war," Roosevelt said. "Let us mobilize to meet it."

NEWSREEL II

April to June, 1932

On April 1, the Dow Jones Industrial Average closes at 72.2 points, slightly below the 74.6 level at the start of the year ... More than fifty thousand coal miners are out of work in Illinois and Indiana after their labor contract expires. Mine operators offered $5 a day as a base wage; the miners demanded the previous $6.10 rate be maintained, despite dropping coal prices and increased competition from nonunion mines ... Amelia Earhart arrives in Ireland, the first woman to fly solo across the Atlantic. The first man to achieve that feat was Charles Lindbergh ... Jack Benny's radio program debuts ... Poet Hart Crane heaves himself overboard from a ship in the Gulf of Mexico; his body is never found ... Author Pearl S. Buck wins the Pulitzer Prize for The Good Earth ... Richard Halliburton and pilot Moye Stephens arrive in Oakland with their plane, aboard the USS McKinley, ready to begin the final leg of a global trip—to Los Angeles, where they had begun eighteen months earlier ... New York Times journalist Walter Duranty, an apologist for the Stalin regime, wins a Pulitzer Prize for his reporting from the Soviet Union ... Al Capone, the face of Prohibition-era gangsters, arrives at a federal prison in Atlanta to serve his sentence on tax evasion charges ... Laura Ingalls Wilder publishes her first novel, The Little House in the Big Woods ... Paul Gorguloff, an anti–Soviet Russian émigré angry over his perception that France had not done enough to *oppose Bolshevism, assassinates Paul Doumer, France's president, in Paris... In Germany, Adolf Hitler and General Kurt von Schleicher strike a secret deal that begins to undo German democracy and paves the way for the rise of the Nazi Party... About a dozen young military men, working with nationalistic military leaders seeking to undermine civilian rule and force a more aggressive stance toward China, burst into the residence of Inukai Tsuyoshi, Japan's prime minister, and assassinate him in a hail of gunfire. "The political consequences of the assassination will be watched with close interest, however, particularly as to its possible repercussions on Japanese policies in Manchuria,"* The New York Times *reports. "A military-Fascist government in Japan with the consequent breakdown of parliamentary government would be the cause of considerable disquietude." Shortly afterward, Japan formally recognizes the puppet state it established in Manchuria.*

CHAPTER 7

"Wets, Drys, and Hypocrites"

I N SPITE OF THE 1929 Stock Market Crash, the intersection of
Wall Street and Nassau Street in lower Manhattan remained
the symbolic, if arrhythmic, heart of American capitalism. The
New York Stock Exchange, where fortunes were made and lost,
occupied the southwest corner; the J. P. Morgan Building, home
to one of the world's most powerful banks, stood on the southeast
corner. Federal Hall—which for a time held a fortune in government gold as the sub-Treasury Building—occupied the northeast
corner, and the Bankers Trust Building, whose namesake banking
tenant was closely linked to the Morgan financial empire, filled
the fourth corner, directly across from the Stock Exchange.

On May 18, a sun-drenched but cool Wednesday afternoon,
a small group of well-dressed women gathered in the canyon
formed by the massive buildings and immediately drew a crowd.
Led by Helen Astor, the wealthy wife of Vincent Astor, the
women began handing out pamphlets and seeking donations
and new members for the Women's Organization for National
Prohibition Reform (WONPR), founded three years earlier by
socialite and former Republican activist Pauline Sabin. Passersby outside the New York Public Library, more than three

miles to the north, similarly encountered Polly Lauder Tunney, heiress to a portion of the United States Steel fortune and wife of the former heavyweight boxing champion, Gene Tunney. Other street meetings were held elsewhere in the city and around the country.[1]

If contributions are a measure of success, the women did just fine, raising more than $16,000 in Manhattan alone over the first three days of what the organization billed as "Repeal Week," with more money coming in from most of the rest of the forty-eight states. For Sabin, though, donations mattered less than the number of new members signing up—critical, she believed, to proving to the nation that the powerful Women's Christian Temperance Union, or WCTU, didn't speak for all women. Sabin also believed that organized women, who won the right to vote eight months after Prohibition began, would be a potent political force for its repeal. And by that spring her group had doubled its membership to six hundred thousand over the previous year, simultaneously feeding and surfing a wave of national discontent over Prohibition, which countless Americans observed about as well as they did speed limits.[2]

On the evening of the first day of Repeal Week, the New York campaigners came together at the posh two-thousand-room Hotel Commodore, just east of Grand Central Station at Forty-Second Street and Park Avenue, for a fundraising gala and, of course, speeches. The main voice belonged to Sabin, the face of the organization and a critical engine within it. Sabin lived with her husband, Guaranty Trust Company chairman Charles H. Sabin, at One Sutton Place South, a new luxury building overlooking the East River between Fifty-Sixth and Fifty-Seventh Streets, and across the street from the homes of J. P. Morgan's daughter Anne, and the former Anne Harriman, the widow of Cornelius Vanderbilt's grandson. There were few richer circles in Manhattan in which to travel, even with the financial hits delivered by the depression.[3]

Blond, lithe, and tall at five feet ten inches, the forty-five-year-old Sabin spoke with an easy, practiced confidence, her voice increasing in pitch as she sought to make herself heard deep into the corner of the ornate ballroom, and over the clatter of people still finishing their dinner.

"The question is not one of drink," Sabin said. "This is a national emergency, in which the security of our institutions is at stake, and the choice is between law and order, and organized crime." She decried politicians who publicly supported Prohibition while drinking in private, a cynicism she felt undermined political legitimacy. And timing mattered. More and more onetime supporters of Prohibition were "rapidly climbing upon the great American bandwagon. But even so, if the Prohibition question is not settled at the next election, it is my sincere belief that the great cause to which we are pledged will suffer a severe setback."

Sabin followed that with a speech the next night at the Brooklyn Academy of Music in which she made the financial case for repeal. At a time when the federal government faced a $2 billion deficit and increasing demands for aid to the impoverished, repealing Prohibition and enacting taxes on beer, wine, and liquor would raise nearly $1 billion a year and save the government the $40 million a year it spent trying to enforce laws that had proven to be unenforceable. Sabin didn't mention Al Capone by name, but just two weeks earlier, the Chicago gangster and bootlegger, who had never been convicted of any of his reported scores of murders (let alone his lesser crimes), had finally arrived at federal prison in Atlanta to serve an eleven-year sentence for the most mundane of crimes: tax evasion.[4]

The question, Sabin told the crowd that night, was "whether the enormous amount of money now flowing into dives, dens and speakeasies should be diverted to better purposes. The absurdity of sending gangsters to jail for failure to pay income taxes when their incomes are derived from liquor should, it seems to me, make us realize this economic farce. Prohibition has divided the United States, like Gaul, into three parts: Wet, Dry, and hypocrites."[5]

The depression, of course, defined the times, but Prohibition—its failures, social and political reverberations, the growing demands for its repeal—didn't lag far behind. Sabin embodied the nation's changing views of the ban. Born in 1887 into a wealthy and politically connected Chicago family—her father, Paul Morton, was a railroad executive; her uncle Joy founded Morton Salt—Sabin grew up in Washington, D.C., and New York City. Her father served as President Theodore Roosevelt's navy secretary when Pauline was seventeen (a scandal over illicit shipping rebates forced him out after a year), and a grandfather served briefly as Nebraska governor and four years as President Grover Cleveland's agriculture secretary.

Initially, politics didn't interest the young Pauline. After graduating from boarding school, she made her formal society debut at age seventeen; at age twenty, she married J. Hopkins Smith Jr., generally described as a Manhattan sportsman. They had two sons before she took the unusual step of divorcing him in 1914 and, with another woman, opened what became a successful interior decorating business. Ads for the Waldorf-Astoria highlighted town houses she had decorated through her Eighteenth Century Inc. business at 572 Madison Avenue.[6]

Two years after divorcing Smith, Pauline married Sabin and soon joined several charity boards, an experience that led her to realize that "in New York City you had to have political pull to get things done." Although her husband was a Democrat, Sabin became active in Republican politics, hosting fundraisers at the couple's Bayberry Land estate in Shinnecock Hills, just west of Southampton on Long Island. Sabin also raised funds for the Harding-Coolidge ticket in 1920, and the next year became the founding president of the Women's National Republican Club, serving until 1926. She also broke a barrier by becoming the first woman to serve on the Republican National Committee, the party's leadership group. These were not idle pastimes. Sabin threw herself deeply into the work and developed a reputation for "charm, gaiety, and wit," strong organizational skills, and a graceful approach to small-room politics. Those abilities would come to serve her well.

Sabin had been a lukewarm supporter of Prohibition, seemingly as a function of class and expectation. Women—particularly conservative rural and Southern church folks—were one of the driving forces behind the constitutional amendment to ban alcohol, arguing that drunken men frequenting saloons kept their families impoverished and posed a physical risk to wives and children. Women who frequented saloons similarly threatened the stability of marriages and the American family, not to mention the image of women in general, at least from the perspective of the Women's Christian Temperance Union and other Prohibition advocates, such as the Anti-Saloon League, or ASL.

In the struggle between proper social behavior and immorality, Sabin, as a wealthy socialite, embraced propriety and "favored prohibition when I heard it discussed in the abstract." She thought that a ban on alcohol would be good for her two sons by protecting them from drunkenness. But as Prohibition went on, Sabin became convinced that rather than reducing lawlessness, Prohibition promoted it. Violent gangs fought each other over bootlegging operations, and widespread resistance to sobriety simply supplanted saloons with off-the-books speakeasies.

Wording of the Prohibition amendment proved problematic, too. The amendment prohibited making, importing, and selling of alcohol, but not drinking it; and while statistics suggest overall consumption decreased, Prohibition failed to make a serious dent. There was a point of political philosophy to be made, too. Among the nineteen constitutional amendments extant at the time, only the Eighteenth regulated personal behavior, anathema to those devoted to the concept of individual liberty.

For Sabin, it was all too much. In the June 13, 1928, issue of *The Outlook* magazine, and while she still served on the Republican National Committee, Sabin issued a call to arms to the women of America to take up the repeal cause, declaring, "I am now convinced that it has been proved a failure." And not just a failure, but a broken promise.[7]

"In my opinion, the majority of women with young children favored prohibition because they felt that when the Eighteenth Amendment was enacted drinking to excess would never be a problem in their children's lives, that temptation would be completely eliminated," Sabin wrote. "They have found that their children are growing up with a total lack of respect for the Constitution and for the law."

Noting that a women's movement deeply influenced the adoption of the Eighteenth Amendment, Sabin argued that a women's movement would be equally capable of amending or repealing it.

Sabin remained loyally within the Republican fold through the election, believing that Hoover, for whom the debate over the Eighteenth Amendment was a distraction, "would do something about Prohibition" as president. Instead, Hoover's March 3, 1929, inaugural address infuriated Sabin when he doubled down on Prohibition, arguing that bootlegging exacerbated the nation's crime problem and arose from the failure of Americans to respect the law. He pledged to create a commission to explore "the whole structure of our federal system of jurisprudence, to include the method of enforcement of the Eighteenth Amendment and the causes of abuse under it." In other words, Hoover wanted to make Prohibition work better, not get rid of it.

Five days later, Sabin resigned from the Republican National Committee and began laying the groundwork for the WONPR. At an informal gathering in Manhattan, she formed a committee of her peers, drawing in socialites with such names as Cortlandt and Van Rensselaer and Whitney; then she expanded it to include other leading female socialites from around the country.

Over two more similar gatherings, the group adopted a decentralized structure dividing the country into fourteen regions, then drafting leaders responsible for putting together state-level organizations. The women worked quickly. Even before the structure was set, Sabin urged simultaneous demonstrations be organized in four or five large cities around the country to draw attention to Prohibition's failures.[8]

Sabin convened the inaugural national meeting of the still-developing women's group in Chicago on May 28, a little more than two months after the first small gathering in Manhattan. Some two dozen women delegates (contemporary news accounts doubled the number) from seventeen states gathered at the Drake Hotel to finalize the structure and plan for a national conference in the fall.

Under Sabin's leadership they mapped out a multiprong strategy, creating an investigations office to gather data on drunkenness and "the effect in Prohibition on the younger generation," along with statements and analyses from within the criminal justice system; a publicity bureau to push the agenda and counter Dry arguments through a battery of letters to the editor of newspapers around the country; a speakers bureau to make advocates available; state and federal level tracking of all legislation related to the issue; and an office to drum up membership.[9]

News coverage of the Chicago meeting appeared in more than five hundred newspapers, mostly a mix of local editorial comments and wire service reports. Battle lines fell in place quickly. Dr. Clarence True Wilson, in charge of public morals for the Methodist Episcopal Church, denounced Sabin and her allies as "a little group of wine-drinking society women who are uncomfortable under prohibition."[10]

Over the next three years, Sabin and her fellow wealthy socialites would put together the most unexpected of social movements, drawing together servant-dependent urban elites with small-town housewives, the latter enjoying their brushes with high society women. In addition to regular local and state meetings, the national executive committee held quarterly sessions in different cities around the country, serving the dual purpose of keeping the momentum moving and making the organization geographically inclusive.

By the summer of 1932, the WONPR claimed nearly 1 million members, who together mounted a sophisticated political and publicity campaign—one that, in fact, picked up on the tactics the Anti-Saloon League had used to back the Eighteenth Amendment.

THE ODDS AGAINST repealing the Eighteenth Amendment were so long because the politics were so difficult. Few people—even among those actively seeking it—thought repeal possible. For beginners, the nation had never repealed an amendment. And Prohibition had gone into effect just twelve years earlier with overwhelming bipartisan political support, though that did not necessarily reflect popular support. No state put a binding ratification vote before the people, and none held conventions of elected citizen representatives; ratification came through votes by state legislatures, and many of those were remarkably undemocratic. Legislative districts often were not determined by population, leading to a massive imbalance between rural and urban areas, to the detriment of the cities. Rural areas tended to be more conservative, more religious, and more supportive of banning booze.[11]

New York State offers a good example of that imbalance. New York City's 1930 population stood at just over 6.9 million people, accounting for more than half of the state's 12.6 million people, yet only held twenty-two of the state's fifty-one assembly seats. Upstate urban centers, such as Buffalo and Rochester, shared assembly seats with outlying rural areas, further diluting urban political power.

The main engine behind Prohibition was the Anti-Saloon League, which arose in Oberlin, Ohio, in 1893, and over the next several years put together a single-issue lobbying force that exerted significant power and quickly surpassed the WCTU and the Prohibition Party in influence. The ASL benefited from a couple of realities. The WCTU and the Prohibition Party looked at a ban on alcohol and the shuttering of saloons as one of several social policies they supported, which led to internal distractions and a diffuse approach to lobbying. The ASL intentionally focused on one issue, creating a template for modern single-issue pressure groups. And it had the churches to draw from.[12]

Some three-quarters of the leaders of the ASL were clergymen, mostly Methodist and Baptist, and they developed a "capillary network of churches," in the words of historian Daniel Okrent, which gave them a considerable communications and organizational advantage. As a result the league could generate a tsunami of letters and telegrams in short order from all corners of the country, inundating targeted elected officials. The ASL also enjoyed the support of wealthy individuals, including noted abstainer John D. Rockefeller (who helped found the University of Chicago in hopes of creating a Baptist counterpart to Harvard College).[13]

But there were more forces behind Prohibition than the ASL and the WCTU. For rural and small-town America, the saloon represented the sins of city life, and represented the cultural tensions between traditional concepts of American life—home and farm—and the growing, immigrant-heavy urban centers. In fact, the 1920 Census for the first time showed more people living in urban areas than in rural parts of the country; the urban population grew by 19 million people over the previous decade, while the rural areas had lost 5 million residents. The political fallout from that would lead Congress to skip the decennial reapportionment of the House of Representatives for the only time since the nation's founding.[14]

Progressives also embraced Prohibition as a means, in their view, of bettering the lives of others. Many, sometimes correctly, saw the saloon as the power base for urban political machines, such as Tammany Hall, and thought eliminating saloons would lead to a more responsive democratic system. Nativists backed it on racist and xenophobic grounds. Alcohol, in their eyes, was the purview of Jews, Catholics, and immigrants from Ireland, Italy, and, worse yet because of the timing of the Great War, Germany.

The Great War led to a range of limitations in the United States, including food—the program that cemented Hoover's reputation as a logistical genius. The ASL, the WCTU, and the other Prohibitionists tied banning alcohol to the war effort, often ginning up statistics about how much grain went into making alcohol that instead should feed soldiers overseas and their children at home. Patriotism demanded sacrifice. Billy Sunday, whose alcohol-denouncing sermons drew thousands of people as he barnstormed across the country, added momentum to the cause.

Congress finally adopted the Eighteenth Amendment in December 1917, eight months after the United States entered the war, by bipartisan margins far exceeding the required two-thirds majority of each house. The measure then went to the states for ratification, a process that required approval by three-fourths of state legislatures or state conventions that were called for the purpose to approve the amendment. Just three weeks later, the Mississippi state legislature became the first to consider the amendment, approving it by near-unanimous votes, and without debate. A year later, Nebraska became the thirty-sixth state legislature to ratify, adding the Eighteenth Amendment to the Constitution.

Because of internal Wet-Dry divides, the major political parties had sat out those battles. But over time the Republican Party became viewed as the Dry party, in part because it held political control in Washington and thus was tied in the public mind with its enforcement. The Democrats, while split, became affiliated with the Wet movement. The lines were solidified with the 1928 presidential election and Hoover's open embrace of Pro-

hibition after outpolling Al Smith, whose Catholicism and support for repeal cost the Democratic Party crucial votes in its
traditional stronghold in the Bible Belt, presaging the eventual
political realignment of Southern conservatives to the Republican Party.

THE FRAMEWORK FOR Repeal Week, the event that brought Sabin
and other socialites to the heart of Wall Street on that May day,
had been set at the Women's Organization for National Prohibition Reform executive committee meeting on February 29 in
Charleston, South Carolina. It included directives for local organizers to cast a wide net by seeking out newspaper and magazine
editors, hotel managers, musicians, and local women's clubs and
unions, with a special focus on trying to enroll supporters among
immigrants, union members, and local businesses, including secretaries and clerks.

In April, the organization held a full conference in Washington to settle plans for the summer. Key among them: persuading
both major political parties to adopt anti-Prohibition planks during their upcoming June presidential nominating conventions.
The organization even drafted suggested wording and, through
their state affiliates, pressed local elected officials and party delegates to come out for repeal by the time they reached the
conventions in Chicago. As Sabin and other group leaders repeated in public speeches, they felt the political moment was ripe.
Political polling was in its infancy, but the *Literary Digest,* a weekly
magazine of current events, routinely canvassed its subscribers
on various issues. In a survey taken in 1930, about 40 percent of
readers who responded said they favored repeal. A new survey reported in April 1932 that support for repeal had nearly doubled to
74 percent, a tidal change in the national mood.[15]

But the women gathered at the Washington conference remained uncertain over whom the organization should endorse
for president. Hoover was expected to easily win the Republican

nomination, and while he defended Prohibition, he still might be endorsable, in the women's eyes, if the Republican Party added a repeal plank to its platform. On the Democratic side, while the party was increasingly viewed as Wet, Roosevelt—the front-runner, but not the assured nominee—had been noncommittal on the issue. So the women decided to wait until after the June conventions and leave the endorsement to their own executive committee, scheduled to meet in July.

But internal fractures were emerging. The women were united in their support for repealing the Eighteenth Amendment, but politically they ranged from left to right, and many could never see themselves voting for a Democrat or, conversely, a Republican, regardless of their stance on Prohibition. Margaret Damrosch, part of the New York delegation, and wife of long-time New York Symphony Orchestra conductor Walter Damrosch, rose to ask whether the executive committee would "decide which one we stand for," and whether that would commit members to "give up our individual vote."[16]

That was the plan, replied Marion Booth Kelly, of Bronxville, a group leader, arguing that she trusted the political judgment of the women on the executive committee to endorse a candidate whom those "who put our patriotism above party loyalty, will be able to support." It was not a unanimous viewpoint. "I am already pledged to a potential candidate," said Florence Whitney, of New York. "I know he is Wet. I am perfectly loyal to this organization, but I never could subscribe" to subjugating her vote to the orders of the executive committee.

But then, asked another member, what good would the Women's Organization for National Prohibition Reform be if it didn't vote as a bloc? They argued back and forth for a bit, debating whether they should vote as a bloc just for the presidential candidate and leave it to the individuals to decide on state-level candidates, and what would happen if, miraculously, both Hoover and the Democratic nominee came out for repeal. They decided that if all the options were Wet, then they should vote for whomever they wished. But absent that, it would be silly after three years of organizing, lobbying, and fighting, to dilute their electoral power just when it mattered most.

Grace Bagley, a longtime Republican activist and devoted suffragette from Boston, sought to put the moment in a broader context than traditional political partisanship. Some issues were party matters, some were not.

"We are in the presence of a great moral issue such as only comes once in a lifetime," she said. "If we are going to save our country from the disastrous results that are now being felt from one end of our country to another, if we are going to keep ourselves from being submerged by the gangsters and the underworld, we have got to put this great issue ahead of every other until it is accomplished."

Loud and prolonged applause erupted, and after a few more minutes of discussion, the question went to a voice vote. An avalanche of "yeses" overwhelmed the solitary "No." But it left unaddressed the fundamental issue: How would anyone know whether the women would, indeed, vote as a bloc? And whether that would be enough to change history?

CHAPTER 8

The Bonus Army Marches

THE U.S. GOVERNMENT OWED Walter Waters money; of that, he was certain. And the government, in fact, agreed. What was in dispute was when exactly that money should be paid— now, as Waters and thousands of other Great War veterans were starving for work and food; or in another thirteen years, as Congress had promised when it passed the Bonus Bill in 1924.

The veterans had their supporters in Washington for making the payments now, including Representative Wright Patman, a Texas Democrat who himself had served in the army during the war. Patman made obtaining "a square deal" for veterans the prime issue in his first run for the House in 1928; shortly after being sworn in, he introduced a bill that would have made the bonus payments immediately. The measure went nowhere, but it cemented Patman as Congress's top advocate for the pro-bonus movement.

Patman tried again in January 1932, but still had trouble finding political support. The Veterans of Foreign Wars were with him—some one thousand members paraded to the Capitol steps on April 8 to deliver a petition—but the much larger and more politically connected American Legion was not. Its leadership felt widows and children of fallen soldiers should be helped before putting money in the living veterans' pockets. Newspaper editorials roundly dismissed the proposal as fiscally dangerous, simultaneously adding to the existing $2 billion federal budget deficit and, by simply printing more money to pay the bonuses, risking devaluing the dollar. The Republican Party, which controlled the Senate, also opposed the measure on fiscal grounds, making it unlikely the bill would pass. And even if it did, President Hoover—like his predecessor, Calvin Coolidge—staunchly opposed spending $2.4 billion in federal funds on what he saw as a relief program.[1]

"Such action would undo every effort that is being made to reduce Government expenditures and balance the budget," Hoover said in a March 29 statement. "The first duty of every citizen of the United States is to build up and sustain the credit of the United States Government. Such an action would irretrievably undermine it." He followed that up in an April 15 press conference arguing that, somehow, consideration of paying the bonus early eroded public faith in the economy, and pointing out that the politics were arrayed against it. "Any canvass of the Senate will show that it is impossible for the bill to become law," Hoover said. "A possible canvass of the House would indicate the same thing at the present stage, and so the public alarm on that is entirely ill-placed."[2]

Hoover read the political tea leaves correctly, at least at the moment. After weeks of delays, the House Ways and Means Committee finally killed the bill in May 1932. For Waters and his fellow veterans, frustration over the bill's death "brought the nucleus" of the march "into a reality." Daily gatherings in Portland about how to force Congress's hand began attracting more people, and Waters and other organizers quickly created a command structure. A former sergeant named Chester A. Hazen emerged as the leader, and organizers required march participants prove they had served during the war and "agree to be law-abiding and to submit to proper discipline as administered by the elected officers." They set May 10 as the date of departure for Washington.[3]

Men signed up by the scores. On the day of the march, they numbered about 280, which the march command divided into units of about forty men each—the Bonus Expeditionary Force, a play on the name of the American Expeditionary Force under which they had served in Europe. Behind a banner that read PORT-LAND BONUS MARCH—ON TO WASHINGTON, the BEF made for the Union Pacific freight yard in Portland. Despite all the attention to self-organizing, mirroring the military structure under which they had served, the Bonus Army had no plan beyond leaving Portland. "Friends were furnishing trucks to take us from the city to the Union Pacific freight yards," Waters wrote. "From there, our plan, on paper, seemed simple, almost childish. We were going to Washington."

The first wrinkle: Nobody could afford train tickets. Union Pacific's managers learned the veterans planned to hop a daily eastbound freight train as it stopped at the Portland yards and ordered the engineer to pass through without slowing, let alone stopping, leaving the men stranded.

And no one arranged to feed the marchers, so as they stretched out that first night in the freight yard, volunteers fanned out to nearby restaurants and stores, seeking food donations. It was, to say the least, an inauspicious start, with veterans ignoring their recently elected commanders, "every man now became a general... and started to issue orders," and in the morning many sleeping through a four o'clock "Reveille." Some men deserted.[4]

The remainder, after an hour of marching drills on "a big sandy flat" near the yard, spent the day getting to know each other and playing cards as they awaited that evening's eastbound freight train. Union Pacific officials arrived and told Waters and the others that they would not be allowed to board cars, and if they stayed in the area, "we'll run the train right through the yards again without stopping." The veterans said fine, they'd line up across the track in a human blockade. They haggled back and forth, threats underscoring the intensity, before the rail officials relented and let the men clamber aboard empty cattle cars parked in the yard that would then be added to the evening train.

"These cars were far from clean—about six inches of dirt on the floors. We searched for a shovel and cleaned it out," one of the veterans, John Steven Murray, wrote in an unpublished diary. Around 8 P.M., the train began its slow roll out of the freight yard. "There were a lot of people down at the railroad to see us off."[5]

At stops along the way veterans' groups donated food and other supplies, but the expedition was less military—or former military—than a rolling mob of the discontented. An advance team under Hazen was supposed to raise money and find food, but ineptitude won out. By the third day the main contingent had traveled only 530 miles—reaching Pocatello, Idaho—with nearly 1,900 more miles to go. "Fortunately, the nation's eyes were not yet on us," Waters recalled. "Had they been, they would have seen a dozen groups of ragged men standing around a dusty lot in a little Idaho town on a cold windy, spring day."

Hazen finally showed up at Pocatello but without money or provisions. As some of the men accused him of pocketing donations, Hazen pulled out a gun, which drew the attention of police monitoring the ragtag band of brothers. The police confiscated Hazen's gun, and his relationship with the marchers ended, so he returned to Portland.

At the start of the expedition, Waters had been appointed as a second-tier commander under Hazen, but in Pocatello, fearing the collapse of his march, he effectively took charge. Waters convened a meeting during which he harangued the veterans over the general disorder into which they had fallen. The men responded and elected the amiable A. F. Taylor as the new commander to take over Hazen's original role as the advance man and put Waters in charge of organizing the motley crew into a more focused and disciplined outfit. Waters appointed a half-dozen men to serve as a security force and another half-dozen men to serve as a "transportation committee," which centralized their efforts to find train schedules and other means of moving eastward. He also established a commissary of sorts, appointing a chief steward—former army supply sergeant Jim Foley—to keep track of supplies and donations.

Once Waters reorganized the group, he arranged for permission from Pocatello municipal officials for a parade that served several purposes. First it gave the men a sense of pride and mission. But it also began to raise their public profile and their funds. As the veterans marched to "the beat of a borrowed drum," Waters dispatched four men to stroll through the small crowd, collecting donations; they picked up $20.

That night, aided by sympathetic rail crews, the veterans switched to the Northern Pacific Railway line headed to Cheyenne, Wyoming. They were greeted that evening with a hot meal prepared in mule-drawn kitchens from a nearby army post, arranged by a veteran who worked for the railroad; then they held another parade, where they were cheered on by a couple of thousand locals. A few hours later, the men reboarded the same railcars, now coupled to another train, and rolled eastward through Nebraska to Omaha, then across the Missouri River to Council Bluffs, Iowa, arriving around six o'clock in the morning, where they hoped to shift to the Wabash line and continue to East St. Louis, Illinois.

Newspapers had yet to take note of the Bonus Expeditionary Force, but, clearly, messages were being sent ahead to veterans' groups about its status and arrival times. At Council Bluffs, Waters had been led to believe the Wabash line would be just as accommodating as the Northern Pacific. But over the course of the day, cooperation by local train workers was trumped by orders from higher-ups to not let the men board the freight cars.

When he got that news, Waters took a couple members of the transportation committee with him to meet the rail line's local trainmaster, who reiterated that the men would not be allowed aboard the freight train. Waters returned to the men and filled them in. They discussed climbing atop the cars, anyway, and ride on the roofs as far as they could, but decided that tunnels and bridges posed too serious a danger. As midnight neared, bringing the departure of the train, the men gathered along the tracks. At a signal the engineer gave two blasts on the horn and began to move forward, but "suddenly there was the blatant hiss of escaping air and the train parted in the middle." Some former rail workers among the veterans had uncoupled part of the train.

The yard crew hurriedly reattached the cars and the engineer tried again, but once more, the sound of hissing air broke the night and the train separated. And again. And again. The engineer gave up and said he wouldn't move the train unless the marchers were allowed to board, and Waters and the trainmaster walked off to the office, where a hurried telephone call was placed to higher-ups to whom the trainmaster reported the standoff and relayed that his calls to the police and the local sheriff to intervene were fruitless. The trainmaster hung up and led Waters to four empty freight cars on a siding and told him to board the men. After which, the cars were coupled to the train, and in the early hours of morning, the engineer tried once again to head east. This time the train chugged off into the darkness.

THE BEF HAD been on the road for more than a week now, and news reporters had finally picked up the scent. On May 20, the *St. Louis Globe-Democrat* reported that four hundred veterans were "in virtual possession of a Wabash freight train, having compelled the crew to add five extra cars at Council Bluffs" and would arrive that very morning at the Wabash rail yard in the North St. Louis neighborhood. The article, citing unidentified railroad officials, described the travelers as "a semi-military organization under the leadership of W. W. Waters of Portland" headed to Washington, D.C., "where a hearing before President Hoover will be sought in an effort to bring about payment of the soldiers' bonus."[6]

The men intended to shift to the Baltimore and Ohio line at East St. Louis and continue their eastbound journey. The industrious reporter spoke with C. C. Farmer, the local freight manager for the B&O, who said he had wired his superiors in Cincinnati and doubted the rail line would take any steps to try to keep the men from boarding their freight cars.

"How can you arrest 500 men?" Farmer told the reporter, noting that countless drifters were already riding the rails in search of jobs and food. "After all, why should we discriminate against veterans? Why, I counted almost that many on a freight the other day, and I guess the men will ride free if they are lucky enough to find spaces."

A version of the *Globe-Democrat*'s story, including its inflated numbers of men and description of "commandeered" cars, and augmented in some cases by reporting from a United Press reporter in St. Louis, went over the national wires. In city after city the details were too delicious for wire editors to resist. Variations of the article appeared in more than five hundred newspapers that same day, and nearly four hundred more newspapers the next day. Overnight the quixotic effort by some three hundred hungry and broke Portland veterans became a national cause.[7]

Farmer did not, in fact, speak for the B&O line when he said it would not interfere with the men. B&O officials arrived at the marchers' makeshift camp in North St. Louis armed with an injunction barring the veterans from boarding their freight cars, which Waters and the other veterans dismissed as just another hurdle.

The veterans spent the night of May 22 sleeping in the Wabash box cars in which they had arrived, and the next morning were summoned by a bugler to gather. The plan, they were told, was to march some twelve miles from the North St. Louis freight yards across the Mississippi River to the East St. Louis yards where B&O operated its trains. A local veteran with a truck had been enlisted during the night to move the expedition's baggage and supplies, enabling the men to march unencumbered.

They faced two options for crossing the river: a toll bridge, or a free public bridge that would add two miles to the march. Waters opted for the toll bridge, even though they didn't have toll money for three hundred men.

They set out a little after 7:30 A.M. under partly cloudy skies and marched, six to eight abreast, some three miles south to the entrance of the massive McKinley Bridge. As they neared the toll booth, they picked up their pace and, "looking neither to left nor right," moved in a silent block past the toll collector, who did nothing to try to collect the fees. On the Illinois end of the bridge, a motorcycle slipped in front and escorted the marchers seven miles southeast to the B&O freight yard, where the men set up camp on a nearby vacant lot and under the gaze of some two dozen railroad police officers.

As local veterans arrived to deliver food and other supplies—and, in some cases, to present their discharge papers and join the march—Waters spent portions of the day negotiating with B&O security chief P. J. Young, though the talks were one-sided. Waters promised that his men would stay out of the rail yard until an eastbound freighter was ready to move and kept trying to find ways to gain permission for the men to board the cars. At one point he offered to pay $75 a car; Young said the fee would be $5,000 a car.

Waters returned to the camp and arranged yet another parade, this one in the heart of East St. Louis, while Young added more officers to his security force. Activity within the rail yard itself slowly picked up—a tactic, it turned out, to obscure the assembling of an eastbound freighter, which rail officials hoped would go unnoticed amid the broader shuffling around of railcars.

The ruse didn't work. An informant in the yard alerted the marchers that a train was about to pull out, and Waters hastily arranged the men into a line, two abreast, and they moved into the rail yard, their numbers overwhelming the rail police detachment. In short order they were spread out over the train, perched on the top of sealed boxcars, and sprawled over open-top coal and cinder cars. Young approached Waters and demanded the men get off the train; Waters refused; the train stayed right where it was, and no other trains left the yard that night. The veterans may have captured the train, but it may as well have been a tree.

In the morning the veterans finally climbed down. "I, for one, was nearly froze as the cinders were wet so it was pretty cold towards morning," Murray wrote. The men returned to their camp in the vacant lot. The confrontation had drawn more police attention, with the rail force now numbering about 150 men, including local police standing watch over a growing crowd of occasionally belligerent supporters of the Bonus Marchers. The next day the men saw another train being assembled and made for it. "The boys went over this bank and across them tracks and it looked just like going over the top in France," Murray wrote. After another stalemated discussion between Waters and Young, the uncoupled engine pulled away, leaving the railcars standing on the track. The men once again climbed down.

B&O officials turned to the state for help, and Lieutenant Governor Fred E. Sterling, temporarily in charge while Governor Louis Emmerson was out of state, deployed six companies of the Illinois National Guard to East St. Louis. The order, and the arrival of armed troops, increased both the tension and speculation, particularly in the newspapers, of a pending violent showdown. The violence at Ford's Rouge Plant in Detroit two months earlier remained fresh in the nation's mind.

B&O tried one last gambit. Using smaller engines designed to shuttle cars around a yard, and generally lacking the power to move full trains long distances, they began moving a few cars at a time out of the rail yard. The veterans noticed the activity, but dismissed it as routine car shuffling, until a full engine coupled to a tender and a caboose roared to life and began moving out. Some of the transportation committee men hopped aboard the tender, the open-top car carrying coal to fuel the train, and learned that the engine was headed for Caseyville, seven miles away, where it would couple itself to the single cars that had already been moved out and form the eastbound train.

A madcap scene ensued of disheveled veterans running down the tracks, then getting picked up by cars driven by supporters, who sped them on to Caseyville, arriving around the same time as the engine. The first few arrivals were the front edge of a tide; eventually all the men, now numbering well over three hundred, with fresh volunteers, once again clambered aboard a train.

And, once again, the engine shut down and the train didn't budge.

WATERS MISSED THAT scene. Exactly what happened to him remains murky. In his memoir Waters claimed that he resigned as part of a ruse. On the second day of the showdown with B&O, he approached Young and delivered an ultimatum, with two reporters conveniently within earshot: If B&O did not relent by 3 P.M. and let the men board a freight train, Waters would "quit as leader and take no more blame for anything that happens. You can take your choice of letting a responsible group ride a freight on your road, or, if you wish, of having three hundred [leaderless] individuals to deal with."

Unsurprisingly, Young ignored the ultimatum, and Waters quit and disappeared. Waters wrote in his memoir that he had already arranged an alternative resolution with local American Legion officials. If the men couldn't ride the rails, they would ride the roads in a caravan of trucks and cars, two hundred miles east, to another rail hub at Washington, Indiana. Waters wrote that he moved ahead to ready Washington for their arrival, but George

Alman, a former lumberjack and infantryman who helped organize the departure from Portland, said that Waters had simply disappeared, leaving the expedition in the lurch. And as one of the expedition organizers, Alman, presumably, would have been among those who were in on Waters's ruse. Another explanation was floated that Waters simply sought to avoid arrest. Three days after Waters left, the *St. Louis Post-Dispatch* reported that he was in Indiana awaiting the men.[8]

Regardless, the veterans were about to resume their travels. Despite Waters's assertion that he arranged with local American Legionnaires for the escape from East St. Louis, news accounts credited St. Clair County sheriff Jerome Munie with finding cars and trucks to ferry the men across Illinois to the Indiana state line. The convoy pulled out of Caseyville around 9 A.M., to cheers of a crowd of several hundred people, many of whom had driven in from elsewhere in the region to support the marchers and see the spectacle. "It was the most exciting time Caseyville had experienced in years," the *St. Louis Star and Times* reported. "The streets were jammed with automobiles."[9]

The showdown in East St. Louis was natural newspaper fodder; and as word of the Bonus Expeditionary Force spread across the nation, the cause became contagious. Small groups formed in different cities and began their own plans for heading to Washington, first as a trickle, then as a wave. Thirty veterans from Utah arrived in Chicago aboard boxcars en route to Washington. In Camden, New Jersey, calls for up to one thousand veterans went out, though only a couple of hundred would eventually join. Four hundred veterans in San Francisco moved out, and another one hundred veterans awaited them in Sacramento. An integrated group of some two hundred veterans formed in and around New Orleans and, despite initial interference from segregationist police, made their way to the capital, too.[10]

In Washington, officials began trying to figure out how to handle the expected arrival of several thousand veterans, few of whom had any money or access to food or even basic shelter. Much of the response fell to Police Superintendent Pelham D. Glassford, a retired Great War brigadier general, who, after his November 1931 appointment, liked to ride around the city on a police motorcycle. He initially sought to head off the veterans by meeting with White House and congressional officials in a vain effort to persuade them to act on the Bonus Bill. If the veterans got their bonus, they would turn round, he reasoned. He also sounded out the Department of War, and other military offices, for financial help in buying tents, food, and other supplies, and stated publicly that unless the federal government agreed to provide support for the veterans, he would order the men out after forty-eight hours. Still, Glassford was rebuffed at every turn.

Some space remained available in the city's existing shelters, and Glassford arranged to use several vacant commercial buildings to house the vets. Realizing that demand would quickly outpace that meager supply, Glassford designated an open field in Anacostia, across the river in Southeast D.C., to be the site of a makeshift camp to be built by the arriving veterans themselves. And Glassford worked with local supporters to arrange fundraisers, including music revues and boxing matches. Most significantly, Glassford had attended a meeting of the marchers already in the District, who had named themselves the Bonus Expeditionary Force, following the lead of news articles about Waters's group. Glassford addressed the men twice and ended up getting elected secretary-treasurer in charge of a small food budget. More radical minds in the bonus army read that as a sign that the protest had been co-opted by the authorities.[11]

Elsewhere in the capital plans of a different type were being made. Inside the ornate Department of War building, to the west of the White House, chief of staff General Douglas MacArthur and his top aide, Major General George Van Horn Moseley (whose own top aide was Major Dwight D. Eisenhower), were receiving intelligence reports about the flow of men to Washington, D.C., and about possible communist involvement.

MacArthur directed Moseley to oversee arrangements to defend federal installations, should the march evolve into something more insidious. And he directed Moseley to revise "Emergency Plan White," which the military drew up in 1923 in response to political unrest and labor strikes that fueled overblown fears of revolution by Bolsheviks, anarchists, and other radicals. With the rise of fascism in Europe, fear of a leftist insurrection was joined by fear of violence from the right. Though Plan White focused on quelling domestic disturbances, it also was a "carefully crafted contingency plan intended to meet and crush a radical revolution." Under its parameters Moseley ordered several tanks and troop transports be repositioned to military sites close to the capital in case they were needed.[12]

Waters and his Bonus Expeditionary Force knew nothing about the preparations under way in D.C. At each state line the men were greeted by state or local police and convoys of cars and trucks—often provided by state highway departments—to move them forward, a combination show of support for the politically popular marchers and a desire by state leaders not to let an encampment on their soil become a financial burden. From Washington, Indiana, the men were trucked to Zanesville, Ohio, and from there through West Virginia to Pennsylvania, where national guardsmen took charge of the convoy, intending to speed them through the state in five hours to the Maryland border.

At Zanesville, Waters had received a telegram from Representative Patman asking him to get to Washington a few hours before the rest of his contingent to "confer with the officials with regard to the program there." A Cincinnati-based Secret Service official also summoned Waters to a hotel meeting and questioned him "about my men, who was who, what their motives were in coming to" Washington, D.C. The Secret Service had kept the marchers under surveillance, fearing they might pose a threat to

Hoover's safety, but the agent informed Waters he believed they were not a threat.[13]

Late on May 28, the caravan stopped for the night at an ice rink in Cumberland, Maryland, planning to arrive in Washington, D.C., the next day, a Sunday. "We had traveled across three thousand miles in 18 days," Waters wrote. "I had left Portland with no intention or desire to do anything more than to bring the company across the continent. That was done. But the response from ex-servicemen in other states now made the problem a far different one . . . Seemingly some common chord that moves men had been touched."[14]

CHAPTER 9

On the Fringes

ERBERT HOOVER WASN'T A POPULAR nominee among Republican leaders before the 1928 election, and as president he
did little to curry their favor. He saw himself as outside—or
above, even—the traditional political world, and distrusted the
compromisers and dealmakers who made Washington, D.C.,
run. He viewed patronage as unethical, though he wasn't so pure
that he wouldn't find an appointment for a political friend or potential rival if he saw his own advantage in it.[1]

For instance, by early 1932, wealthy Pittsburgh financier Andrew Mellon, whom Hoover held over as treasury secretary from
the Harding/Coolidge administrations as a sop to Wall Street,
had become a lightning rod for progressive Democrats. Texas
congressman Wright Patman—the veterans' Bonus Bill advocate—had gone so far as to sponsor an impeachment movement
in the House over allegations that Mellon's government policies
and decisions directly affected his own business and financial interests. At the same time Hoover wanted the U.S. ambassador to
Great Britain, Chicago businessman and former vice president
Charles Dawes, to return and lead the Reconstruction Finance
Corporation. So Hoover gave the seventy-six-year-old Mellon an

international plum and packed him off to London, ending the impeachment process and removing a potential political liability from Hoover's cabinet ahead of his reelection campaign, and adding Dawes's business acumen and power of persuasion—he was a noted desk pounder—to the work of the RFC.[2]

Still, no sitting Republican president had failed to win nomination in the party's history, so the 1932 nomination appeared to be Hoover's for the asking. And despite moments of pique in which he disavowed interest (usually after someone criticized him), Hoover was, indeed, asking for the nomination. Theodore G. Joslin, the press secretary, noted that while Hoover blanched at the prospect of campaigning, he "wants another term more than he wants anything else. He wants to demonstrate his ability under favorable conditions." In fact, Hoover's inaugural address had laid out two terms' worth of proposals, many of which—such as reorganizing the executive branch, including the criminal justice system, and expanding public health services—had been sidetracked by the economic collapse.[3]

By February, Hoover had begun to focus more on the coming election. He ordered Joslin to oversee the compilation of extensive research on more than thirty issues that he had dealt with during his years of public service and prepare reports on each, then send them to congressional supporters to enter into the Congressional Record, the extensive index/record/journal of daily congressional activity. Hoover believed that if the voters considered his full record, they would give him their support, a remarkably naïve reading of the political landscape.[4]

Internal Republican opposition festered. Hoover had been aligned with the progressive wing of the party, embodied by the late Theodore Roosevelt, who favored a more active government than did the Old Guard traditional conservatives. Early in his presidency Hoover backed initiatives to improve the health of children, investigate the roots of poverty, and assess the nature of crime and policing. He also introduced what he perceived to be a sense of professionalism in how the White House operated, running it like a business instead of a political enterprise. Hoover's progressivism, though, had its limits. He fundamentally believed in a minimal role for government and thought most social problems should be addressed by leaders of the communities in which they occurred.[5]

The Republican Old Guard, which included powerful members of Congress, never accepted or trusted Hoover. As president he issued relatively few vetoes—thirty-seven altogether—yet each one made it more difficult to attract support for his own initiatives. After the Republicans lost control of the House in early 1931, and maintained control of the Senate only through Vice President Curtis's power to cast tie-breaking votes, key party leaders' dissatisfaction with Hoover as the party's standard-bearer only deepened.[6]

In late April, Thomas Lamont, a partner and key figure in the J. P. Morgan banking operations, and investment banker Otto Kahn, a Wet liberal Republican who described Hoover's handling of the depression as "persistently unskillful," invited about twenty "financial and industrial leaders" to a secret gathering in New York City. Lamont and Kahn played significant roles in the Old Guard and feared that Hoover was unlikely to win reelection, opening the door for Democrats to increase government regulation and involvement in their business affairs.[7]

The party needed a new candidate, they argued. Someone in whom the nation could have more faith than Hoover. Someone like former president Calvin Coolidge, whose decision not to seek reelection four years earlier had left the party—and the nation—with Hoover. They urged the group to send a delegation to visit Coolidge at his home in Northampton, Massachusetts, to talk him into answering the call of party and country and challenge Hoover for the nomination.

They didn't appreciate exactly how far Coolidge had removed himself from political life. When Coolidge left the White House, he and his wife returned to their half of an in-town Northampton duplex they had rented for more than twenty years. The duplex sat close to the sidewalk, and quickly became a tourist draw, especially when Coolidge tried to relax on the front porch. On some days thick traffic blocked the street, causing a ruckus and annoying neighbors who had their own daily lives to lead.

A year later, Coolidge and his wife bought a twelve-room house on nine acres of land outside of the town center, overlooking an oxbow of the Connecticut River. The new house, called The Beeches, sat at the end of a long private driveway, hidden from prying eyes and ensconcing the couple in easily controlled privacy. And if the physical distancing wasn't clear enough, Coolidge published an article in a September 1931 issue of the *Saturday Evening Post* saying that he had no intention of running again, urged the Republican Party to stay the course with Hoover, and emphasized the "necessity of standing by its principles and supporting its loyal leaders."[8]

It's unclear whether any of the financial elites summoned by Lamont and Kahn accepted the challenge to try to woo Coolidge back from The Beeches, but two participants in the meeting, stunned at such an audacious act of betrayal, called Hoover intimate Henry M. Robinson, a California banker, who, in turn, called the White House.

Joslin, the president's secretary, reported that Hoover was "irate" over the plot. "That shows how much of a friend Lamont is," Hoover steamed. "Of course, Kahn would do anything, but I didn't think it of Lamont." Hoover described the effort as a "stupid action and if it bears any fruit at all, it cannot but make for further trouble. It is unthinkable Coolidge would even consider it." It was unthinkable—Coolidge had no intention of giving up his quiet routine of answering letters, writing an occasional newspaper column, napping, and walking his dogs.[9]

The only direct challenge Hoover faced for the nomination came from former U.S. senator Joseph I. France, of Maryland, who announced in April 1931 that he would run as an alternative. France had served one term in the Senate from 1917 to 1923, where he aligned with the so-called "irreconcilables" opposed to the U.S. joining the League of Nations. But France focused primarily on Prohibition. A strong Wet, he decided to challenge Hoover because he felt the president "lacked the candor and the courage to state boldly and clearly where he stands upon this." The *Baltimore Sun* noted that France's candidacy, while not likely to succeed, could at least roil the Republican waters. "When anyone asks that direct question" on Prohibition, "he makes things embarrassing for the Republican politicians."[10]

Nationally, the Republican state-level primaries received scant attention, primarily because Hoover had a presumed lock on the nomination. And primaries were largely advisory: party leaders would select most of the delegates to the national convention. But the contests still drew attention as a barometer of where the party faithful stood. In the March 8 New Hampshire primary, Hoover's slate of delegates, the only ones on the ballot, took a sweeping victory in a surprisingly heavy turnout for an election with no drama. But over the next two months, France, financing his own campaign, won delegate slates or nonbinding "presidential preference" votes in North Dakota, Nebraska, Illinois, and Pennsylvania (in some he was the only candidate), with Hoover winning only Massachusetts. What seemed at first a gnatlike presence was becoming quite bothersome to Hoover, so he and his circle decided to give it a swat.[11]

France's adopted home state of Maryland, where he lived on a farm owned by his wife, the widow of a wealthy businessman, loomed next on the primary calendar. Hoover filed for the primary just minutes before the deadline, and two and a half weeks later trounced France, taking 60 percent of the vote at a time when "favorite son" candidates usually prevailed. The gnat was done for, and what little wind France had behind him dissipated. "Please, just one more reference to the forgotten man," *The New York Times* wrote after the primary, playing off Roosevelt's now-famous speech. "He has been identified . . . He is Joseph Irwin France."[12]

Hoover also kept a close eye on the field of Democratic candidates, carefully weighing how he might fare against each in the November election. Like other observers, he saw the early rise of Franklin Roosevelt as a wild card mixed into the deck and greeted Al Smith's emergence as a possible contender as "my first real break" in his chances for reelection. A scramble among several well-supported Democrats for the nomination could only help the Republicans, Hoover believed, by forcing the Democratic candidates to take and defend public stances on such divisive issues as Prohibition, tariffs, and farm policies. And it would require the Democrats to spend campaign funds much earlier in the cycle, tasking the eventual nominee with simultaneously reuniting a divided party, replenishing cash reserves from donors who had supported his rivals, and mounting a national campaign against an incumbent, even one severely weakened by the national crisis.[13]

FRANKLIN ROOSEVELT HELD deep confidence in his chances for the Democratic nomination. Beyond the family name, Roosevelt's warm and usually engaging disposition came across in public as confident and reassuring, a sharp contrast to the wooden Hoover. Press coverage of Roosevelt's anti-depression policies in New York was mostly favorable, and his political popularity in the state—the nation's largest with forty-seven electoral votes—gave him added appeal among Democrats tired of losing presidential elections. And the letter-writing campaign by James A. Farley and Louis McHenry Howe had created an impressive network.

Not everyone had the same confidence in Roosevelt as he had in himself, though. In December 1931, influential newspaper columnist and political analyst Walter Lippmann derided Roosevelt's lack of specific policy proposals. The economic crisis was "paramount" for the nation, but Roosevelt avoided offering solutions and proposals, which frustrated Lippmann and others in the intellectual class. "Governor Roosevelt belongs to the new post-war school of politicians who do not believe in stating their views unless and until there is no avoiding it," Lippmann wrote.[14]

A few weeks later, and just days before Roosevelt's January letter publicly acknowledging his candidacy for the Democratic nomination, Lippmann took aim again, dismissing Roosevelt as an inconsequential intellect, the embodiment of upper-class privilege, and a man "without a firm grasp of public affairs and without very strong convictions." To Lippmann, Roosevelt was a glad-hander whose ability to drift around issues without taking a stance left him as amorphous as the face of the Cheshire cat. "He is not the dangerous enemy of anything. He is too eager to please ... He is no crusader. He is no tribune of the people. He is no enemy of entrenched privilege. He is a pleasant man who, without any important qualifications for the office, would very much like to be President."[15]

It was an eviscerating take that stunned Roosevelt's inner circle. They had joked darkly among themselves about earlier Lippmann columns, but couldn't figure out a response to the new one. Howe, in New York City, clipped the article from the *New York Herald Tribune* and sent it to his boss in Albany, advising him that the column had run widely around the country. "I do not think that there is anything we can do about it, but I would advise you to read the article." In the end Roosevelt said nothing publicly and left no record of his private thoughts. The response was silence, deciding to focus the campaign on the parts they could control.

Roosevelt got the politics right, and, despite Lippmann's frustrations, detailed policy proposals really didn't matter for most voters at that point. Roosevelt knew there would be proposals later, birthed by his Brain Trust. For now, the nation was ailing, Hoover's limited response to such broad and deep need made him vulnerable, and Roosevelt was selling *himself,* and his track record as New York governor, as the solution.[16]

Publisher William Randolph Hearst, though, had another solution in mind: Speaker of the House John Nance Garner, of
Texas. Hearst, owner of the largest newspaper chain in the country, had made his own run for the Democratic presidential
nomination in 1904, while serving in the House of Representatives (he and Garner entered at the same time). Despite his role
as a leading cheerleader for the United States to go to war with
Spain in 1898 over Cuban independence, Hearst was a long-
standing isolationist. He opposed the United States entering the
Great War and argued through his newspapers against joining
the League of Nations. And as he looked at the field of potential
1932 Democratic candidates, he saw an array of affirmed or suspected internationalists.

Garner was not an internationalist. But he also wasn't interested in running. Recently installed as House Speaker, Garner
had a thin Democratic majority and a legislative program he
wanted to push through. He had spent years jockeying for the
Speaker's chair, and he feared entering the presidential campaign
would jeopardize his legislative ambitions. Also, as a delegate
Garner had witnessed firsthand the 103-ballot fiasco at the 1924
Democratic convention and had a keen appreciation for the risks
the party faced if it descended into another fratricidal war. He
privately told journalist Bascom Timmons, a fellow native Texan
who ran his own news service from Washington, D.C., that the
Roosevelt-Smith rift already strained party unity, which would
face a further challenge from the number of favorite-son candidates in different states. "I don't want to jeopardize our cohesion
and the legislative program by a presidential candidacy of my
own," Garner said.[17]

But then came Hearst. He arrived at the KFI-Radio station in
Los Angeles on the evening of January 2, 1932, to deliver a speech
broadcast nationwide, to be reprinted the next day in his newspapers, denouncing Woodrow Wilson's internationalist policies
that had "cost the nation thousands of lives and thousands of

millions of dollars and contributed no material benefit to any single citizen who was not a war contractor." The Democratic Party, Hearst complained, had followed Wilson "up a political blind alley, and everyone who has followed in his footsteps has crashed against the stone wall of defeat" in ensuing presidential elections. He went on to argue bizarrely that Hoover's unpopularity arose from his history in the Wilson administration, conveniently overlooking the current economic crisis. The leading Democratic candidates, including Roosevelt and Smith, "are all good men in their way, but all internationalists" and "disciples of Woodrow Wilson."[18]

But not Garner, "a loyal American citizen, a plain man of the plain people," whose "heart is with his own people. His interest is in his own country." Hearst concluded that he wasn't telling Democrats whom they should support, but he clearly intended to propel Garner as a candidate without having first discussed it with the Texan. And he followed the endorsement up with a serialized biography of Garner that ran in all of Hearst's California papers, then collected and republished as a nationally distributed pamphlet, *The Speaker of the House.*[19]

Reporters pestered Garner with questions about his intentions and his chances, much to the Texas Democrat's annoyance. Some of the reporters were from the Hearst papers and radio stations under orders from Hearst himself to push Garner's candidacy as hard as they could, even as Garner refused to take part. "Our friend refuses to talk politics or devote any attention to any campaign or allow any manager to be appointed to coordinate efforts being made on his behalf," Hearst wrote in a telegram to Victor Watson, one of his crusading editors in New York. Garner's presidential future lay in their hands, Hearst said. "If Garner gets in the way he will be run over by his own boom. The people do not care what he wants. It is a question now of what they want."[20]

In mid-February, after Smith announced that he would answer his party's call if it came at the convention, two Texas senators pledged to put Garner's name forward at the convention. That took the Texas delegation from the Roosevelt column, at least in the early balloting, making it harder for him to reach the two-thirds majority required for the nomination under party rules.

On the West Coast, where Hearst had significant influence, former Wilson treasury secretary William Gibbs McAdoo also backed Garner, after failing to win the presidential nomination himself in 1920 and 1924. He remained deeply distrustful of any New York Democrat who had ever touched Tammany Hall, and that included Roosevelt. But his support for Garner was also opportunistic. McAdoo hoped that by leading a successful charge for Garner in the California primary, he might also position himself to win a Senate seat in the general election.[21]

The early Democratic primaries revealed the depth of the Democratic Party rivalries. Roosevelt won New Hampshire, which had been considered solidly behind Smith, who dominated the urbanized area around Manchester, while Roosevelt prevailed in the rest of the mostly rural state. With the backing of its powerful party machine, Smith easily took Massachusetts, a state in which his Wet stance helped and his Catholicism barely mattered. The victory, Smith claimed, had the effect of "putting a chock under the wheels" of the Roosevelt bandwagon.

Illinois followed by backing its own senator, James Hamilton Lewis, in a race Roosevelt sat out, part of a shrewd strategy to let the favorite sons have their runs in their home states, in hopes of picking up their delegates in later ballots at the convention. Next up was Pennsylvania, which Roosevelt won by a margin less than predicted, leading newspaper coverage to frame it as a win for the Stop Roosevelt faction. But it also galvanized Roosevelt supporters in the Midwest and South, states that initially planned to send unaligned delegations to the convention began to maneuver to send them as Roosevelt delegates.[22]

Pennsylvania officials were still counting ballots when California Democrats went to the polls for their primary on May 3, and, in a major upset, Garner won with 41 percent of the vote to Roosevelt's 32 percent. Smith trailed badly with 26 percent. The result meant that the Democratic National Convention would indeed be a political brawl. Garner, with Texas and California behind him, and Smith picking up states here and there, meant the Stop Roosevelt movement had a path to victory.[23]

Hoover watched the Democratic scrum from the White House and debated with aides and advisors over how to read the results. Despite their earlier friendship Hoover shared Lippmann's low regard for Roosevelt and believed the New York governor would be the Democrat he could most easily beat. But after the Massachusetts and Pennsylvania primaries, Hoover thought Roosevelt's campaign was in trouble, and after California, Hoover said, somewhat ruefully, that this "just about ends Roosevelt. He can't get the Democratic nomination now."

Hoover anticipated that the convention would turn to someone like former Wilson war secretary Newton D. Baker, a force in the Democratic Party, or Maryland governor Albert Ritchie, both of whom, in Hoover's eyes, had the gravitas and seriousness Roosevelt lacked and thus would be much more difficult to beat.[24]

THROUGH THE WINTER and early spring, Milo Reno and other farm advocates had traveled across Iowa, meeting with farmers and speaking at meetings, picnics, and any other gathering where they found a willing audience. Patience with Washington, D.C., and with a political solution to the farm crisis, had long ago dissipated, and they felt they embodied Roosevelt's notion of "the forgotten man."

On May 4, the farmers convened a daylong meeting at the Iowa State Fairgrounds on the east side of Des Moines. Nearly all sectors had representatives—the dairy producers, men and a few women raising crops, and livestock farmers trading in hogs, beef cows, and chickens. The crowd, numbering around two thousand, mostly belonged to the Iowa Farmers Union, but other attendees, including Farm Bureau members and a few labor union organizers and veterans, hailed from Illinois, Minnesota, Missouri, Montana, Nebraska, Oklahoma, and Wisconsin.[25]

Over the course of the day and amid endless demands for action, the attendees organized themselves into a new Farmers' Holiday Association. They elected Reno to serve as its president, a choice that seemed inevitable, given Reno's years of evangelizing the concept of a farmers' strike. In an overwhelming voice vote taken after hours of pleas and condemnations of banks, the Eastern establishment (with a thinly veiled undercurrent of anti-Semitism), and governmental inaction, the farmers followed Reno's lead and agreed to a monthlong holiday during which they would neither sell their products nor buy material to support their businesses.

"Our object and aim is to give to the farmer the right to production costs, a right that is fundamental and necessary to his future existence," Reno wrote later. "We demand a right to the same exemption from . . . evictions as has been conceded to the banks of the nation." The farmers would be patient as the federal government developed programs to alleviate the farmers' suffering, but only "if they will stop the confiscations of the farmers' homes and property until the present deplorable condition is corrected."[26]

```
      ┌──────────────────────┐
      │      CHAPTER 10      │
      └──────────────────────┘
```

The Bonus Army Arrives

THE OREGON BONUS MARCHERS REACHED the Washington, D.C. border around 5:30 P.M. on Sunday, May 29, aboard sixteen trucks supplied by the state of Maryland and sporting a range of American flags. The Associated Press described the trip as "a transcontinental hitchhike" of "weather-beaten, travel-stained and dog-tired men" who were greeted by three hundred or so people drawn to the curiosity of it all. Among the greeters, somewhat surprisingly, was Walter Waters, who had once again slipped away from his men while they slept in Cumberland, Maryland, and took a 2 A.M. train to meet with Representative Patman at 8 A.M. and Police Superintendent Glassford at 9 A.M.[1]

In Waters's retelling in his memoir, Patman sought assurances that the marchers would not credit Patman with drawing them to D.C., seemingly to avoid political fallout, should the march turn violent or if the national opinion, now favorable, turned against them. "He was so nervous, so very, very nervous," Waters wrote. The commander assured the congressman that he had nothing to fear, he would tell everyone the truth: The men had come on their own volition.

The Glassford meeting was more useful. Waters found him to be "friendly, courteous and above all humanly considerate." Glassford told Waters he had arranged for the Oregon men to billet in a shuttered department store at the corner of Eighth and I Streets SE, less than half a mile north of the Navy Yard on the Anacostia River, and a mile southeast of the Capitol Building. After he toured the building, Waters took a nap among other veterans camped out on the lawn of the District of Columbia courthouse across from Glassford's office in the police headquarters. In the late afternoon a police detachment picked him up and drove him to the district line to greet his arriving men. After a hot meal, provided by a national guardsmen mess, the three hundred men crowded into the department store for the night.

The next day Waters met with contingents from the one thousand or so veterans who had already arrived. They agreed to fold their loosely organized groups under Waters's Oregon unit in part because, they said, they had been drawn to the capital by news reports about Waters and his men. Waters was at a bit of a loss—he knew none of the other groups or their representatives. He was skittish about putting them in positions of significant authority, but "I could not put members of the Oregon group in every leading position."

Waters appointed George Alman, who had come with him from Portland, as his chief aide, in charge of figuring out where to shelter the men, and a former boxer named Mickey Dolan as his personal bodyguard, though Waters didn't spell out why he felt he needed one. He then asked the other groups to send him a couple of names each for leadership roles, and after interviewing a dozen men, he selected F. A. Ross, of Texas, as supply officer and Owen Lucas, of the Bronx, as a second aide. In an ominous turn Waters also designated a handful of men, whose identities would not be widely known, to lead a secret service and "inform me of any radicalism growing beneath the surface; they were to keep their eyes and ears open for Communists or for any agitators trying to turn the B.E.F. to their own uses."

It was not an irrational fear, but the designs and presence of communists constituted a minor part of the whole. As part of its efforts to organize class struggle in the United States, the Communist Party USA had formed specific groups to insinuate themselves into demonstrations. The party's Unemployed Councils had played significant roles in organizing hunger marches around the nation, including the fatal confrontation at the Ford Rouge plant in March. It also had created the Workers Ex-Servicemen's League to organize veterans into a political force, which, in turn, had made agitating for early payment of the veterans' bonus one of its objectives.

But the league had yet to make much of a showing. Communists were scattered among the marchers, but most weren't there as an organized unit. Rather, they tended to be people drawn individually to leftist beliefs in part as a response to the economic collapse and/or their war experience. To many people on the left, the United States entered the war mainly to ensure the European combatants paid their debts to American companies. In fact, the Communist Party struggled to keep what it saw as a golden opportunity from slipping away.

"The spontaneous outburst of the Bonus March created a crisis in the central committee of the Communist Party, because the party, although working for the creation of such a movement, had, as it were, missed the boat in getting it started," Joseph Kornfeder, a top party official, later recalled. "So it started by itself and the problem then arose as to what could be done to get hold of this runaway movement and catch up with it."[2]

In fact, there may have been more undercover Secret Service agents intermingled with the different groups of veterans than there were communists. The agency, responsible for protecting the president and his family since the 1901 assassination of President William McKinley, reacted to the hunger marches—

including one that ended on the Capitol Building steps—by directing its operatives to join groups as they could. They found few radicals among the veterans. "They had little influence on the men," Edmund W. Starling, who had joined the White House security detail during the Wilson administration, recalled in his memoir. "The veterans were Americans, down on their luck but by no means ready to overthrow their government."[3]

The not-so-subtle distinction between communists and "Americans" reflected a broad view among federal authorities that communists were mainly foreign agitators. And the main exception to Starling's observation was a veterans' group being organized in Detroit by John Pace, a Kentuckian by birth, who joined the Communist Party USA in the winter of 1930 through 1931, and almost immediately was assigned to organize workers' councils in Michigan, including a May 1931 hunger march in Lansing, and then the Michigan Workers Ex-Servicemen's League in early 1932.

On May 23, 1932, as word spread about Waters and his Oregon marchers, Pace and Judge Edward J. Jeffries, of Detroit, an alumnus of the Coxey's Army 1894 march on Washington and "a violent radical" in the eyes of local newspaper editors, addressed some 1,500 people summoned to Cass Technical High School, just north of downtown Detroit, to organize a veterans' group. Just over a week later, some 450 men—most likely not aware they were being led by a communist organizer—braved a relentless rainstorm to hop streetcars to the Pennsylvania rail yard, where they were allowed to board open-top coal cars for Toledo. Then they transferred to ten freight cars headed for Cleveland, where they intended to skip ahead to Pittsburgh, then Washington, D.C.[4]

In Cleveland, C. B. Cowan, an active communist who had led a hunger march to Akron the previous year (and urged the marchers to "walk into restaurants and take their meals"), had organized a group of several hundred men to join the D.C. protest.

Where Waters demanded volunteers prove they had served in the Great War, Cowan didn't care. If people wanted to march, he'd take them, and he didn't differentiate between fellow communists and anti-communists, either, setting up a tension within the group itself.[5]

Pace's group arrived at the Cleveland rail yards to find Cowan's group already there haggling with rail officials about transport to Washington, D.C. Combined, their numbers exceeded one thousand men, a formidable force for the rail and local police to reckon with. Rail officials had already rerouted scheduled trains to avoid stopping within reach of the marchers, but that did not dissuade the veterans. Twice, men surged into the roundhouse and symbolically took control—a couple dozen men posed atop a locomotive for a photograph that went out over the news wires—but were expelled by the rail and Cleveland police. Several fistfights broke out among the men as well, as Pace, clearly lying, denied that communists filled the Detroit contingent. "I am not a communist and most of these men are not communists," Pace said. "I don't believe in it and we're all loyal to the government." Still, the violent skirmishes, combined with the striking image of unemployed men seizing control of private railroad property, with its shades of a Russian-style workers revolt, added to convictions among top federal officials that communists were moving toward an uprising.[6]

The Detroit and Cleveland contingents eventually gave up on the train and made their way by motor vehicles to Pittsburgh; then, without Cowan, who had been detained as a "suspicious person" by Pennsylvania police, they moved on to D.C., where Pace directed the men to condemned apartment buildings slated to be razed for the new Federal Triangle complex, another move that fueled official paranoia about communists seizing property.

In the White House "we were all disturbed by the influx of 'bonus marchers,'" Theodore Joslin, Hoover's press secretary, wrote in his journal. He saw the decision by officials in different states to provide transportation to the veterans as "nothing short of a breakdown of state government." He urged President Hoover to stop the men from crossing into the District of Columbia, but Hoover rejected the idea, fearing violence. "Trouble must be avoided at any cost," Hoover said. The president instructed Joslin that if the veterans sought a meeting with him, he would accept a small committee of representatives, "but I won't receive any communists." He suggested the marchers' fingerprints be matched with military records to ensure the men had served in the war, and any who had not served "should be thrown out," seemingly dismissing the possibility that a man could be both a veteran and a communist.[7]

BY MID-JUNE, more than ten thousand Bonus Marchers had arrived in Washington, D.C., with more arriving every day, many wearing khaki shirts as a visible reminder of their military service. An accurate count is impossible, but at its peak the demonstrators totaled more than twenty thousand people, mostly single men, but also some women and children. The veterans were scattered across at least nine significant encampments and more than a dozen smaller outposts. The most visible was Camp Glassford, named for the police superintendent and located a couple of blocks from the Capitol.

But the largest and most significant stood on the Anacostia flats, just west of the southern end of the Eleventh Street Bridge, where more than half of the total Bonus Expeditionary Force created the largest Hooverville in the nation. The inhabitants eventually named it Camp Marks, after a supportive police precinct captain. The selection of the site by Glassford was strategic. The veterans could see the tops of the Capitol and the Washington Monument, but had to cross a drawbridge to get there. And the site itself was marked on the east by a police station and bordered on the north by the river, on the west by a massive drainpipe, and to the south by a ten-foot escarpment. To

Glassford, it made for a good place to contain a mob, should the veterans get unruly.[8]

Encampment populations were ever shifting as marchers quit or, in the case of suspected communists, were thrown out, and new marchers arrived, which meant the number of people involved over the span of the protest in the city far exceeded the twenty thousand or so demonstrators at its peak. On June 11, the *Evening Star*, citing registration records by the BEF, reported 9,361 people at Camp Marks alone.

A month later, the short-lived *B.E.F. News*, produced by the executive committee of the BEF, reported that Camp Marks had 14,576 registrations that included eighty families and more than two hundred children. Camp Glassford held another 2,100 registrants, with two hundred more at Camp Simms. Uncounted others were scattered around the District of Columbia.

The registrations didn't include a racial breakdown, but the veterans, despite camping in a segregated city, were an integrated force—an ironic twist, given that the men served in segregated units during the Great War. In 1913, President Woodrow Wilson, a Democrat, a Southerner, and a segregationist, had directed federal facilities in the District of Columbia to adopt strict segregation codes. At one point during the Bonus March, one hundred Black marchers from Louisiana complained that they had been passed over in food distribution, while their white counterparts had meals. Waters directed that all food arrivals be delivered to the communal canteen, ensuring a more equitable distribution.[9]

Drawing on their military experiences, the veterans laid out Camp Marks "divided up into regimental units with corners and streets, same as in the training camps of 1917 and 1918." As it grew, different sections became dominated by people from the same state. Some veterans had tents, a few lived in cars, but much of the housing was cobbled together from whatever the veterans could find, with a nearby city dump serving as a supply depot. A discarded automobile bumper became a roof; egg crates became walls; one resident "built himself a lean-to shelter from a child's broken blackboard with the babies' scrawling chalk marks still on it. Another had made himself a tent out of an American flag." One man built a sod house. Several wove long grasses through rusted bed springs for walls, while others harvested broad leaves from wild burdock plants and overlaid them on frames for a rain-resistant roof.[10]

"Dismantled automobile bodies, considered the choicest of all treasures to be salvaged from the junk heaps, ancient double-decker bed frames, with boards stretched across them, bags of dried grass—these kept sleeping men out of the mud," Waters wrote. "One man found a casket and set it on trestles for his bed. Another found a piano box and put up a sign, 'Academy of Music.'"[11]

Protecting from rain above was one problem; protecting sleeping veterans and their families from the wet ground was another. Throughout June, regular rains made the camp a muddy mess. The settlement had none of the usual urban infrastructure. Veterans assumed shifts cooking for the masses at field kitchens set up around the encampment; latrines served as bathrooms (as did nearby gas stations); water came from two long hoses attached to fire hydrants. Medical care was offered at first through a small Marines-run clinic on Indiana Avenue, then a full-fledged Army field hospital at the unused Fort Hunt, on the west bank of the Potomac River, about twelve miles downstream from the Capitol. Some three hundred men a day eventually would receive medical care for everything from body lice to severe maladies that required hospitalization. Men also turned to the Anacostia River, described as little more than an open sewer, as a source for doing laundry, bathing, and washing utensils; mosquitoes, flies, and other insects swarmed the camp.[12]

George A. Hastings, a director of the White House Conference on Child Health and Protection, visited the camp with his wife and wrote to the president's aide French Strother about what they had seen. He described a car arriving from Texas with two parents and ten children. "Their only shelter was a tarpaulin fastened to the rear of the car and spread out eight or ten feet behind the car. The children, including a baby about three months old, lay on the ground."

The father of another family of five children told Hastings he had been jobless for more than two years and relief help in their hometown in Pennsylvania had run out. During their month in the camp, they survived on a daily loaf of bread, a quart of milk and "some loose skimmed milk in the afternoon. One of the children has been sick of diarrhea" and had been hospitalized. While dismissing "the misguided single men who wish to endure the hardships and squalor of the camp," who had "come as a result of red propaganda," Hastings urged the administration to find some way to get the families out of the camp and back home.[13]

The "frightful" conditions under which the veterans were living also drove a spike of fear through the heart of William C. Fowler, the city's health officer, that an outbreak of typhoid or other serious disease might ravage the campers and spread through the rest of D.C. Fowler had no solution short of abandoning the campsite, and the veterans refused to budge. Officials at one point sent trucks around to the various sites and offered free transportation to anyone who wanted to leave, but few did.[14]

The marchers were in Washington to create a spectacle, and so they did. Washingtonians made regular visits to gawk at the bedraggled veterans, and many brought food and useful items to make camp life a bit easier. Regular deliveries of food arrived from different states to support their contingents, and the U.S. Post Office set up a mail center. The marchers themselves established a publicity bureau to try to control some of the public perceptions of the campaign. They arranged sporting events, including prizefights, and occasional musical performances. Father James R. Cox flew from Pittsburgh to D.C. and delivered a speech at the camp backing the men's demands and urging them to hold strong. Father Charles E. Coughlin, the right-wing

Catholic radio priest from suburban Detroit, sent a $5,000 donation earmarked for food and shelter, so long as it didn't benefit any communists.

From Iowa, the leaders of the Farmers' Holiday Association offered help, too. In a telegram signed by Milo Reno and other members of the executive committee, they said the association "is ready and willing to send carloads of food to the veterans now camped in Washington. We are prepared to go on strike July 4 and withhold our products from the market and would like to use this method to dispose of our surplus." The only hitch: Someone would have to underwrite the costs of shipping the goods. It's unclear whether any shipments were sent.[15]

Waters and the other leaders insisted on no drunkenness or panhandling among the men, and an outright ban on radicalism, which was generally effective, though not completely. A security force of veterans kept watch and D.C. police stopped by daily to size things up. The veterans generally remained orderly, despite a few frictions. One marcher was stabbed to death in a fight with another, who was hustled off to the city jail. Most of the arrests, though, appear to have been of communists handing out leaflets or giving speeches, including a man named William Powell, age fifty-three, detained and charged with disorderly conduct after giving a speech to a small gathering of mostly Black people at the corner of Seventh and P Streets. His topic: denouncing the Alabama courts for the death sentences imposed on eight young Black men railroaded in Scottsboro for the alleged rape of two white women.[16]

CAMPS AND PARADES drew the attention of the public, but persuading members of Congress to vote for speeding up the bonus payments would take more effort. So the BEF dispatched men to visit the offices of their own elected representatives and senators. The halls of Congress, usually filled with the sartorially conscious, now added the disheveled and the downtrodden.

"The veterans, frankly, made a nuisance of themselves," Waters said. "A couple of veterans were always sitting in each representative's waiting rooms. The representatives were solicited outside the building as well." The perception that their ranks were filled with communists unsettled many members of Congress. A group of about 125 veterans seeking a meeting with Representative Isaac Bacharach, an Atlantic City, New Jersey, Republican, was ejected from the Capitol Building by D.C. police, who believed (without apparent evidence) that they were communists. Another throng of about one hundred men arrived at the east entrance planning to meet with Representative Frank Crowther, a Republican representing the Schenectady, New York, area, but were also stopped by the police, who eventually admitted a delegation of three, while the rest waited on the plaza outside.[17]

The audaciousness of thousands of veterans descending on the capital demanding attention to their specific issue proved to be too much for some politicians. A group of veterans roaming the halls of the Capitol Building ran across Senator James Hamilton Lewis, an Illinois Democrat, described in an Associated Press report as "the pink-whiskered senator noted for his courtesy and courtly manner," and began to berate Lewis over a speech he delivered the previous day urging the veterans to go home. Several of the veterans were from Illinois and said they had voted for Lewis.[18]

"If you are from Illinois, you are dishonoring the state," Lewis said. In a brief contentious discussion that drew onlookers, including fellow senators, the veterans replied that they intended to stay until Congress had approved the bonus payment. "You know where you'll go, won't you?" one of the veterans said. "I don't know what you mean," Lewis replied, "but you can go to hell, and I will go back into the Senate to do my duties."

The veterans had a specific goal. Representative Patman's bill to award the bonus payments immediately had died in the House Ways and Means Committee in May, but under House rules if

145 members signed on to a rehearing, the bill could be revived and sent to the floor for a vote by the full House. Patman worked on colleagues sympathetic to the bill and obtained eighty-two signatures before the veterans arrived in D.C. He continued to buttonhole colleagues, while the veterans worked on any representative they could reach. On June 4, the 145th signature was obtained in what can only be seen as a victory for the veterans. The House had shelved the bill; the veterans marched and demanded and cajoled; the House decided not only to give it another look, but support for the bill grew in part by some House members' desire to be seen as allied with the down-and-out heroes of the Great War.[19]

After its planned June 13 adjournment, the House remained in session under Speaker Garner so the measure could be considered. After a procedural vote the main bill came to the floor on June 14. Waters initially announced that the BEF would stay away from the Capitol Building during the vote, hoping to dampen accusations that the men intended to coerce by their presence. But when the debate began, several hundred veterans were seated in the gallery and thousands more arrayed themselves outside the Capitol, resting on the steps and the lawn.

As if the vote wasn't already framed by sufficient drama, early in the floor debate Representative Edward E. Eslick, a Tennessee Democrat not given to making floor speeches, went to the podium to deliver an impassioned defense of the Bonus Bill, and to urge his colleagues to pass it. So rare was a floor speech by Eslick that he arranged for his wife and some friends to be in the gallery to witness what he presumed would be a historical moment. After pointing out that America's allies in the Great War had already provided bonus payments to their soldiers, Eslick said, "I want to divert from the sordid. We hear nothing but dollars here. I want to go from the sordid side." With that, he gasped, grabbed for the edge of the podium, and then a nearby desk, as he slumped to the floor, dead.[20]

The death stunned the chamber, and, as word circulated outside, the veterans. It took forty minutes for the House to gain enough order to adjourn for the day. Across the river from the Capitol Building, Camp Marks lowered its flags to half-staff in honor of a House member the veterans considered an ally, and Waters issued a statement describing Eslick's death as "a personal loss."

"His passing is the more poignant in that at the moment death called him he was fighting for justice for the men who offered their lives in defense of our country and now find themselves destitute," Waters said, though the words sound as though the camp's publicity bureau may have done some polishing. "On behalf of the Bonus Expeditionary Force I wish to express both to his family and colleagues our grief at the loss of a distinguished statesman and friend of the war veterans."

The House somberly resumed the Bonus Bill debate the next day, again under the watchful eyes of the veterans. As anticipated, the House passed the measure by a significant margin, 209-176, sending the bill to the Senate, where the measure had little support. Regardless, the veterans diligently lobbied the senators, and on June 17, the day of the Senate vote, an estimated eight thousand veterans thronged the Capitol complex as the senators debated. Most remained outside, but some walked the hallways, leaving muddy footprints on the floors, and a few obtained seats in the gallery. There was little question what the Senate would do; the big concern was what the veterans would do.[21]

Runners kept the veterans outside informed of the goings-on inside. Field kitchens were brought to Capitol Hill to feed the men as they waited. Some joined in half-hearted songs, while most sat in silence or quiet discussions awaiting the next update. Police and reporters pressed Waters over how the men would react when the bill lost. They would do nothing, Waters said, other than return to their camps and continue to wait and lobby.[22]

But the mood shifted when word came that Glassford, the police superintendent, had ordered the Eleventh Street drawbridge to be raised, preventing any more veterans from moving from the camp to the Capitol. Police had also barricaded the Pennsylvania Avenue Bridge and a rail bridge, scuttling efforts by the veterans on the south side of the Anacostia River to join their comrades at the Capitol.[23]

"There were eight thousand angry men over there at Anacostia," Waters said. "I did not want the eight thousand now around the Capitol to fly into rage when they heard of this seeming act of provocation."[24]

An emissary from the Senate emerged, tracked down Waters, and quietly asked him to come inside the building, where he was told the Senate had killed the Bonus Bill. Waters came back out and climbed atop a pedestal footing so he could address the crowd and informed them of the defeat.

"This is only a temporary setback," he shouted. "We are going to get more and more men and we are going to stay here until we change the minds of these guys."

No noticeable response came at first, as though the men were trying to process the defeat. Despite the political reality many had still held out hope the Senate would come through. Then they started to boo, a few at first, then others joining in. A reporter for the Hearst newspapers, Elsie Robinson, standing behind Waters, urged him to tell the men to sing "America," and then to return to camp.

And that's how the night ended, in disappointment and a song.

CHAPTER 11

Scottsboro and Atlanta

DAWN HAD JUST BEGUN TO break over the Yazoo and Mississippi Valley Railroad yard in Baton Rouge on July 25 when John Pierre, a Black train fireman, ended his shift. As Pierre left the yard a few blocks from the State Capitol Building, a white man walking up the street raised a rifle, aimed at Pierre, and fired. The bullet missed its mark but delivered its message: Pierre ducked and ran as his assailant took off in another direction. This was far from a random attack, and authorities quickly linked the shooting to other assaults over the previous few months in a "reign of terror" intended to kill or scare off Black railroad workers to make way for unemployed white men.[1]

It was a bloody campaign. At least seven Black men had been killed, and more than twenty others wounded or, like Pierre, targeted and missed. Aaron Williams, the "oldest negro fireman on the Vicksburg route division," was killed late at night by a single shotgun blast as he stood in an engine window. The shot came from an automobile without lights that pulled up alongside the parked train. In an even more dramatic incident, a train approaching a bridge, about three miles south of the Yazoo and Mississippi Valley passenger terminal in Vicksburg, Mississippi, halted suddenly when F. W. Behrnes, the white engineer, spotted a burning fuse—a railroad danger signal—on the tracks ahead. The fuse sputtered out, so Behrnes, seeing no danger, tried to restart the train. Before he could, a man in a light overcoat and carrying a shotgun clambered aboard. Wilbur Anderson, the train's Black fireman, saw the gun, leapt from the locomotive, and began running, but the gunman took aim and hit Anderson in the neck and back with two blasts of buckshot, killing him.[2]

The violence drew wide condemnation and prompted a rare response from law enforcement, though not until after a four-month investigation by railroad authorities. Five men were arrested and accused of being part of "a carefully planned and well-financed murder plot." Some of the accused were former railway men themselves. None of the men were charged with murder in any of the shooting deaths. Two eventually pleaded guilty to assault-related charges, though the sentences—five years for one man, six months for the other—paled compared to the crimes. Juries found the other three men innocent, unsurprising verdicts in a time and place in which Blacks rarely found justice within the court system.

Lynching, a decades-long force of intimidation and extrajudicial killings, still occurred as Southern Democrats stymied efforts in Congress to pass a federal anti-lynching law. In April, a white woman living near Crockett, Texas, about one hundred miles north of Houston, told her family that a Black man, Dave Tillis, a fifty-two-year-old sharecropper, had entered her bedroom. Tillis's landlord, Arch Maples, a candidate for sheriff in an upcoming election, detained Tillis, put him in his car, and drove toward the sheriff's office in Crockett, about fifteen miles away, when he said two armed men appeared in the roadway. He stopped, and as one of the gunmen kept watch over him, two others emerged from the woods at the side of the road, and the three of them dragged Tillis into the woods. The remaining gunman ordered Maples to drive off. He fetched the current sheriff and they returned to the site and found Tillis's body, with a gash in the forehead, hanging from a tree, strangled to death. Police later arrested a brother and the father of the woman and three other male relatives, but it's unclear whether any of the men were ever convicted of the crime.[3]

Elsewhere, both public and private pressure arose to dismiss Black workers from a range of jobs and replace them with unemployed whites. In January, the city of Charlotte, North Carolina, dismissed Black employees—many with long tenure in their public service jobs—and replaced them with white men. In February, a mob of some two hundred unemployed white men descended on a building under demolition in Jacksonville, Florida, and demanded the project manager fire the Black crew and replace them with members of the mob. The manager refused and the white men rioted, chasing the Black workers from the site. One of the rioters was stabbed after several of them cornered a Black worker, who lashed out with a knife, then made his escape. In April, the South Carolina railroad commission ordered that no trains could operate in the state unless a white man oversaw passenger care, a response to the Pullman Company's practice of appointing Black porters to oversee train services.[4]

The criminal justice system offered little hope. During the spring of 1931, nine young Black men—uneducated teenagers, mostly—had been accused of raping two young white women on a train near Scottsboro, a rural hamlet of some 2,900 residents on the west bank of the Tennessee River in northeast Alabama. The incident began with a fight between Black and white hoboes riding in an open-topped car partially filled with gravel, and it ended with the Black men forcing all but one of the white men and two white women, who were unemployed mill workers, off the train. The white men reported the incident to a station house, claiming they had been beaten by a Black gang. A sheriff's posse intercepted the train, arrested all the Black drifters they could find, and took them to Scottsboro, where the young men were nearly lynched.

Four days later, a grand jury indicted the nine teens and young men, and a week after that, the trials began as national guardsmen protected the courthouse building from a throng of thousands gathered outside. Some of the defendants' families hired Chattanooga lawyer Stephen Roddy, who mostly practiced Tennessee real estate law, to travel to Scottsboro to help, and after he appeared to watch a court proceeding, the judge tried to assign him to defend all nine. Roddy, unfamiliar with Alabama criminal law procedures, demurred, until a local lawyer, eighty-year-old Milo Moody, who hadn't handled a criminal defense in years, offered to assist.

Four separate trials took place with remarkable speed and injustice over three days, with the two women, Victoria Price, twenty-one, and Ruby Bates, seventeen, the key witnesses, though Price took the lead in relating the events, clearly relishing the spotlight. What didn't emerge in the testimony was that both women had histories of prostitution, and that they likely concocted the rape story to distract investigators from their possible violation of the Mann Act, which banned interstate travel for sexual purposes. All the jurors were white, under a system that effectively barred Blacks from jury pools, and with the defense counsel lacking the time, resources, and drive to investigate the elements of the alleged crime, and the victims' backgrounds and reliability, the verdicts were a foregone conclusion.[5]

By the end of the fourth day, eight defendants had been pronounced guilty and sentenced to death, but the jury couldn't reach a verdict on the ninth defendant, a thirteen-year-old, who was subsequently held for retrial. The death sentences were later stayed, pending appeals to the Alabama Supreme Court, which on March 24, 1932, upheld seven convictions and sentences, but overturned the eighth because of the youthful age of the defendant. But two months later, as the Bonus Army slowly filled up public spaces in the capital, the U.S. Supreme Court announced that it would hear an appeal that the defendants had been denied a fair trial through the exclusion of their peers from the jury, and through denial of adequate counsel.

The Scottsboro Boys case, as it became known, was notable for many reasons, not the least of which was the continuing American injustice against Black men, particularly in the South. Even before the Alabama Supreme Court upheld the verdicts, Bates recanted her story and said neither of the women had been raped. Medical examinations of the two women just after the arrests found no evidence of rape but did establish that they had engaged in intercourse hours before the purported attack. Yet, the defendants were still found guilty, and state appeals courts upheld the all-white jury verdicts.

The National Association for the Advancement of Colored People, under new leader Walter White, monitored the case, but reacted slowly—"dithered" is how White biographer Kenneth Robert Janken described it—and failed to comprehend the level of outrage among Black communities across the country. White's blatant classism also hindered the NAACP. In a meeting with the defendants and their families, White couldn't conceal his disregard for their education level and presumed lack of intellectual abilities. White sought to project an image of the NAACP as a respectable middle-class organization fighting for equal rights and racial equality, and believed the path to progress would require alliances and cooperation with liberal whites. He did not relish defending uneducated alleged rapists, even if the underlying issues were, in fact, racism, inequality, and injustice.[6]

So International Labor Defense, a legal arm of the American Communist Party, stepped into the void. After the Scottsboro Boys were arrested, representatives of the ILD began contacting their families, part of a broad effort to attract disenfranchised Black Americans to communism. The CPUSA was, in fact, one of the few organizations at the time to both pledge and follow a race-neutral policy of inclusion (though even it was not immune to prejudice). The struggles of Black Americans were rooted in race, but also in class, the party believed. Impoverished Blacks had this in common with impoverished whites: Both were the victims of an oppressive capitalist system that exploited workers for profits. The Communist Party, its adherents advocated, offered a different approach, and a different system. And they made some headway with those arguments.

The presence of communist organizers in the South, particularly as they worked in Black neighborhoods in places like Birmingham and among Black sharecroppers in rural regions, jolted the white power structure. Police and white posses stormed into meeting houses rousting the attendees, beating and arresting many of them. In Birmingham, communist-organized neighborhood councils took root, also sparking a backlash by political leaders and police. Rumors swirled, fed in large part by local newspaper coverage warning of the Red menace riling up Black residents.

Then three women were shot, two fatally, allegedly by an armed Black man, who had jumped on the running board of their car, as they returned home from the movies. The crime fed fears of Black radicals in their midst after the lone survivor told police the man forced them into the woods and held them hostage while "he blamed the white race for the negro's conditions and declared that the white people are forever heaping injustice on the negro." Posses formed to chase down the attacker, while white mobs burned Black businesses, dragged sleeping Black residents out of their beds, and jailed men who supposedly resembled the man the survivor described.[7]

The ILD's efforts to woo the Scottsboro Boys' parents were simple, but effective. They sent small amounts of money for financial support, and occasionally provided bus fare so the families could visit their sons in prison—all aimed at gaining their trust and support. White, meanwhile, at the prodding of other activists (including Roy Wilkins, who would eventually succeed him as president of the NAACP), decided that the NAACP should step up.

A bitter and public dispute broke out between the NAACP and the ILD, with the NAACP accusing the communists of duping the defendants' parents to push communist propaganda, and the ILD accusing the NAACP of being part of the capitalist system that aimed to electrocute the young men. The parents held firm and stuck with the ILD. "I don't care whether they are Reds, Greens or Blues," one mother said. "They are the only ones to put up a fight to save these boys and I am with them to the end." In January 1932, the NAACP announced its withdrawal, leaving the Scottsboro Boys, and the ILD, to their fate.[8]

The ILD confounded its critics, though, by hiring nonparty member George W. Chamlee, a former county solicitor based in Chattanooga, to handle the appeals. Chamlee was part of a respected Tennessee family and had once written an essay defending lynching in certain circumstances. Hardly the kind of Northern radical that white Alabamans feared, though the ILD did also hire Walter H. Pollak, a Manhattan attorney in private practice who had a history of defending radicals, including Benjamin Gitlow, one of the founders of the American Communist Party. It was Pollak's appeal that the U.S. Supreme Court granted in May, setting oral arguments for October.[9]

ANGELO HERNDON, WHO grew up in abject poverty after the death of his coal-mining father when Angelo was nine years old, ranked among the Communist Party's more active Southern representatives. Angelo's mother worked as a housekeeper for a white family in their hometown of Wyoming, Ohio. When Angelo was thirteen, he and his sixteen-year-old brother, Leo, hopped a freight train to Lexington, Kentucky, and began working in coal mines themselves.[10]

It was brutal work done by a segregated workforce, with managers often cheating the workers by underweighing the cars they loaded and charging exorbitant rates for substandard housing and food. Herndon quit and floated around the South for a while, trying his hand at other jobs, including working a cement mixer on a dam project, but found the experiences were numbingly similar: dangerous working conditions, poor living standards, no recourse to worksite abuses, and a special level of misery for Blacks.

He wound up in Birmingham, back working in a coal mine and living under Jim Crow conditions, experiencing daily indignities, and witnessing anti-Black violence. As angry as all that made him, he found himself angrier still at his fellow Blacks for ceding so much power to their white tormentors. Herndon was only sixteen, but the experiences began to radicalize him: "The more I reflected upon the grave injustices inflicted upon my people, the more the spirit of rebellion surged up in me."[11]

In June 1930, Herndon spotted "some soiled handbills" on the ground with the headline WOULD YOU RATHER FIGHT OR STARVE? The question struck him as a revelation and led him to a meeting that afternoon of the Birmingham Unemployed Council. Herndon passed through a gauntlet of police outside arrayed to both keep watch and intimidate attendees, but inside he found whites and Blacks sitting together, sharing a dais, and alternating speeches about the need for communal action to counter both the power of capitalism and the power of white society. At the end of the meeting, Herndon joined the Unemployed Council and began moving ever leftward.[12]

Over the next several months Herndon sought to persuade fellow miners to join the National Miners' Union, but only succeeded in getting himself arrested for vagrancy, despite having a full-time job. After seven days in the Birmingham city jail, a judge sentenced Herndon to twelve months on a chain gang because, as the judge explained, Alabama didn't have a state law against insurrection, as did neighboring Georgia, so that was the maximum sentence he could impose. The conviction was tossed out on appeal, but Herndon emerged from jail blacklisted at the coal mines.

So Herndon went to work as a union organizer with no set wage. He was routinely rousted by police and Klansmen and often jailed and occasionally convicted. He traveled to Camden County, Alabama, about one hundred miles south of Birmingham, after being invited to help organize sharecroppers. Within days he fled for his life after being tipped off that white landowners were organizing a lynch mob.[13]

At times police arrested Herndon, not for his politics but because of his race. He was among the scores of Black men rounded up and beaten by police as they searched for the man who had shot the three young women coming home from the movies. His politics added another layer of suspicion. Police tried to beat a confession out of him in the jail, and when that didn't work, they took him by car to a wooded area, some twenty miles outside the city, chained him to a tree, and threatened him with death if he didn't confess. Herndon still refused and suffered abuse for hours with fists, feet, and rubber hoses before the officers hauled him back to the jail and dumped him, face and body bloody and swollen, onto the floor of his cell. Police released him and the others a few days later when the survivor failed to identify any of them in a mass lineup.

Herndon's activism and arrests made him a recognized figure among Birmingham's radicals, as well as among the police. Partly for his safety and partly because his skills were needed elsewhere, the Communist Party sent him to Atlanta in early 1932.

In the middle of June, Atlanta cut more than twenty thousand people from its overextended relief rolls, deepening the misery of those already on the brink. Many who had moved to the city from farms were rounded up and sent back home. But Herndon and other activists were particularly stirred by a claim by Commissioner Walter C. Hendrix, of Fulton County, made during a public hearing that he had seen no evidence of significant hunger and need in Atlanta and told leaders of relief agencies that "if you have evidence of such a condition, I think that we should have it from you."[14]

So Herndon and others organized a protest by hundreds of unemployed and needy people outside Hendrix's office, a gathering that remained peaceful, despite antagonism by police. It was the evidence that Hendrix claimed he wanted, though few involved thought the demonstration would change his views. But it did attract police to the organizers. The day after the rally Herndon stopped by a post office to pick up mail from a box he had rented and was nabbed by two police detectives under orders from county solicitor-general John A. Boykin. In the box were stacks of flyers about an upcoming meeting, and in his rented room police found communist tracts and more flyers advocating labor cooperation among Blacks and whites.

Nothing in the literature or pamphlets that police seized from Herndon advocated insurrection or revolution. Still, a movement of communists (often perceived as Jewish radicals) and oppressed Blacks instilled fear among Atlanta's leaders. When Herndon had been convicted in Birmingham on charges related to his union organizing, the sentencing judge lamented that Alabama didn't have a state law against insurrection. But Georgia did. After being held *in communicado* in jail for eleven days (during which his jailers beat him and threatened to electrocute him with a lamp wire), a grand jury handed down an indictment charging Herndon with attempted insurrection in violation of a Georgia law initially enacted to criminalize slave rebellions. The maximum penalty: death.[15]

CHAPTER 12

The Conventions

AFTER WEEKS OF PRIVATE CORRESPONDENCE and meetings, leaders of six anti-Prohibition organizations came together on the morning of June 7 in Manhattan's Empire State Building to finalize plans for what they would call the United Repeal Council, or URC. The goal: to marshal their forces and pressure both major national parties to adopt repeal planks at their upcoming conventions.[1]

Those attending included Pauline Sabin, of the Women's Organization for National Prohibition Reform, and Pierre S. du Pont, of the Association Against the Prohibition Amendment (AAPA), two of the nation's best-known campaigners for repeal. There were joined by leaders of the Voluntary Committee of Lawyers, the Crusaders (an organization of men under age thirty that preached education and moderation instead of a federal ban), the American Hotel Association, and the Republican Citizens Committee Against National Prohibition. Combined, the groups claimed some 2.5 million members, a formidable bloc.

It wasn't entirely clear that the different organizations would find sufficient common ground to work together. They shared a common goal but differed in approaches, and additional friction came from personality clashes among leaders of the Crusaders that spilled into the broader meeting. But after several hours behind closed doors, the leaders of the organizations hammered out the final wording of their mission statement demanding each major political party call for full repeal of the Eighteenth Amendment through state conventions, ensuring the public had a say in the decision.[2]

The URC also elected officers, beginning with du Pont as president, a nod to the primacy of the AAPA, but also a likely reflection of cultural male dominance. Sabin, who had drawn hundreds of thousands of women to the repeal cause and made the WONPR a political force on the issue, became one of the five vice presidents—the other four spots divided among the other member organizations.

Even before the meeting was held, the groups had been planning a mass showing in Chicago for both the major party conventions, including a parade and rally on the eve of the Republican gathering. Sabin's group had compiled names of delegates from each state and crafted suggested language to be included in letters from their members to the delegates, engineering a grassroots campaign to press for repeal planks. The letters were to be tailored to delegates of each party, but embraced the same basic argument: growing public opposition to Prohibition and reinforcing "the unquestionable right of the people in the several states to express their will as to whether the 18th Amendment shall be repealed or retained."[3]

The Wet movement was buoyed by the near-simultaneous announcement by John D. Rockefeller Jr., a lifelong teetotaler and one of the leading Dry voices in the nation, that he considered Prohibition to be a failed experiment. It was a stunning shift of position. In a letter to Columbia University president Nicholas Butler, supporting the academic's proposal for repeal, Rockefeller noted that he was a third-generation teetotaler, that he and his father had been backers of the Anti-Saloon League, and that they had spent about $350,000 getting Prohibition passed.[4]

Yet, in the years since Prohibition went into effect, he wrote, consumption had increased, saloons had given way to off-the-books speakeasies, the black market had given rise to a violent gangster underworld, and—echoing Sabin's position—respect for the law and law enforcement had declined. "It is not to be expected that the repeal of the 18th Amendment will in itself end all these evils," Rockefeller wrote, adding that "repeal is a prerequisite to the attainment of that goal." The announcement drew vicious responses from some of his former allies, who called him "naïve" and "misled," but words of welcome from the anti-Prohibitionists. "We are all more than delighted," Sabin said. "He is our most powerful recruit so far."[5]

The URC wasted no time in getting to work. Over the next couple of days, members traveled to Chicago to set up a temporary headquarters in the Sherman House Hotel, at the corner of Randolph and Clark Streets, near City Hall, about a mile west of the lakefront, which they would maintain through both major conventions. Sabin, though, took rooms in the Blackstone Hotel, across South Michigan Avenue from the lakeside Grant Park; it was an ironic choice, given that gangster boss Al Capone, who controlled Chicago's bootlegging trade, regularly patronized the hotel's barbershop before he went to prison. But that also put her one block from the Congress Hotel, where the Republican Party leadership—of which she used to be a member—had its headquarters.

Edgar Rickard, long-standing friend of Herbert Hoover's from his London days, and a central figure in the circle of President Hoover loyalists, took rooms there, too. He questioned, at first, whether he could do "the Chief" much good by going to Chicago, since the president would have seven members of his cabinet there, as well as two of his secretaries and a dedicated telephone line from the Hooverites' war room in the Congress Hotel to Hoover's desk in the White House.[6]

"Office matters need attention," Rickard noted in his diary as he waffled. The depression imperiled his financial interests in the Maine-based Pejepscot Paper Company, the Pitney Bowes Postage Meter Company, and a Great Lakes–Atlantic shipping company, the Erie and St. Lawrence Corporation. He also served as Hoover's business agent, overseeing the president's investments and trust funds he had established for Lou Hoover and the couple's two sons. So he had plenty to do at his office at 42 Broadway in lower Manhattan.[7]

But even as he seesawed, Rickard reserved a suite with Lewis L. Strauss at the Congress Hotel, just in case, and on June 11 wrote that he had "succumbed to the urge to attend the convention." He boarded a special train booked for New York's Republican delegation that made stops to pick up more party members in Albany, Syracuse, Rochester, and other cities along the line that paralleled the Erie Canal, before continuing westward to Chicago.[8]

With President Herbert Hoover's nomination assured, only two convention issues offered the potential for drama: an intraparty fight over what the party platform should say about Prohibition, followed by a question of what to do with Vice President Charles E. Curtis. The New York contingent shared a broad party belief that Curtis, a former congressman and one-time Senate majority leader, would not, at age seventy-three, have the stamina to travel the country campaigning on behalf of Hoover. "It is going to be a hard campaign, and they want a real campaigner . . . who can influence money contributions," Rickard wrote. Charles Dawes, who served as Coolidge's vice president, would be acceptable to the traveling delegates, but a contest for the number two slot carried risks. If Hoover stood any chance at all in the general election, it would have to be with the party united behind him.[9]

Rickard arrived at the hotel on the morning of June 12 and checked into the suite that over the next few days would be the late-hours gathering spot for Hoover's close supporters as they analyzed the day's events and strategized on Hoover's behalf. "We had all arrived at the definite conclusion that there existed a well-planned conspiracy to take control of the party machine," Rickard noted. The goal wasn't the looming election, but the one four years hence, suggesting that some of the party leaders had already written off 1932—and the Hoover administration—as a lost cause.[10]

The United Repeal Council dogged Republicans wherever they could find them. Raymond Pitcairn, of the Republican Citizens Committee Against National Prohibition, tried to organize a donation boycott. Speakers at the convention-eve rally at the Coliseum a few blocks south of The Loop told some eight thousand attendees, which included many Wet delegates, that if the Republicans did not push for repeal, there would be a Democrat in the White House in the spring. In large part it would occur because the repeal proponents would work to make it happen if the Democrats adopted a repeal plank at their convention and the Republicans didn't.

Other lobbying efforts were more subtle. Sabin took her dinners at the Blackstone dining room with Ione Nicoll, another executive of the WONPR group, where they "were holding forth on their favorite topic," Rickard reported. Grace Roosevelt, wife of Teddy's son Archie, invited Republican National Committee treasurer, and Hoover intimate, Jeremiah "Jerry" Milbank to dinner, "where they heckled him a lot on the Prohibition question and his backing of the Chief and made it very uncomfortable for him."

In the end the drama died away. Hoover's supporters won the platform debate with a banal and seemingly contradictory compromise that did not call for repeal—Hoover feared losing support of the Drys if they did—but backed the idea of offering a new amendment that would let states make their own decisions, while retaining Congress's ability to legislate enforcement of federal protections for states that decided to continue Prohibition.

Arthur Krock, of *The New York Times,* wrote that "it is Wet and it is Dry; it opposes repeal and proposes it, and it provides those safeguards and that 'alternative' which Drys have been demanding. Word came from Washington that the President thought well of the document." He should have, because it came at his direction. Separately from noted Wet H. L. Mencken: "The Hoover plank at least has the great virtue of being quite unintelligible to simple folk. Even the specialists here on the scene continue to dispute it."[11]

A last-minute effort to force a plank backing repeal died in a 681 to 472 floor vote. The convention then, by voice vote, approved the full platform, including Hoover's straddling approach to Prohibition. And the effort to supplant Curtis as vice president also dissipated as the main alternative, Dawes, declared himself uninterested.

The only other potential moment of drama involved former senator Joseph I. France. Because he had won a few preference polls in the West, the convention was obligated to take a motion from the floor for his nomination, which came from the delightfully named Lawritz B. Sandblast, an Oregon lawyer and delegate. But hardly anyone knew what he said because just after he began speaking, the microphone went dead. When he finished, France climbed the stairs to the stage and strode toward the lectern, demanding to be recognized to deliver comments.

Bertrand H. Snell, a member of Congress and the chair of the convention, intercepted France and told him he would not be recognized because he was not a delegate. France waved proxies from two missing delegates that he argued entitled him to be recognized. As the two men went at it, four uniformed Chicago police officers surrounded France and forced him from the stage, propelling him awkwardly down the steps, then hauled him off to a nearby station house before releasing him. France told reporters afterward that he had prepared a 1,500-word speech arguing that the party could not win in the fall with Hoover as its candidate and announcing that he would withdraw his name from consideration to offer up a replacement challenger: Calvin Coolidge.[12]

And so the only real excitement of the convention was hustled off by the cops, and reduced to a historical footnote.

SABIN AND THE rest of the United Repeal Council had a much easier time with the Democratic delegates. Al Smith was a longtime Wet, John Nance Garner solidly Dry, and Franklin Roosevelt, after some waffling, had come out for repeal. But for strategic reasons Governor Roosevelt didn't think the Democrats should focus much attention on the issue. Doing so, he feared, would lose the party support of Southern Drys. The stronger and less divisive issue, he believed, was the economic collapse and the failure of Hoover and the Republicans to come up with a plan for fixing it, and for not sending sufficient relief to those suffering the most. Roosevelt's "forgotten man" embodied both the Drys and the Wets.

Sabin and the other Prohibition activists remained in Chicago as the Republicans cleared out and the Democrats flowed in—among them Sabin's husband, Charles, a party fundraiser and delegate. James A. Farley and "the office force," as he called his colleagues working for Roosevelt's nomination, left New York City by train on the morning of June 18 and set up shop in Suite 1702 of the Congress Hotel days before representatives of the other candidates got established.

Chicago's foul air deeply affected Louis Howe, Roosevelt's top advisor, who often would be found on the floor of his suite several floors up from the campaign offices gasping for breath. Yet, he still managed to pull his usual number of strings. The campaign brought along a telephone operator and installed a direct line from Howe's suite to Roosevelt's office in Albany through which they "kept in close contact with the Governor at all times so that he knew everything that was going on." They also used the setup to let Roosevelt speak directly with delegates, often selected by Farley, which was a "psychologically effective" strategy, according to Bronx political boss Edward J. Flynn, "to acquaint these people with the candidate." And Farley scattered loyalists among the various hotels, creating "a regular system for getting the news."[13]

By Farley's count, Roosevelt had the commitments of around 690 delegates, more than a simple majority, but well short of the 770 votes needed to win the nomination under the party's two-thirds rule. As the Stop Roosevelt movement came together, some Roosevelt supporters began advocating for a floor fight to drop the rule, which could be done with a simple majority vote. But to do so would likely prompt an intra-party split; Southern delegations long supported the rule because it gave them veto power over the ultimate nominee. In early April, Roosevelt, who saw the two-thirds rule as an "anachronism," had decided to put off making a public stand. Much like advocating for repeal of Prohibition, Roosevelt feared losing Southern support if he pressed the two-thirds issue. Plus, trying to change the rule could be read as a sign of weakness, a tacit confession that Governor Roosevelt didn't think he could win the nomination through the traditional path.[14]

A couple of days before the convention, Farley convened what he expected to be an informal meeting of some of Roosevelt's campaigners and loyal members of each state delegation. Farley quickly lost control of the gathering, though, as Louisiana political kingpin Huey P. Long delivered an impassioned speech that persuaded the group to pass a resolution "pledging the Roosevelt forces to fight for the abolition of the two-thirds rule." The move "hit" Farley "like a blow on the nose. My confidence was badly shaken for the first time." Farley returned to the hotel offices and called Roosevelt in Albany, who talked him down. "The governor told me not to worry, to let things drift along, and that he was confident a way out of the mess would be found without doing us any damage."[15]

Roosevelt's strategy for winning the nomination was about to get its acid test. He had avoided entering primaries in states that had favorite-son candidates to give them their moment in the sun. But he, mostly through Howe and Farley, maintained regular contact with key delegates in those states, hoping to win their support after the first ballot. And he had for months been working behind the scenes to place loyalists on key convention committees.[16]

Measures of Roosevelt's strength would come in early showdowns over various issues, led off by the two-thirds rule. Roosevelt had sent a telegram to Farley to share with the convention backing off the rules change. Roosevelt stuck to his argument against the two-thirds rule, but said "the issue was not raised until after the delegates to the convention had been selected" and thus, out of a sense of fair play, it should remain in place for the convention. He called on his supporters to "cease their activities."[17]

But Long and J. Bruce Kremer, a national party committeeman and William Gibbs McAdoo's floor manager at the 1924 convention, continued to push the issue, leading the Rules Committee—run by Kremer—to adopt a measure on the eve of the convention that would scrap the two-thirds rule if, after the sixth ballot, the convention had not settled on a nominee. An instant uproar followed among the Stop Roosevelt forces, leading Farley to issue a hasty statement disavowing the move. He then met privately with Kremer and persuaded Kremer to drop the change. While news accounts viewed this as a loss for Roosevelt, in the end he got the resolution he wanted.[18]

The next test involved competing slates of delegates from Louisiana and Minnesota. Long, as it happened, had yet to be recognized as a convention delegate. Louisiana had sent two delegations—Long's, which had been selected at a state committee meeting, and a second one selected at a state convention. The national convention sided with Long. Similarly, a rebel slate from Minnesota sought to replace one led by Einar Hoidale, a congressional candidate, citing arcane rules. Roosevelt had sided with Long and Hoidale, and the victories established that Roosevelt had the backing of a majority of the convention—but not two-thirds.

The next battle came over the appointment of a "permanent" chair of the convention. Jouett Shouse, John J. Raskob's ally running the Democratic National Committee, had been jockeying for the appointment for months. Roosevelt, unsurprisingly, balked at putting a key figure in the Stop Roosevelt movement in such a powerful decision-making role at the convention. The governor supported Montana senator Thomas J. Walsh, chair of the infamous 1924 convention, who had led Senate investigations into the Teapot Dome Scandal. Walsh won by a 626 to 528 vote, another display of Roosevelt's strength.[19]

Ironically, the biggest political fight of the era, Prohibition, didn't play as much of a role in the Democratic convention as the Republicans'. Roosevelt, in typical fashion, remained out of the fray and instructed his supporters to vote their consciences. Senator Cordell Hull, of Tennessee, a stalwart Roosevelt supporter, spoke from the dais in favor of maintaining Prohibition, but to little effect. Smith's passionate argument for repeal earned him sustained ovations from the Wet crowd. In the end the convention voted 934¾ to 213¾ to put the Democratic Party on record calling for outright repeal. It also demanded immediate amendments to the Volstead Act, which guided enforcement of Prohibition, "to legalize the sale of beer and other beverages of such alcoholic content as is permissible under the Constitution."

The biggest fight, of course, would be over the nomination itself. The convention heard ten hours of nominating speeches for nine candidates, including the favorite sons, which didn't end until early Friday morning, July 1. Sensing an opportunity, Farley and the rest of the Roosevelt forces—a majority of the delegates—pressed for an immediate first ballot vote, anticipating that if Roosevelt didn't win it, then he would on a second ballot.

After several hours of seconding speeches for each of the nominees, balloting began about 4:30 A.M., and lasted nearly two hours, including the tallying. The result: Roosevelt had 664¼ votes, far more than second-place Smith, with 201¾ votes. A second ballot after sunrise showed little change: Roosevelt picked up eleven votes, while Smith lost seven. In both ballots Garner came in a distant third at 90¼ votes, while the other candidates remained in the low double-digits.

Farley and the Roosevelt contingent decided it was time for a break, but the Stop Roosevelt forces, angry at being forced into an all-nighter and hoping to embarrass Roosevelt with a third straight failure, refused and forced another ballot, which began shortly after 8 A.M. Again, little changed, so the convention adjourned as the campaign managers caught naps between backroom lobbying sessions.

William Randolph Hearst found himself in position to be kingmaker. Shortly after the adjournment, Joseph P. Kennedy, a Roosevelt man and friend of Hearst, reached the newspaper baron at his San Simeon estate and warned him that if Roosevelt didn't win in the next few ballots, the deadlocked convention would likely turn to a compromise candidate, with the internationalist Newton Baker the inside favorite. Boston mayor James Michael Curley reached Hearst with the same analysis (it's unclear whether he worked in tandem with Kennedy and the campaign). Baker, who had served as Wilson's secretary of war, and had spent years urging the United States to join the League of Nations, "was little less than an enemy of his country" in Hearst's eyes. But the publisher also couldn't stand Smith. So he went with Roosevelt by default.[20]

Hearst sent word to Garner to release his delegates. But that was only part of the battle. A released delegate is not necessarily a delegate committed to Roosevelt. In hurried and secret negotiations in a borrowed Congress Hotel suite, Farley told Sam Rayburn, Garner's campaign manager, that Roosevelt could "swing the vice-presidential nomination for Speaker Garner if Texas threw in their lot with us." Rayburn demurred. "We'll see what can be done."[21]

Over the next few hours the nomination fell into place. Rayburn spoke over the telephone with Garner, still in Washington, and they agreed he would step aside and support Roosevelt. Rayburn stood before the Texas delegation at 6 P.M. and told them about Garner's decision. After some bitter back-and-forth, the delegation voted narrowly, fifty-four to fifty-one, to back Roosevelt. When word of that began spreading, McAdoo, controlling the California delegation pledged to Garner, called Hearst and made an unsuccessful play for his support as a compromise candidate, then agreed to align the delegation behind Roosevelt.[22]

The convention reconvened at 9 P.M. The Stop Roosevelt forces were expecting to see some erosion of support for Roosevelt, particularly the Mississippi delegation. But there were also murmurs of a change from Garner. As the fourth alphabetical ballot got under way and reached California, McAdoo strode to the dais and announced that because Roosevelt had three times won a majority of the delegate votes, he deserved the nomination, and that California would shift its forty-four delegates to Roosevelt. Boos rang down from the galleries stuffed with Smith supporters, but they held no sway. McAdoo also spoke for Texas, saying the two delegations "are acting in accord with what we believe best for America and for the Democratic party." Invoking the 1924 convention in which he went one hundred ballots, just to lose, McAdoo told the delegates that "I would like to see Democrats fight Republicans, not Democrats."[23]

The switch by California and Texas gave Roosevelt the delegates he needed to win the nomination, and as the roll call continued, other states fell in behind. Candidate Albert Ritchie himself announced that he and Maryland now supported Roosevelt. When the roll call reached Utah with its eight votes, the nomination was sealed. The only holdouts were New York and seven other states loyal to Smith; the former governor, sensing the battle was lost, listened to the results over the radio. The final tally: Roosevelt, 945 votes; Smith, 190½ votes; 9½ votes scattered among three other men, including 5½ for Baker.

Someone else was listening to the balloting over the radio, too: Roosevelt, back in Albany. Shortly after the victory he dashed off a telegram to the convention. Roosevelt had decided as far back as April that if he won the nomination, he would break with tradition and fly to Chicago to address the convention and then convene a meeting to reorganize the party ahead of the fall election. He wired his intentions to Walsh, and Walsh read the telegram from the dais in the Coliseum.

Roosevelt, Eleanor, three of their children, several top staffers, and Sam Rosenman boarded a chartered tri-motor airplane in Albany the next day and took off, about 7:30 A.M., for the bumpy ride to Chicago. They landed about 4:30 P.M., to find Howe, Farley, son James Roosevelt, and a few others waiting to greet them. The entourage piled into cars, Howe and James jamming into the back seat of the lead car next to Roosevelt, and drove through a throng of cheering supporters as they left the airport.[24]

Howe had read a draft of the acceptance speech crafted by Roosevelt, Rosenman, Raymond A. Moley, and other members of the Brain Trust, and as the car moved, he told Roosevelt he objected to several sections. Roosevelt "listened to him with one ear, argued back out of the side of his mouth—all the while smiling and waving at the wildly cheering crowd." Howe pressed Roosevelt heatedly, until Roosevelt "suddenly exploded—'Dammit Louie, I'm the nominee!'" It was, James said, "one of the few times I ever heard him get really rough with Louis." But Roosevelt also incorporated the first introductory passages of the speech his old friend and advisor had drafted.[25]

Some two hours later, Roosevelt, using a cane and leaning on James's arm for support, haltingly made his way to the stage at the Coliseum, thunderous applause and cheers raining down. The acrimony of the previous few days had disappeared—though, so had Al Smith, who was already on his way back to New York, along with supporters, leaving gaps here and there on the floor.

Roosevelt spoke for forty-six minutes, his words echoing through the cavernous hall and across the airwaves. He had little new to say and offered a distillation of his view that the Republicans had led the nation into crisis and had no road map for the way back out. He reemphasized the nation held interconnectedness of national interests: If farmers can't afford products made by factory workers, there are fewer factory workers, who, in turn, have less money to buy food.

"That is why we are going to make the voters understand this year that this Nation is not merely a Nation of independence, but it is, if we are to survive, bound to be a Nation of interdependence—town and city, and North and South, East and West," Roosevelt said, sweat streaming down his face. "That is our goal, and that goal will be understood by the people of this country no matter where they live."

He again promised a "new deal" for the nation, and a fresh way of doing things—symbolized, he said, by his decision to scrap tradition and fly to Chicago to address the convention. "Let it be from now on the task of our Party to break foolish traditions. We will break foolish traditions and leave it to the Republican leadership, far more skilled in that art, to break promises." Pushing back at Republican efforts to paint him as a radical, Roosevelt noted that the economic crisis "has produced but a few of the disorderly manifestations that too often attend upon such times," conveniently overlooking the deadly hunger marches in cities, the unrest and threatened farmer strikes in the Midwest, and the presence of thousands of unemployed Great War veterans encamped in the nation's capital demanding early bonus payments. "The way to meet that danger" of political radicalism "is to offer a workable program of reconstruction, and the party to offer it is the party with clean hands."

The crowd of twenty thousand interrupted Roosevelt numerous times with cheers and applause, but none matched the outpouring when Roosevelt addressed the other major issue of the day.

"I congratulate this convention for having had the courage fearlessly to write into its declaration of principles what an overwhelming majority here assembled really thinks about the 18th Amendment," Roosevelt said to the roaring crowd. "This convention wants repeal. Your candidate wants repeal. And I am confident that the United States of America wants repeal."

DIARIES III

Tuesday, June 7

NELLIE COWLEY, GLENDORA, CALIFORNIA

John D. Rockefeller Jr. comes out for the repeal of Prohibition. Perhaps it will be best to go back to the saloon and let people see what it really is. If it is repealed, I look for an orgy of drunkenness to sweep the country, and an appalling number of auto accidents.

Friday, June 10

FAY WEBB GARDNER, RALEIGH, NORTH CAROLINA

A busy, hot day. Helped Lizzie and Miss Wise put away all [of our] winter clothes, coats and all blankets. Oversaw cleaning the third floor, assorted magazines, cleaned bureau drawers, etc. Madge to dentist at eleven to have bad tooth x-rayed—may have to pull. Mama read the papers all morning. Ralph and Max Jr. rode to town, and to movies after lunch. Read papers and some magazines in afternoon. Atmosphere politically warming up ... the move to stop Gov. Roosevelt ... collapsed—predicting he will be nominated on first ballot at Convention in Chicago June 27. The G.O.P. chiefs are meeting at Chicago next Thursday. Prohibition will be a big issue to both parties. Raining tonight—soft and gentle. Will read some, then to bed. Somewhat tired out.

Thursday, June 16

NELLIE COWLEY, GLENDORA, CALIFORNIA

The Republican platform comes out with a plank favoring an amendment to the Constitution, which will turn the liquor question back to the states to decide as they wish, but if a state wishes to be dry, the Federal government will aid it in keeping liquor out. It seems a step backward, but perhaps it is the wise thing to submit it to the people and have it settled once and for all. The Wets made a very noisy demonstration and would not let Garfield speak for the Dry side. I cleaned Mamma's room.

Monday, July 4

EMILY A. C. RICH, OGDEN, UTAH

This morning Dr. and I drove to Salt Lake City to see his sister Lubbie Pratt. We found her very sick. She has well developed cancer of liver etc. and cannot live long. She is now 82 years old, very bright & hopeful, wishing to live longer. Viola her daughter came from New York yesterday to be with her. We ate lunch with Dr.'s brother Fred and his wife Em Rich and had a nice visit. Called to see my brother, Oren, and his wife Mae. He was just leaving for the mines where he and Mark are trying hard to make a living these times of depression as neither have had work for a year. We came home about 3 p.m. having enjoyed a lovely cool ride. Quite a change in the weather from yesterday. Cool all day and night.[1]

CHAPTER 13

Hoover Rousts
the Bonus Army

THE DEMOCRATS HAD JUST BEGUN their convention when, back in Washington, the Senate voted to shelve the Bonus Bill. Until then, the Bonus Marchers had been tolerated, if not openly welcomed, in the capital. But the end of the bill also marked a shift in how Washington, D.C., perceived the veterans, and within the ranks of the men themselves. Officials and newspaper editorials began urging the men to pull up stakes and go home. The *Evening Star*, which opposed the payment of the bonus as unaffordable, urged the leaders of the Bonus Expeditionary Force and their allies in Congress to "strive together to turn these good men toward the homes they left to come here." The editorial praised the veterans' behavior during the at-times emotional demonstrations, but said that "cool heads should take control of the situation and bring about the only appropriate conclusion of this demonstration. The conclusion would be an exodus from the city as orderly and as dramatic as the gathering of the army in the beginning."[1]

Pelham Glassford, D.C.'s police superintendent, floated a plan under which Congress would establish a homesteader program for unemployed vets, giving them land and work, seemingly oblivious to the fact that farmers had been struggling to feed themselves and their families since the end of the war. (It paralleled a suggestion by Governor Franklin Roosevelt that the unemployed in cities be given access to abandoned farms around the country.)

Readers, too, sent in suggestions on how the veterans should be handled, including a proposal by retired army major (and prolific writer of letters to the editor) Alexander Sidney Lanier that the men be mustered back into the military for a year under Glassford's command and deployed to a base in Maryland, free to be discharged if they found a job. "These men," Lanier wrote, "instead of being a potential menace to peace and order would then be supporters of the government and defenders of the public order."[2]

Some veterans had had enough. BEF leader Walter Waters repeated his vow that the veterans would remain in D.C. and continue lobbying until they received the bonus, even if that meant camping out until the due date in 1945. But many men decided to go home. D.C. police estimated up to one thousand veterans departed a day or two after the Senate vote; Waters put the number of those who gave up at around two hundred. A Washington-based correspondent for *The New York Times* observed that the day after the Senate vote "a survey of the camps showed the men generally standing fast in their determination to stay." And men continued to trickle in daily by the handful, occasionally by the dozens. Instead of slowly shrinking, Camp Marks slowly grew. Statistics compiled by the army's Military Intelligence Division estimated eighteen thousand veterans in Washington two days before the Senate vote; a few days later, it estimated, the bonus army had grown to twenty thousand people. By July 20, the BEF counted 23,674 men, women, and children scattered among the camps.[3]

Ignoring the sting of the Senate defeat, Waters issued a call for 150,000 veterans to come to D.C. by fall to build on the summer campaign and increase the pressure on Congress. Official Washington, already concerned about the massed men, became even antsier. Glassford floated the idea that if the railroads agreed to provide transportation, many of the men would welcome a free ride home. The Pennsylvania and Baltimore & Ohio lines offered tickets at a fare of one cent a mile for individual veterans—the Oregon marchers' trips would cost about $28 each—but no level of government stepped forward to pay, so the idea fizzled.

From the early successes of the Bonus March, there had been some power moves by various veterans who sought to play a larger role in the BEF, or in some cases to take over. Waters himself was learning how to lead a political movement on the fly and seemed to know intuitively that the BEF was a one-issue crusade. The demand for early payment of the promised bonuses united the veterans, from the jobless factory workers in Portland, Oregon, to the impoverished farmers in Louisiana, to the white-collar workers in New York or Boston. It was, at heart, a nonpartisan mission. Waters realized that if the BEF began to make demands on other issues, it ran the risk of internal divisions. The only political endorsements he approved were those backing members of Congress who supported the Bonus Bill— and opposing those who did not. The day after the Senate vote, the BEF's executive and legislative committees voted to formalize that position and try to portray the veterans as a united bloc on that single issue.

The fringe presence of communists posed a special concern for Waters and other leaders, even though one of the unifying elements for the rank and file was their opposition to communism. In fact, the men harangued and sometimes beat radical agitators when they came by to proselytize; and even in informal conversation, someone espousing anything perceived to be radical thought could be hounded out of camp. Still, overt efforts by people such as John Pace, of the Michigan contingent, fed the Hoover administration's belief that communists organized the march; and despite the veterans' diligent efforts to keep them out—including Waters's shadowy military police unit—it's likely some managed to remain within the main body of the BEF.[4]

But in the wake of the Senate vote, the communist group began agitating for the men to "turn out" Waters and join them in a broader movement by returning to their hometowns and band "with other workers of which we are a part for immediate relief and unemployment insurance." Waters rebuffed the effort, warning the men that "there will be many factions and groups with pet hobbies and crazy ideas of government" trying to influence the BEF.

"I will not allow myself to be influenced by their oratory, or the beautiful picture of their special heavens," Waters said sarcastically. "I will ask you to pledge yourselves to me, as red-blooded Americans, not to listen to them, because we are Americans in principle and can only join that which is wholly American and that represents true American ideals."

Waters began organizing the BEF for the long haul. On June 25, the first issue of the *B.E.F. News* appeared, an eight-page newspaper published by the veterans under editor Joseph L. Heffernan, a journalist, lawyer, and former municipal judge and mayor of Youngstown, Ohio. It aimed to keep the veterans informed about the march efforts and camp life, and to serve as an information conduit for those outside Camp Marks and the other campsites. "In it you will read the thoughts of the veterans camped at Washington," the *B.E.F. News* wrote in announcing its own birth. "It is a composite outcry, and behind it a seeing eye will discover anguished heartbeats."[5]

Waters also arranged to have identity cards issued to the men to overlay a stronger semblance of order and organization, but also to control who could claim to be a part of the recognized group. That gave the BEF another tool to try to keep the radicals on the outside. They proved to be a persistent bunch.

WATERS HAD A habit of quitting as the BEF commander, but, in his telling, always with a purpose. On the road to Washington, D.C., Waters disappeared during the showdown at East St. Louis, leaving a power gap that other marchers, led by George Alman, filled by forming a workers' committee to make the major decisions. That group fell away after Waters resurfaced a couple of days later when the caravan reached Indiana.

Then a week after arriving in the capital, Waters again stepped down, this time over health and stress issues. "After four days of sleepless hurrying from one problem to another, I collapsed and resigned as commander," he wrote later. The *Evening Star* reported that Waters was "ill with a nervous breakdown," and that Alman took charge after a late-night meeting of BEF leaders, who also formed an executive committee.

Despite the illness, by June 10 Waters had returned to power with a vote of the executive committee after co-leading a parade of seven thousand veterans "in motley uniforms but ordered ranks" from near the Washington Monument, down Pennsylvania Avenue, to the Capitol. Yet Waters's single-mindedness set up tension with executive committee members, who "sought constantly to displace my tactics of passive resistance with some vague program of their own."[6]

Waters was under significant pressure. He was the main contact point and negotiator with Police Superintendent Glassford, but he also bore responsibility for finding food for the men and trying to keep them organized and on good behavior. Waters oversaw regular purges for leftist beliefs, including ousting Alman, suspected of aligning with radicals. And Waters faced sporadic dissent among men who resisted the centralized command, arguing that they were no longer in the U.S. Army and needn't follow orders. In a group that exceeded more than twenty thousand people in Washington, D.C., with countless more supporters and sympathizers nationwide, there were plenty of competing ideas about strategy, camp management, and public relations.

There also was growing unrest in some quarters about Waters's leadership.

"A half-dozen plots and fights for leadership broke out," Waters wrote, adding that his "secret service" brought him reports of "camp commanders and other officers meeting mysteriously in hotel rooms around town. The only difficulty they seemed to be having in all their plotting was in deciding just which man was to succeed me." Demands increased to align the BEF behind the Democrats in opposition to the Hoover administration's intransigence, which ran counter to Waters's recognition that focusing the BEF on anything other than the early bonus payment would undermine its appeal and power. Communists following the lead of Pace, New York City organizer Emanuel Levin of the Workers Ex-Servicemen's League, and others created a parallel Central Rank and File Committee headquartered at Thirteenth and B Streets SW, hoping to peel away followers of "the mincing, strutting puppet generals of the Waters' group."[7]

The mounting internal criticism and second-guessing led Waters once again to quit. In his letter to the executive committee that had installed him, Waters painted himself as someone upon whom leadership was thrust. "I did not, nor do I now, seek the tremendous responsibility of this position" and that "it is my frank opinion that the rank and file of the B.E.F. now in Washington should be permitted at this time to choose their permanent national commander." He said he had no intention of leaving the BEF or trying to force a vote of confidence for himself, and that he would fall in line behind whomever the men selected.[8]

In his memoir Waters framed his June 25 resignation as an act of altruism, and democracy. The dynamics of the BEF and its members had changed since he and the Oregon contingent first arrived in the nation's capital and "I felt that they should have a chance to choose their commander." If the rank and file thought the purpose of the BEF should be expanded, they should be able to choose that path. But elsewhere in the memoir Waters occasionally wrote disparagingly of some of the men who resisted his directives as malcontents and whiners.

This new resignation set off a leadership crisis, which seems to have been Waters's intent all along. But it also may have just been a fit of pique. On June 24, Waters had issued a call for the BEF to "come to the Capitol to show the Senate that we are here," but only a relative handful of veterans responded. Waters had also cut off the supply of food to Pace's contingent to try to force that group to oust Pace. Pace stepped down temporarily; food was delivered; the men reinstalled Pace. In a third rebuke Waters had agreed to Glassford's request that no more men be sent to a small shantytown at Camp Meigs, north of Union Station, which he wanted closed, but the Executive Committee voted to overrule him. The commander also was heckled as he addressed veterans at the Thirteenth and B Street SW encampment.[9]

In the wake of Waters's resignation, Alman worked the Anacostia flats, drumming up political support, and aligned himself with Pace, while the "more conservative element" among the veterans sought ways to get Waters back as commander. Camp Bartlett and squatters at 645 C Street SW voted to reinstate Waters, a symbolic move given that there was no election at hand. Meanwhile, representatives from all the camps met to plan a convention to chart the future of the BEF, including its leadership.

The executive committee selected Thomas Kelly, of New Jersey, to fill in as interim commander, but he almost immediately resigned and was replaced by George Kleinholz, another Portland marcher. Glassford, the sympathetic police superintendent, also washed his hands of formal involvement with the BEF, resigning as treasurer. Food was running low and moves began in Congress to appropriate $100,000 to help the veterans get home.

On June 29, four days after Waters resigned, some ten thousand veterans met at Camp Marks to return him to his command. Waters, addressing the men from atop a shed roof, had his terms:

"On one condition only. If you are willing to give me complete dictatorial powers." They were, and by acclamation he resumed his position as commander, an act described by both the United Press and the communist *Daily Worker* as a coup. Almost immediately Waters disbanded committees, purged perceived nonloyalists from official positions, announced he would appoint another five hundred MPs, and ordered daily hourlong military drills for the men, in part to give them "something to do other than sitting around feeling sorry for yourselves."[10]

But Waters also saw the drills as an act of warning.

"I believe it will make some other people worry," Waters told his men. "What will it look like to our people uptown to see 20,000 men doing squads, right?"

As Waters reasserted his control over the Bonus Army, General Douglas MacArthur planned for bedlam. Shortly after the veterans began arriving in the capital, MacArthur wired military leaders around the country seeking intelligence on whether communists were involved. Only one response hinted at potential links; the rest noted that the veterans pointedly sought to bar communists or other radicals. A separate summary of the veterans already in Washington, D.C., alleged that three of the twenty-six identified leaders may have had radical ties, though it's unclear how well-sourced the military commanders were among the unemployed veterans. Yet, there also were reports and rumors of a group heading to the nation's capital from Central New York with military-grade weapons supposedly supported by some marines already stationed in Washington.[11]

MacArthur, egged on by his virulently anti-communist top aide, George Van Horn Moseley, convinced himself that the veterans were being controlled, or had been infiltrated, by communists who planned to use the Bonus March as a Trojan horse for an uprising in the capital. Orders went out for active-duty soldiers at Fort Myer, in nearby Arlington, Virginia, to begin drills on riot control, and for an experimental armored car and a self-propelled seventy-five-millimeter gun to be redeployed there from Fort Meade, in case they were needed.

Under the revised White Plan for defending the nation's capital from insurrection, the army would first use tear gas and other nonlethal steps to persuade noncommunist "veterans to be given the opportunity to disperse," presuming that the communist agitators would remain and be subject to more stringent actions. Under a second revision to the White Plan in late July, if the army was deployed, MacArthur would oversee the D.C. police, and, should they fail to quell any disturbance, would send in regular troops to arrest the remaining demonstrators and place them under armed guard on military trucks for the trip home. Notably, there did not seem to be a law that allowed for such a merger of military and civilian responsibilities.[12]

As Congress moved to adjourn in the middle of July, the veterans increased their demonstrations, demanding that the House remain in session until it passed some form of a bonus bill. One contingent from California, unaffiliated with Waters's BEF, drew headlines and onlookers with its "death march," in which veterans shuffled silently around Capitol Hill for several days, pausing briefly on July 15 to make way for a protest by the BEF, in which Waters was twice detained by Glassford and his men until they reached yet another compromise allowing the BEF to remain at the Capitol, so long as they did not block access to the building.

On that same day, yet another group, this one led by communist leader Pace and comprised of some two hundred men, gathered at Eighth Street NW and Pennsylvania Avenue around 10 A.M., and began to move toward the White House. One hundred D.C. policemen, many bearing tear gas guns, hastily joined the usual security detail and shut down the area around the White House. A small contingent led by Inspector Albert J. Headley confronted the demonstrators near the Treasury Building, just east of the White House, and demanded they disperse. An argument with Pace, an assistant, and several of the protesters ensued and Headley grabbed Pace by the throat and tried to push him back. With Headley's contingent outnumbered, and the veterans responding with angry shouts, Headley let Pace go and retreated.[13]

The veterans pressed on, skirmishing with small police detachments along the way, until they reached the main body of police. There, Pace and his assistant were arrested and bundled into a police car. The body of the demonstrators remained for a bit, jeering and insulting the police, but, leaderless, they eventually dissipated. As protests go, it was fairly minor and reminiscent of the dozens of similar confrontations communist organizers had engaged in around the country over the previous few years, most of them under the mantle of fighting for jobs, food, or general relief. But this set-to, so near to the White House, carried a shroud of menace to it, at least in the perceptions of MacArthur and his aides. Communists marching on the White House was, to them, yet another harbinger of insurrection.

From the early days of the march, veterans had found squatter space in condemned buildings along Pennsylvania Avenue between the White House and the Capitol, most of them dating to the Civil War era and slated for demolition to make way for the planned Federal Triangle. In mid-July, with upward of two thousand men still squatting in and around the buildings, the Treasury Department sent word to the D.C. police commission that it needed the veterans evicted so the demolition, long delayed, could commence. On July 21, Waters received an order from Glassford to begin evacuating the buildings by noon the next day and be finished by midnight, on July 24.[14]

Waters saw the order as an act of provocation—an effort by the government to "stir them up, and no better way could have been improvised than to give twenty-four hours' advance notice to 'get out,'" truncating the time for rhetorical effect. The BEF also had to leave the rest of their encampments in parks and on public land by August 4, a directive that would limit the BEF to

Camp Bartlett, on thirty acres of private land that was provided by a sympathizer, along Alabama Avenue between Twenty-First and Twenty-Third Streets SW. "The orders stirred up the camps, naturally, as we had no time to prepare them for it," Waters wrote.

Waters told Glassford he would order the men out of the condemned buildings, once they found a new place to go, and that in the meantime he intended to direct hundreds of men at Camp Marks to make daily visits to the site to "increase the numbers of passive resisters." The deadline was extended by a couple of days as the police commission and Glassford argued over how and when to move the men out, and negotiated with Waters, who finally agreed to move the men in small stages—two hundred the first day, then groups of forty or more over the ensuing days—until the squats were cleared.

In the interim another demonstration by Pace's group moved toward the White House on July 25, a midday effort to rally support from office workers on their lunch hours. Glassford's force formed a more muscular defense this time, and the march turned into a violent confrontation along New York Avenue at Fifteenth Street, near the White House. Police waded into the throng, swinging clubs and chasing people down the street. They targeted individual demonstrators, clubbing and subduing them and dragging some into cars and off to the police station. One demonstrator punched a *Washington Times* photographer and was arrested amid utter confusion, with curious onlookers roughed up along with the demonstrators. In all, nine people were detained, and Pace—who was not present—and two other men were charged with inciting a riot.[15]

WATERS THOUGHT HE had a deal with Glassford on a slow retreat from the squats, but the police commission had no intention of letting the evacuation drag out, a decision Glassford had withheld from Waters. On the morning of July 28, Glassford led a meeting of his officers to lay out the day's game plan for cordoning off several blocks around the squats and then supporting Department of Treasury officials as they delivered eviction orders. The goal: to remove all the veterans immediately.[16]

Waters didn't learn of the double cross until after he arrived at Pennsylvania Avenue, and not long before a half-dozen Treasury Department agents showed up with Glassford's men and began ordering people out of the first building. They cleared the street-level floor without incident as veterans gathered up their few possessions and filtered out. On the second floor the agents encountered some resistance, and Glassford's police eventually dragged out two veterans, one of whom took a few swings at the police officers.[17]

As the evictions continued, more veterans began arriving on trucks from Camp Marks and thronged around the outside of the building. Accounts differ on whether the new arrivals included some of Pace's more radical agitators, but tensions increased dramatically, with veterans hollering at the police.

At the rear of the building, a small contingent, led by a man carrying an American flag on a pole, crossed a rope line draped by the police. Glassford ordered the veterans to stop, but they surged forward, one of them ripping the badge from Glassford's shirt (another veteran soon recovered it and returned it to Glassford). Bricks began flying and officers began falling, four in all, one of whom suffered a fractured skull. Glassford managed to restore order within minutes, and the police and the veterans settled into a fraught standoff—with hundreds more men moving in from Camp Marks and more police arriving from around the city.

Around 2 P.M., Glassford and a small contingent of police officers entered a building adjacent to the one already cleared of veterans to gain a higher-elevation view of how the veterans and police were arrayed on the streets below. A group of veterans, curious to see what Glassford was up to, followed them in and up the stairs. A melee broke out between the police and veterans already in the building, who battered the officers from above with a garbage can and a nightstick grabbed from a police belt. Amid shouts from veterans below of "let's get him," one of the officers on the stairwell pulled his service revolver and began firing into the men below, killing William Hushka, a thirty-nine-year-old Lithuanian immigrant from Chicago, with a bullet to the heart, and mortally wounding Eric Carlson, thirty-eight, of Oakland, California. Glassford shouted from above to stop firing, but the damage was done.

Despite the violence—three police officers also were injured in the building melee—Glassford believed he had control of the operation, and that the veterans would be removed. But his over-lords on the police commission disagreed and appealed to the White House for military help. Hoover gave it, directing the army to "assist the District authorities to restore order," clear the Pennsylvania Avenue sites, and force the veterans back into the established camps, where local authorities could begin criminal investigations. Patrick J. Hurley, Hoover's secretary of war, dis-agreed with Hoover's plan for limited involvement by federal troops, and chief of staff MacArthur, who had been preparing for this moment for weeks, had his own more ambitious plans for dealing with what he perceived to be a leftist insurrection.[18]

Soldiers and equipment already in waiting moved to the El-lipse between the White House and the National Mall, the first detachment of cavalrymen on horseback arriving about 2:30 P.M., soon followed by infantrymen ferried up the Potomac on a steam-ship. Tanks and self-propelled artillery cannons arrived on flatbed trucks.

Glassford, who believed his department still had control of the situation, learned of the military callout and rushed to meet with General MacArthur at the Ellipse. MacArthur told the po-lice superintendent that his troops would remove all veterans by that night, beginning with the squatters along Pennsylvania Ave-nue, then on to the other camps, including the massive village on the Anacostia flats. Glassford sped off to Pennsylvania Avenue to warn the veterans of the impending sweep and sent word of MacArthur's plans to the other encampments.

At MacArthur's direction the army, whose officer corps included future national heroes Major Dwight D. Eisenhower and Major George S. Patton Jr., began moving about 4:30 P.M., down Pennsylvania Avenue. They made for an imposing force: More than two hundred cavalrymen, swords drawn, were in the lead, filling the broad boulevard; they were followed by tank-laden trucks, some four hundred marching infantrymen, and staff cars bearing MacArthur, Eisenhower, Brigadier General Perry Miles (in charge of the army troops usually stationed around the capital), and Captain Thomas Jefferson Davis, MacArthur's close aide.

Many of the veterans had already fled, but hundreds remained. The soldiers issued a three-minute warning, then donned gas masks. One of the veterans threw a stone. The soldiers returned fire with tear gas canisters. The veterans—"animated by the essence of revolution," MacArthur would say later that night—replied with more stones and bricks, and a few grabbed the tear gas canisters and heaved them back among the soldiers.[19]

It was a mismatch by any measure. The active-duty soldiers moved forward; the former soldiers scattered. Fire erupted among the sidewalk shanties; each side blamed the other for the arsons. In short order all that remained was burned debris. MacArthur's men moved on to Camp Glassford, near the Capitol, and cleared that site, too, by five o'clock, and then moved on to the Red camp at Fourteenth and C Streets SW, but Pace and his men had already fled. The troops continued to clear small encampments, took control of the National Mall—including marching through the Botanic Garden—as members of the public joined in with the veterans in yelling at the soldiers. By 7 P.M., the work was all but done.[20]

MacArthur ordered his men to take a dinner break, and then around 9 P.M., he moved to the Eleventh Street Bridge leading to

Camp Marks, pausing at the north side. There he received a directive from President Hoover not to cross the bridge and clear out the veterans on the Anacostia flats. MacArthur ignored the president's message and ordered the U.S. Army to continue its work. The men crossed the bridge, turned to the right, and "entered the area at the eastern tip, descending into the flats through a steep, poorly conditioned road," MacArthur later reported. That part of the camp was nearly empty, and several of the soldiers torched a handful of shanties "to illuminate the immediate surroundings and permit orderly disposition of the troops." A camp leader carrying a white flag approached MacArthur's staff car and asked if the troops could give the remaining veterans time to evacuate. MacArthur agreed, and after an hour's pause ordered his men to resume pushing the remaining veterans, occasionally at bayonet point, out of the camp.[21]

As the Bonus Army retreated, some began setting fires, including burning the main stage from which they heard speeches and received orders, and the gospel tent, site of religious services. The soldiers used their matches as well, setting backfires to try to keep the conflagration from moving beyond the camp. By morning the temporary village of U.S. veterans had been reduced to ashes.[22]

NEWSREEL III

July to September, 1932

On July 1, the Dow Jones Industrial Average closes at 44.4 points, some 40 percent below where it began the year . . . Hitler's Nazi Party wins a plurality of seats in the German Reichstag, but can't attract enough support among rival parties to form a government; another election is scheduled for November . . . Fire begins in a rubbish heap beneath the Coney Island Boardwalk and, fanned by an ocean breeze, grows rapidly to incinerate five blocks of the wooden walkway, an adjacent three square blocks of buildings, including at least two amusement rides and six bathhouses, and two hundred automobiles, many owned by sunbathers visiting the crowded urban beach resort. Miraculously, no one is hurt . . . Vice President Charles Curtis officially opens the 1932 Summer Olympic Games before a crowd of 105,000 people at Olympic Stadium in Los Angeles . . . Union miners in Illinois, out of work since their previous contract expired on March 31, overwhelmingly reject a new contract supported by United Mine Workers of America president John L. Lewis that would drop their daily wage from $6.10 to $5. The union immediately schedules a new vote for August, which also appears to go down to defeat, but before the ballots can be certified, one of Lewis's vice presidents spirits them away and Lewis imposes the $5 contract on the members. The ploy exacerbates a long-running rift between members and union leaders and feeds a wave of fistfights on picket lines, gun battles at marches, *and the dynamiting of activists' homes. Several people are killed in the violence. On September 2, the more radical miners meet at Gillespie, Illinois, and form the breakaway Progressive Miners of America, aiming to supplant the UMWA . . . A Washington Star correspondent reports from Tokyo that Japan's "arsenals are working full blast, some of them overtime, in the manufacture of munitions; chemical factories are increasing their output, the Japanese air force is being enlarged and there is considerable activity on all spheres of military action" . . . Seven inches of rain falls in the Tehachapi Mountains, about seventy miles northwest of Los Angeles, causing the Tehachapi Creek to rise twenty feet in ten minutes, sweeping away a service station, a length of railroad track, including a bridge, and a freight train waiting out the storm on a siding; some forty people, mostly itinerant men riding the rails, are swept away with it.*

CHAPTER 14

The Farmers' Strike

WELL BEFORE DAYLIGHT BEGAN CREEPING into the Iowa sky on August 12, scores of dairy farmers had fanned out along the darkened main roadways of Woodbury County. Some arrived in cars, others in farm trucks, and they established informal checkpoints to hail passing traffic. The mission was straightforward: They were to stop any of their fellow dairymen from passing through with milk, butter, and other products destined for distributors and markets in Sioux City, a rail and farming hub on the eastern bank of a bend in the Missouri River.

The Farmers' Holiday Association members had set the Fourth of July as the start date for its long-awaited strike, though they left themselves an out. Milo Reno, the president, and the rest of the unpaid executive committee could delay the start if they felt that conditions warranted, such as a rise in prices or Washington coming through with new policies. And for a few weeks it seemed like that might happen. A few key commodities prices did rise slightly, and farm bills were discussed in the Capitol, so they delayed the holiday. But those potential winds of change turned out to be a light and short-lived breeze, and by early August, with no government relief and prices dropping again, the strike began.

While the Farmers' Holiday Association catalyzed the protest, events quickly took on a life, and an order, of their own. From the start, Reno and his fellow leaders didn't offer much strategic leadership. They developed no plan for how to conduct the strike, other than for the producers to withhold their products. And they offered no formula for establishing the cost of production that would set the foundation for the prices they ultimately would demand. By one estimate the difference between what they were being paid, and what would amount to a reasonable profit, was significant. The cost of production alone for a bushel of corn was ninety-two cents; farmers were paid a dime. For hogs the livestock men would break even at eleven cents a pound; they received three cents. Butterfat cost sixty-two cents a pound to produce; the payments were eighteen cents. So to make a reasonable profit, at a time when consumers themselves were broke, a noticeable hike in consumer prices would be required.[1]

The farmers, for the most part, organized themselves, crafting their own game plans, making their own demands. It was as though the farmers, after listening to the speeches by Reno and reading regular exhortations in the *Iowa Union Farmer* newspaper, thought "good idea," then ran with it. In fact, Reno and the others didn't anticipate picketing, nor did they seem to understand that a farmers' strike would succeed only if the farmers left their land to fight. Staying home and neither buying nor selling for a month would only get them so far, especially if the farmers were not a united front, and they were not. There also was no talk of enforcement mechanisms to ensure solidarity, though peer pressure was significant. A farmer on the outs with his neighbors has a lot of trouble getting help during harvests and other labor-intensive times. "I've got to stay on living here," one unidentified farmer told *The New Republic.* "I guess I'll leave the truck in the shed for a while."[2]

Picketing had more impact than simply disrupting commerce. Conflict and drama make for good headlines. After the blockades had been in effect for several weeks, Reno wrote to a friend that he opposed picketing "because of the danger of loss of life and property," but conceded that "the action of the boys on the picket line has done more to focus the attention of the powers that be to the real facts of the situation than any other thing."[3]

The first to act were dairy producers in the northwestern corner of the state who sold their products in Sioux City, primarily to the J. R. Roberts Dairy Co., the largest processor and distributor in the region and thus the price-setter. The dairy producers had demanded Roberts raise the price it paid them from $1 per hundredweight of 3.5 percent fat milk to $2.17 per hundredweight. Roberts rejected the demand, and in the early hours of August 12, the dairymen went on strike while pledging to supply free milk to relief agencies, orphanages, and hospitals, in part to fill a moral obligation, but also to win public support.[4]

On a rural road outside of Moville, Iowa, some twenty miles east of Sioux City, picketers stopped a dairy truck operated by Mike Hanna and Pete Malcolm, two of the largest dairy farmers in the area, and demanded they turn around. Hanna and Malcolm refused, so the picketers dumped four hundred gallons of their milk onto the roadway. Dozens of other trucks encountered similar barriers, and while many heeded the order to turn around, others sought to evade the blockade by taking side roads, or just motoring on through, only to find themselves chased down by picketers in cars.[5]

No clear numbers indicate how effective the blockades were. By the second full day of the strike, police detachments monitored the picket sites and escorted those who wished to proceed to protect them from harassment. The Woodbury County sheriff deputized around one hundred unemployed men to help escort truck drivers who wished to pass through blockades, ironically giving some temporary job relief. Dan Roberts, who managed the family's dairy processing operations, dismissed the efforts as "a so-called strike ... fomented by a group of radicals and is not supported by the conservative farmers of the territory. In fact, most of the farmers know nothing about it."[6]

While the strike may not have had support from a significant majority of farmers, they all certainly knew about it. It would have been impossible to miss the months of meetings and stories splashed across newspaper front pages. Farmers also used the radio as an electronic lifeline, bringing them news and daily updates on farm prices. The 1930 Census estimated one in five rural families owned a radio and noted that many more people had access to radio programming through stores and other commercial buildings. Many farms had telephones, too, speeding the sharing of information. It's hard to imagine that hundreds of farmers blocking access to markets didn't have a prominent place in some of those broadcasts, or among the news items that neighbors shared with each other.[7]

Roberts, then, engaged in targeted disinformation, a common practice during labor disputes. But he also took significant steps to ensure that his operations were still supplied with milk. On the second full day of the strike, with roads barricaded, a train from Omaha dropped off a shipment of twenty thousand pounds of milk for Roberts and his competitor, the Fairmont Creamery.

As the processors expanded their net for milk and dairy sources, the producers also extended their blockade. By August 14, the number of picketers had grown significantly to an estimated 1,500 farmers, who severely impeded the flow of goods into Sioux City, despite the presence of more than one hundred police officers. The picketers' prey now included produce trucks and those hauling hogs and other animals. Most turned around. Within a week the Dairy Producers Association estimated that dairy deliveries dropped by 90 percent, and hog deliveries were halved.[8]

The picketing lacked any sort of central direction and had no set leader. Once the farmers embraced the tactic, they forged ahead organically. Picket camps served as regional command posts and bivouacs. "This is how it happens," wrote a reporter for the *Omaha World-Herald* early in the strike. Cars and trucks filled with farmers arrive at a post at dusk, but "there are many more men than are needed" at that site. "Word comes that a trucker is trying to evade by going down on the bottom roads. A truckload of pickets goes full speed to that road, stops, opens a camp. They stay all night." Some sleep in the open, or cram into the vehicles if it rains. Others take to nearby barns or haystacks. At dawn some make the rounds of farmhouses in the vicinity scrounging for breakfast donations from willing supporters. The picketers come and go, returning to their farms to catch up on chores, then returning; some devote all their time to it, manning blockades at night and returning home to sleep during the day. Presciently, the writer declared, "If Milo Reno called off the strike today it probably wouldn't close a single picket camp."[9]

The Farmers' Holiday spread like a vine. Pickets went up in an arc from the southwest to the northeast of Iowa affecting Nebraska, South Dakota, Minnesota, and Wisconsin. Then North Dakota joined in, and eventually Illinois and Indiana. Much of the organizing came at Farmers Union picnics, where Reno and other leaders delivered speeches as part of programs that included dancing and games. The movement leapfrogged to parts of Georgia and among potato farmers on New York's Long Island. And everywhere it generated headlines and, in some quarters, a growing fear that smoldering pockets of dissent in the heart of the country could develop into a political wildfire.

THE GAPS IN the blockade at Sioux City were significant and obvious: the rail lines, and a motor vehicle bridge crossing the Missouri River from the Nebraska side. While farmers in northeast Nebraska soon joined the holiday and shut off access to the bridge, the railroads proved more difficult to intercept. And the nature of the strike morphed after the milk producers negotiated a deal with Roberts and the others, settling on $1.80 per hundredweight, an 80 percent jump, but well below the

$2.17 per hundredweight they had demanded. In more recognizable terms the producers would receive about 3.6 cents per quart, up from two cents, pushing the retail price to nine cents per quart, up a penny, with the processors and distributors eating the difference.[10]

That settlement accentuated the difference between the dairy farmers and the rest of the agricultural sectors. Many dairy products had a short shelf life and were hard to stockpile, and so most of the products were distributed in limited regions, fairly near the sources of production. A milk strike could create immediate shortages which gave the dairy farmers more leverage than crop and livestock farmers. But the latter could also store their goods for the duration of a month's stoppage. But a prolonged strike would become more difficult.

Perversely, if the holiday worked and prices increased, the farmers who broke the embargo received higher prices, and when the holiday ended, the flow of stored goods hitting the market at once would drive prices back down again. Thus the Farmers' Holiday was not likely to succeed by itself in bringing higher prices for most of the participants. But it could, and did, draw the nation's attention to their plight.

For the farmers who participated, even tilting at windmills carried an emotional and psychological benefit. And they felt empowered. In Council Bluffs, ninety miles downriver from Sioux City, an armed posse deputized by the Pottawattamie County sheriff arrested more than forty farmers during a violent clash on August 24 as the deputies, supported by Iowa National Guard troops, sought to clear a blockade to markets in Omaha, across the river. Four guardsmen were injured when they drove a tear gas–spewing vehicle through the picket, drawing thrown rocks and boards in return. Hours later, some five hundred farmers and their supporters descended on the county jail to spring their comrades, a showdown that ended without further violence when a wealthy farmer posted the arrested men's bail. The same night police in Sioux City arrested some eighty picketers; hours later, the men won their release, and immediately returned to the picket lines.[11]

A week later, eleven Pottawattamie County deputies suffered cuts and bruises as they escorted hog trucks eastward into Ida County; farmers pelted the caravan with stones and other debris, and at the county line a hand-to-hand melee broke out as the farmers sought to block the trucks. The drivers were eventually chased down thirty miles away, stopped, and persuaded to turn around and return the hogs where they came from, induced in part by farmers opening the doors of some of the trucks and letting the hogs run free.

Then the guns came out.

Several dozen picketing farmers gathered late in the evening at the side of Highway 21, just south of Cherokee, and about forty-five miles northeast of Sioux City, for an update from a farmer named N. B. Cope, who led the Cherokee County Farmers' Holiday efforts. It's unclear what the message was. He spoke about expecting more pickets the next day, maybe as many as two thousand, and it's safe to assume the men were figuring out logistics.

The men kept an eye out for trucks that might try to travel the road, still diligent in maintaining the blockades, but didn't pay much attention to a small caravan of cars. At least not until they slowed to a crawl and began firing tear gas canisters into the gathering, followed by salvos from handguns, rifles, and shotguns. More than a dozen farmers were wounded, one seriously, but the attack focused mostly on their parked vehicles. Bullets riddled the bodies and fenders and radiators and lacerated the tires, making many of them unable to be driven. The caravan then raced around to other barricades in the county and similarly rousted the picketers, damaged the cars, and cleared the roadways at least for the night.

At first, the picketing farmers believed the attackers were county sheriff's deputies, but local law enforcement denied they

Incoming president Herbert Hoover (right) with his predecessor, Calvin Coolidge, during Hoover's March 4, 1929, inauguration, nearly eight months before the stock market crash that heralded the start of the Great Depression.
National Photograph Company, Library of Congress

James Farley (right) ran both of Franklin Delano Roosevelt's gubernatorial campaigns before turning to the 1932 presidential election. The two met on December 7, 1931, at Warm Springs, Georgia, weeks before Roosevelt formally launched his presidential candidacy.
Franklin D. Roosevelt Presidential Library & Museum

Former New York governor and failed
1928 Democratic presidential candidate
Al Smith, a mentor and then rival to
Franklin Delano Roosevelt.
Library of Congress

John J. Raskob, who made his fort
as an advisor and investor
Pierre S. Du Pont, became a major ba
of Al Smith and personally finan
the first full-time staff of a political p
after the Democrats' dismal show
in the 1928 presidential elect
Library of Cong

Former political journalist Charles Michelson,
hired by Democratic National Committee chair
John J. Raskob as the first full-time publicity
director of an American political party,
became a painful thorn in the side of
President Herbert Hoover as he organized
a relentless and highly effective campaign
blaming Hoover and his fellow Republicans
for much of the nation's economic ills.
Harris & Ewing Collection, Library of Congres

Father James Cox speaks at a rally at Pitt Stadium on January 16, 1932, to launch his presidential campaign on the newly formed Jobless Party ticket. He hoped to draw more attention to the interests of millions of unemployed Americans, whom he believed neither of the major parties were serving. *James R. Cox Papers, 1923–1950, used with permission from the University of Pittsburgh Library System.*

Walter Waters (center at table) was an unemployed World War One veteran in Portland, Oregon, when he organized the Bonus Expeditionary Force march on Washington in early 1932, hoping to force Congress to speed up delivery of bonus payments scheduled for 1945. *Underwood and Underwood collection, Library of Congress*

The first rustlings of what would become the Dust Bowl began with a series of smaller dust storms dur
1932. By 1935, massive clouds of dust enveloped communities such as Baca, Colorado, as pictured he
Farm Security Administration – Office of War Information Photograph Collection, Library of Congre

Founder Pauline Sabin (center) in April 1932, flanked by other leaders of the Women's Organizatior
for National Prohibition Reform, which became a leading advocacy group for the repeal of Prohibitio
Second from left is Grace Roosevelt, wife of Teddy Roosevelt's son Archibald.
Second from right is Alice Du Pont, wife of Pierre S. Du Pont. *Library of Congress*

...mbers of the Bonus Expeditionary Force, or Bonus Marchers, occupy the steps of the Capitol Building in ...summer of 1932 as they lobbied Congress. *Underwood and Underwood Collection, Library of Congress*

...hacks built by members of the Bonus Expeditionary Force near the Capitol Building go up in flames ...s active-duty members of the U.S. Army, under the direction of Gen. Douglas MacArthur, routed the ...orld War One veterans from their makeshift encampments. The routing of the Bonus Army fed public ...rceptions of Hoover as cold and indifferent to the suffering of the American people. *National Archives*

Iowa farmer Milo Reno, president of the National Farmers Holiday Association as well as the head of the Union Mutual Life Insurance Company. He was a key figure in organizing farmers to withhold their goods from markets to protest low commodity process.
Union Mutual Life Insurance Company

Nebraska farmers erecting barricades near Omaha as they sought to enforce a Farmers' Holiday – in essence a strike in which they withheld goods from local markets.
Nebraska State Historical Society Photograph Collections

...klin Delano Roosevelt (right) at a table at Hyde Park, New York, with his political mastermind, Louis M. ...e (center), and Bronx Democratic political boss Edward J. Flynn on July 11, 1932, a week after Roosevelt ...on the Democratic presidential nomination. *Franklin D. Roosevelt Presidential Library & Museum*

President Herbert Hoover and his wife, Lou, during a whistle-stop tour in the last weeks of his 1932 re-election campaign. *Harris & Ewing Collection, Library of Congress*

Franklin Delano Roosevelt (right) and Herbert Hoover during the awkward ride from the White House to the Capitol Building on March 4, 1933, where Roosevelt would be sworn in as the 32nd president of the United States. *Library of Congress*

were involved. In the end the attack may have been retribution from a local man who had resented being accosted as he drove through the Highway 21 barricade earlier in the day and returned with friends to do what the police had so far been unwilling to do: use violence to clear the roadways.

Other violent showdowns came in late August, with three days of direct confrontations between farmers and police on roadways outside Omaha. Along a rural stretch of rail line in northeast Nebraska, farmers blockaded the track at a road crossing. When a freight train stopped, they uncoupled the livestock cars. In Danbury, Iowa, forty miles east of Sioux City, farmers slipped into a rail yard and opened the doors of cars holding hogs waiting to be linked up to trains and shooed them to freedom.

Local police, led by county sheriffs, began to lose patience. In the early going they had for the most part maintained an arm's-length distance from the picketers, standing by to intercede when public disorder was threatened, but letting many of the blockades stand. By the end of August, they were engaging in more direct efforts to reopen roads, arresting picketers in small groups and clearing debris, a stance that brought more direct fighting between the picketers and the cops.

With the pickets seemingly spiraling out of control, Reno, head of the national Farmers' Holiday Association, and John Chalmers, who had recently succeeded Reno as leader of the Iowa chapter, ordered a temporary truce. They hoped a pending summit of regional governors could bring about measures that would guarantee a "cost of production" price for farm goods. The farmers largely ignored the stand-down order, signaling exactly how little power the organization had over the strike it had ordered up.

The conference of governors or their representatives from Iowa, Minnesota, North Dakota, Ohio, Oklahoma, South Dakota, Wisconsin, and Wyoming took place September 10 at the

Martin Hotel in downtown Sioux City. As some five thousand demonstrators gathered outside, forty farmers and strike leaders, including Reno, testified inside about the plight of the rural economy, and issued demands for action, including a moratorium on foreclosures and a plan for cost-of-production pricing, including a state-enforced embargo on goods sold for less than the cost of production. The governors and their staffs then convened privately for more than seven hours, finally breaking up a little after midnight.

They released their report the next day—a demand to the Hoover administration and Congress to enact a moratorium on foreclosures, but little else. It pointedly did not endorse the withholding of goods from markets, and essentially said the report "took the burden" for resolving the problem "from the various states, as such, and placed the execution of the proposals squarely before President Hoover and Congress."[12]

Reno expressed guarded satisfaction, while other movement leaders dismissed the governors' report as "a dismal failure," and called for renewed direct actions. Some picketing did continue, but it began to fall off. Yet, with prices still low and farmers still losing their land, the issue, and the tensions, remained.[13]

But a new tactic emerged, one specific to the problem of foreclosures and the forced sale of repossessed farm equipment.

ON PAGE FOUR of the September 16 edition of the *Elgin Review* newspaper, there appeared a short legal notice of a foreclosure sale to be held in three weeks at the farm of Theresa Von Bonn for failure to make good on a $448.90 mortgage she had obtained just ten months earlier from another farmer named John Hemmer. Von Bonn was a sympathetic figure in the area. In May 1930, her husband, Barney, saw a tornado approaching the family farm outside Petersburg, ten miles south of Elgin. As his family scrambled into the tornado shelter, he ran to secure the door of the chicken coop, but the funnel struck before he could get to safety, piercing his body with splintered wood and sending his life-less body cartwheeling through the air before dumping it on the roadway. The tornado also ripped away half of the farmhouse, leaving his wife and their seven children without a place to live, and without the linchpin of their small farming operation.[14]

There is never a good time for such tragedy to befall a family, but coming as it did during the grinding agricultural depression, the effects were magnified. Still, Von Bonn managed to scrape to-gether enough seed money to buy a new farm, just south of Elgin, on a mortgage from Hemmer. When a payment came due, she had more than $500 on deposit in a bank in Humphrey, about forty miles away, but the bank had gone on "holiday." Von Bonn couldn't get her money out; Hemmer refused to give her an ex-tension and foreclosed.

The legal notice coincided with the Antelope County Fair, and there a handful of farmers began discussing what they might be able to do to help Von Bonn and her children. They met again at a local schoolhouse and dispatched a small group to talk to Hemmer, his lawyer, and an official for Hemmer's bank (presum-ably holding some of his debt) and persuaded them to accept $100 to satisfy what Von Bonn owed. Then they arranged for up-ward of three thousand farm families and sympathizers to show up at the Von Bonn farm the day of the sale.

C. J. "Chris" Christenson, who led the Farmers' Holiday As-sociation in the region, addressed the group before the sale began, making no bones about their intent. "This sale ain't going to bring much," Christenson told them. "We got three or four men to bid and we don't want nobody else to bid. And if any-body else opens up their mouth to bid, you know what to do with 'em."[15]

The auction came off as a tense and muted affair, the bidding light and low, as planned. An expensive harness set went for fifty cents, ten cows for $2.50 each, and a few horses for $1.50 a head. After all the items had been presented, the take totaled less than the $100 Hemmer had agreed to, so a hat was passed to make up the difference. "Now that place is Mrs. Von Bonn's." And the buyers turned their purchases back over to her.

Over the course of the next several months, more farmers would engage in similar "penny auctions," and in some instances simply venture to farm supply businesses and make off with repossessed trucks, tractors, and other high-ticket items and return them to the farms from which they had been repossessed. In some places groups of farmers surrounded county courthouses on the day of auctions. As credit holders saw their collateral being lowballed through the collusion of the bidders, they began postponing auctions and sales rather than risk incurring the losses from what were, in effect, rigged markets.

Much like with the Farmers' Holidays, those involved in staving off evictions and forced sales found something satisfying in their efforts. Christenson saw links between banks on holiday freezing the assets of depositors and the demands for farmers' notes to be paid, even though, like Von Bonn, they often lost access to their own deposits to make good. As banks failed, the depositors—farmers and townspeople alike—lost their savings. "We've been eating each other up like cannibals," Christenson observed. "It's time it stopped."

Few thought the related embrace of direct action by the farmers posed a risk to the nation at large, but it also was not just a one-off movement. Hunger marchers had been demanding relief across the nation's cities—sometime, as in Detroit, with deadly results. The Great War veterans had not given up their demands for their bonus payments, with Walter Waters trying to build his "khaki shirts" into a political movement. Father Cox pressed his campaign for president at the head of his blue-shirted Jobless Party. Communists and other perceived radicals continued sowing seeds in the softened political ground. And the Wets were tapping into growing national dissent over Prohibition to push for repeal at the ballot box.

The nation—battered, broke, and angry—wanted change. The presidential campaign would give Americans the opportunity to make it happen. They could decide whether they still had faith in Hoover and the Republicans and their near-religion of self-reliance and limited government, or whether the nation should strike off in a new, albeit uncertain, direction.

DIARIES IV

Thursday, September 22

EMILY A. C. RICH, OGDEN, UTAH

I have spent all morning telephoning, etc., arranging for work at the canning factory. The four Latter Day Saints Stake Relief Societies are arranging to put up fruit as it is so plentiful and can be had for the howling. Our aim is to can 5000 of peaches & 5000 of tomatoes so we may better help the unemployed and those in need. I prepared dinner for Dr. Erashis Murrell, Ralph Cozzens & Margret Cozzens who is living with us. Went to luncheon at Rosella Larkin at three, took part in Pioneer program at 12 Ward at six, had a committee meeting here with Ida Treeseder, Tam Clark & Bishop Terray on the work we hope to put over at the factory canning fruit.

Friday, September 23

EMILY A. C. RICH, OGDEN, UTAH

The weather feels like Autumn. I have been downtown with Myrene looking for a coat but did not get one. Bought vegetables for pickles. Have accomplished very little. Called all Ward Relief Society Pres. in Mt. Ogden Stake asking each one to call six women to give their service peeling peaches next Monday at Greig's Factory. The four Stake Relief Societies expect to can 5000 quarts of peaches. One hundred & twenty women will work all day Monday.

Tuesday, October 4

WILLIAM E. WARFIELD, FORT WAYNE, INDIANA

Miss Pearl Ramsey called to see my wife again today as did Mrs. Carey. They are both out of work and looking for assistance. Our generosity is constantly being drawn upon. We consider it our duty to help the needy. The presidential campaign is underway now and President Hoover is today in his native Iowa making his first major effort—since nomination—to succeed himself. Things look extremely "Democratic" and much depends upon his speech today and subsequent speeches. For the first time since their franchise I believe the majority of negro voters will vote Democratic—but I shall as usual vote a straight Republican ticket. I owe a lifetime loyalty to the party that set my parents and the American Negroes free.

Sunday, October 16

NELLIE COWLEY, GLENDORA, CALIFORNIA

Fog again and cool and damp all day. President Hoover made a fine speech at Cleveland. It was very clear and very convincing. I begin to feel that there is hope of his being re-elected. If he isn't, it will show that the American people do not do much thinking.

Wednesday, October 19

DOROTHY SIMONSON, ISLE ROYALE, MICHIGAN

We had a terrific thunderstorm which rather spoiled the bombastic political speeches! We heard Ogden Mills (Republican) and Roosevelt (Democrat)—and decided to vote for [Socialist candidate] Norman Thomas. It is no wonder people become socialistic, or even Bolshevik in their ideas, when they have to listen to political drivel of the nature we are hearing now. And Mills mentioned all in all some $133.9 million in his speech! And us with $8 in the bank and $65 a month for twelve-hour days of nerve-wracking work—to turn out more boys and girls to become more rotten, grafting politicians. Bah!

NELLIE COWLEY, GLENDORA, CALIFORNIA

I think we're going to have a panic if Roosevelt is elected. I hate his having the name of Roosevelt when he is so different from Theodore Roosevelt. I found "Teddy's" picture a few days ago and have cut it out and put it on the desk. He is standing on the ground by a saddled horse. If only we had him with us now!

Monday, October 31

EMILY A. C. RICH, OGDEN, UTAH

After preparing breakfast & doing up housework I went down to Weber Co & Ogden City Charity building and worked all day assorting clothing. Came home at six p.m., prepared a light supper and retired early. Dr. read aloud to me from Good Earth. *Had letters from Junior and Lucile my sister. Junior had been to see Oertel and family at Columbus Ohio. All were fine. Lucile & family were well but business bad. Dr. went to Salt Lake on business. Came home feeling that conditions are bad regarding his loans from the bank. Received a letter from Thair saying business is bad in LA.*

CHAPTER 15

The Campaign

WITH THE NOMINATIONS IN HAND, and the presidential campaign about to begin in earnest, Herbert Hoover and Franklin Roosevelt found themselves facing a similar challenge: countering lies and rumors.

Roosevelt's problems centered on reassuring the doubtful about his physical stamina. Hoover had barred his advisors from making Roosevelt's physical condition a campaign issue, but that couldn't stop the whispers—and not just among Republicans. In fact, Roosevelt flew from Albany to Chicago to accept the Democratic Party's nomination not only to personify the breaking of political traditions, but to demonstrate his physical fitness to his fellow Democrats and to the nation. Through regular exercise Roosevelt had developed a strong torso enabling him to project an image of health and vigor. In public appearances he invariably entered on the arm of an escort and, while speaking, used one hand on a rail or lectern, while waving with the other, obscuring the strain he endured in simply moving his brace-supported legs. Roosevelt's beaming smile often hid discomfort and pain, as well as occasional indignities involved in just getting from one place to another.

Sam Rosenman, Roosevelt's main speechwriter in Albany, first witnessed the difficulties during Roosevelt's 1928 campaign for governor, which marked the resumption of Roosevelt's political career. "The simple job of getting up and sitting down several times was almost as much exercise as the ordinary man takes during an entire day," Rosenman said. "He could not climb stairs, and often we had to carry him up some back stairs of a hall and down again. He always went through this harrowing experience smiling. He never got ruffled."[1]

Roosevelt believed the best way to prove his fitness was to display it, aided by the acquiescence of reporters and photographers covering the campaign. A week and a half after Roosevelt accepted the nomination in Chicago, he and sons James, Franklin Jr., and John boarded a rented thirty-seven-foot yawl named *Myth II* at Port Jefferson on Long Island for a weeklong three-hundred-mile sailing tour of New England. The cruise would give the governor a chance to rest and spend time with his sons, according to his aides, but there would be a lot of political work done, too. Among Democrats, New England remained Al Smith territory. Delegates from Massachusetts, Connecticut, and Rhode Island stayed true to Smith through the final ballot that gave Roosevelt the nomination, raising questions about whether the party would unite behind its candidate in November. So the trip would also include some fence-mending between Roosevelt and political leaders who, just weeks earlier, were fighting against his nomination.

Roosevelt and his sons, doing their own crewing and cooking, reached New Haven, Connecticut, on the first day, then Stonington on the second, and Naushon Island (owned by the Forbes family, distant relatives) near Martha's Vineyard on the third. From there they traversed the Cape Cod Canal, its edges lined with cheering supporters, and across Massachusetts Bay to Marblehead, finishing up the last day by sailing around Cape Ann and on to Portsmouth, New Hampshire. At each stop, Roosevelt invited aboard local Smith supporters, using his charm in private meetings and public statements to praise them.[2]

The fact that the *Myth II* contained the Democratic nominee for president turned the sailing venture into a waterborne parade. Reporters had rented their own boat, the *Marcon,* to follow along, but agreed to remain a mile or more from the *Myth II,* except for such special circumstances as the daily ship-to-ship press conference. Jesse I. Straus, a Roosevelt intimate whose family was part of the ownership of Macy's, joined W. Forbes Morgan aboard his luxury steam yacht, the *Ambassadress,* where he hosted Joseph P. Kennedy, James Farley, and other politicians and celebrities. Airplanes occasionally joined, too, as photographers were flown in low to use their cameras.

It's intriguing that at a time of great class consciousness, and great suffering at the lower rungs of the economic ladder, Roosevelt didn't suffer much criticism over taking a jaunt on a yacht, a clear symbol of wealth and privilege. His guests were the cream of the financial elite, yet the public embraced him as a "man of the people," even though the economic system he criticized had also richly rewarded him and his family.

News coverage of the trip didn't mention Roosevelt's physical limitations, although there were hints. The *Boston Globe* wrote at the start of the trip that "Roosevelt, on the arm of his son, walked on the long pier where the yawl was moored," then "swung himself down a ramp to the boat." But there were no photographs of Roosevelt in a position that might reveal the uselessness of his legs (in part because Secret Service agents often confiscated film from photographers they thought might have taken a too-revealing photo). Readers saw a hale and hearty man not only ready for a potentially taxing sea voyage, but also primed to take on the world.

The public image of a robust Roosevelt contrasted sharply with Hoover, who had visibly aged during his presidency. Except for occasional forays to Rapidan—carrying work with him— Hoover rarely left the White House, tethered by a sense that

Americans wanted to see their president working. And work he did, usually up by 6 A.M., then not getting to bed until 11 P.M. or so after the daily parade of meetings and crises. By late summer 1932, more than three years after he took office, photographs of Hoover showed a stiff, haggard man warily eyeing the camera.

President Hoover had much to be wary about. As the depression deepened and the pain spread, Hoover became the butt of jokes. One involved Hoover asking Andrew Mellon for a nickel so he could call a friend. "Here's a dime—call all of them." Another said Hoover clearly was a gifted engineer because it took him just over two years to drain the United States. Historian Arthur M. Schlesinger Jr. wrote that vaudevillians incorporated Hoover into their acts. A regular gag involved telling the audience that business is picking up, followed by the observation "Is Hoover dead?"[3]

Hoover was thin-skinned, and rumors gnawed at him. The "smear books" were bad enough, but anti-Hooverites also were reviving false claims from the 1928 campaign: Hoover must be a British citizen, because he had voted in elections while living in London; he refused to hire white employees at a vineyard he owned in California; he drank in private. One accused Hoover of importing slaves from China to work in South African mines, a claim carried in the "Hoover Racketeering Edition" of *The American Freeman* (a successor to *Appeal to Reason*) broadsheet mailed out from Girard, Kansas, by Emanuel Haldeman-Julius, the 1932 Socialist Party candidate in Kansas for a U.S. Senate seat. Hoover supporters sent copies of the paper to the White House, some demanding it be suppressed. Others warned that readers might think that "it must be true because it went through the mail unchallenged," an apparent reference to the post office banning leftist publications from being delivered by mail, a key source of distribution and revenue for the publishers.[4]

The persistence of the rumors that Hoover was a British citizen led the administration to seek a refutation from the State Department, which Secretary William R. Castle did in April 1931, and again in August 1932. Castle, citing British authorities, stated that Hoover had lived in London, but had never voted there nor sought a British passport. Castle also said that Hoover held a valid U.S. passport, and that he had paid annual U.S. income taxes since their resumption in 1913 under the Sixteenth Amendment. "There has never been any taint on Mr. Hoover's status as a U.S. citizen," Castle wrote. But lies are not so easily killed.[5]

One of the most dramatic charges against Hoover was both true and partially self-inflicted: He had ordered the U.S. Army to violently evict thousands of Great War veterans from shantytowns scattered around Washington, D.C. Hoover had, at the request of D.C. officials, sent in the army to help police evict veterans after the initial violent clash. After all, his Treasury Department wanted the federally owned buildings cleared so they could be demolished ahead of a construction project.

Yet, Hoover never mentioned publicly that he had issued a limited directive, and that Patrick Hurley and Douglas MacArthur—perceiving a nonexistent communist plot to commit a coup d'etat—ignored his orders and exceeded the authority he had given them. It was a classic example of a chief executive publicly taking responsibility for the actions of underlings. Further, Hoover ignored his underlings' blatant insubordination even after Hurley and MacArthur rebuffed his request that they issue public statements about their actions. Hoover also let Hurley talk him into dropping a plan to enlist a sympathetic member of Congress to defend his actions and lay bare the failures of Hurley and MacArthur. The public supported the evictions and the president, Hurley told Hoover assistant Lawrence Richey. Why give critics an opening now? "After going over it with his friends and among our people here, we decided that neither myself nor MacArthur should hit the footlights," Hurley said. A more politically savvy president wouldn't have been so gracious and would have demanded the transparency or fired the men. Hoover, instead, presented a unified front and announced "a challenge to the authority of the United States Government has been met, swiftly and firmly."[6]

Despite Hurley's claim, the initial public response to the evictions was mixed, with some people writing the White House to applaud the president's move against "traitors" on the streets, while others condemned the president for using U.S. troops and tanks against war veterans exercising First Amendment rights.[7]

Major newspaper editorials around the country also backed the administration. The *Washington Star,* buying Hoover's description of the veterans as communists and criminals—and the line heavily pushed by MacArthur that they had faced down communist insurrectionists—declared the troops' behavior to be "highly commendable" in routing the order-defying veterans whose march had been "utilized by subversive forces to make trouble and perhaps to precipitate insurrectionary riots." *The New York Times* editorialized that Hoover had shown "great forbearance," but that the initial clashes with police meant "there was but one thing to do" with "violent insurrectionists," and Hoover did it. "We are confident that the decision of the president will be sustained by the great majority of our citizens." The *Los Angeles Times* felt "the federal government could have done no differently" in dealing with the "radical remnants of the so-called bonus army."[8]

It didn't take long, though, for those sentiments to change. Within days newsreels from Pathé News and other outfits began eliciting boos from movie theater audiences as screens showed images of tanks rumbling down Pennsylvania Avenue and U.S. Army troops striding through the veterans' shantytowns. Also, Pelham Glassford publicly denied that he supported calling out the troops, contradicting the police commission for which he worked.

As more people recognized that the United States had used active-duty soldiers to drive thousands of veterans and their families—who had not been involved in the Pennsylvania Avenue violence—from their makeshift homes, veterans' groups, politicians, and others spoke out against what was increasingly seen as an inhumane act. Resolutions were drafted for consideration at regional American Legion conventions condemning the use of the army and opposing Hoover's reelection.

"Owing to the apparent deliberate propaganda and misrepresentations," Hurley issued "a candid statement of the facts" that reiterated the administration's version of events. Theodore Joslin also circulated a private letter among the press corps that summed up the administration's take and admonished his former peers "to do your duty" and "tell these indisputable facts to the American people."[9]

The night the army evicted the veterans, Hoover had declared that many of those in the camps "are communists and persons with criminal records" and directed the attorney general "to investigate the whole incident." In September, that report came out and, unsurprisingly, blamed the violence on an "extraordinary proportion of criminal, Communist, and non-veteran elements" who, after Congress killed the Bonus Bill, hijacked the movement from the "thousands of law-abiding men who came to Washington with full right of presentation of their views to the Congress."[10]

Attorney General William D. Mitchell, relying on a thin sampling of veterans who registered as they arrived in the early days of the march, further concluded that more than 20 percent of the marchers had police records. "It is probable the Bonus Army brought into the City of Washington the largest aggregation of criminals that had ever been assembled in the city at any one time," he wrote. And, of course, there were scads of communists mixed in among them—though the report failed to mention that Walter Waters and his men routinely accosted, occasionally beat, and reflexively exiled suspected leftists.

Notably, the Mitchell report, and earlier investigations, including one by a grand jury, failed to uncover any leading role by communists. And the supposed criminal histories of many

Bonus Marchers were overwhelmingly the sorts of petty offenses one might suspect being committed by starving homeless people, including failure to make child support payments, not to mention Prohibition infractions (hardly an indicator of a life of criminality at the time).

The report's release coincided with an annual American Legion convention in September in, ironically, Portland, Oregon, where the Bonus March had begun. Hurley addressed the convention briefly—where a storm of boos greeted him—but he didn't mention the Bonus Army. Floyd Gibbons, a former war correspondent for the *Chicago Tribune,* and a radio commentator for the National Broadcasting Company (NBC), both covered and addressed the convention. Gibbons had criticized Mitchell's report in his columns and, speaking from the convention stage, reminisced about watching a few months earlier as the ragtag Bonus Army marched down Pennsylvania Avenue seeking the kind of basic sustenance the United States had provided Belgium and other foreign countries. "The thing that I can't understand. . . is how could we do that and send not so much as a hot dog to twenty thousand of them sleeping on the ground and starving three miles from the White House."[11]

The veterans were neither communists nor criminals, Gibbons went on, and to suggest otherwise questioned the patriotism of thousands of men who had risked their lives at war, and of those who were crowded into Municipal Auditorium. "To say that those men are Red, that they are radicals, that they are agitators, casts a slight upon the honorable discharge that all of you carry with pride," he told the convention. "The Americanism, the patriotism, the citizenship of those men is beyond question."

It's unclear how much Hoover's routing of the Bonus Marchers, and the botched efforts to spin it afterward, affected his reelection chances, but it certainly didn't help. Roosevelt, who privately opposed speeding up the bonus payments, wisely stayed out of the fray, keeping the public focus on Hoover alone.

The perceived heartlessness of the action, Hoover's philosophical inflexibility against using federal money to directly help the hungry, and his muted personality, made Hoover seem cold and uncaring and out of his depth, a perception Charley Michelson and the rest of the Democrats were only too happy to bolster.

TO ACCEPT HIS party's nomination in person, Governor Roosevelt broke with tradition and flew seven hundred miles west from Albany to Chicago. President Hoover, adhering to tradition, wired his acceptance after learning of his nomination, but delayed his acceptance speech until after he had received formal notification from the party. So eight weeks after the convention ended, and six weeks after Roosevelt's dramatic acceptance speech, Hoover navigated the 1,500 feet between the White House and the Constitution Hall auditorium to address about four thousand people in person and a national audience via NBC Radio.

It was a dour performance, a recitation of successes that were hard to justify and pledges to return the nation to prosperity, while adhering to concepts of a small and noninterventionist government. "The solution of our many problems which arise from the shifting scene of national life is not to be found in haphazard experimentation or by revolution," Hoover said. "It does not follow, because our difficulties are stupendous, because there are some souls timorous enough to doubt the validity and effectiveness of our ideals and our system, that we must turn to a State-controlled or State-directed social or economic system in order to cure our troubles. That is not liberalism; that is tyranny." And, in a swipe against Roosevelt's charisma: "[O]fttimes the tendency of democracy in the presence of national danger is to strike blindly, to listen to demagogues and to slogans, all of which destroy and do not save. We have refused to be stampeded into such courses."[12]

Yet, he also argued that he had expanded the federal government's role in trying to alleviate the economic crisis, describing his policies as "an unparalleled use of national power to relieve distress, to provide employment, to serve agriculture, to preserve the stability of the Government, and to maintain the integrity of our institutions." Tariffs and the suspension of entry visas for foreign workers preserved jobs by blocking "floods of imported goods and of laborers ... With patience and perseverance these measures will succeed."

Hoover also argued that despite the "unparalleled economic calamity" of the previous three years the government had managed to keep itself running and meeting its financial obligations—as a business, he seemed to say, the government was healthy—as "our people, while suffering great hardships, have been and will be cared for." It was an astounding claim, given that a quarter of the workforce couldn't find jobs, and that uncounted millions were living in Hooverville shantytowns or on sidewalks, trying to keep warm under Hoover blankets of newspapers.

Hoover also discussed Prohibition and managed in just a few sentences to offend the more radical Wets among his supporters—and confuse most everybody else—by arguing that Prohibition had ended saloon culture but, through inconsistent enforcement and "disrespect not only for this law but for all laws," had fueled a rise "in subsidized crime and violence," with illicit speakeasies replacing saloons. "I cannot consent to a continuation of that regime." While Hoover did not call for outright repeal of the Eighteenth Amendment, he went beyond the Republican platform and said "all reasonable people can find common ground" in resubmitting the issue to the states and letting each determine whether it will allow alcohol. That would mean—in practice—the end of federal Prohibition, even if Hoover couldn't move himself to say so in direct terms.

Most Republicans lauded the speech, while Democrats dismissed it as a promise to continue failed policies, with the Drys and Wets split on the Prohibition comments. For the ardent backers of repeal, the speech reflected an adherence to the principle of Prohibition; while for the ardent Drys, Hoover was a turncoat. "President Hoover will be defeated," warned Reverend James K. Shields, superintendent of the New Jersey Anti-Saloon League. "We're not going to be hornswoggled on this proposition. We shall make it very, very embarrassing for Mr. Hoover."

At a convention in Seattle, Women's Christian Temperance Union president Ella A. Boole warned that Drys could neither accept the repeal platform of the Democrats nor Hoover's approach, and that many of them may have to make their decision on whom to support for the presidency based on "convictions on other great issues."[13]

Pauline Sabin's Women's Organization for National Prohibition Reform faced its own internal divisions over whom to support for the presidency. Despite a general stance that the organization's members should base their votes solely on Prohibition regardless of party affiliation, some members couldn't bring themselves to cast a vote for Roosevelt—or any other Democrat, for that matter. After the group's executive committee endorsed Roosevelt in early July, shortly after the conventions, a renegade group of sixty-four Republican members—aided by Hoover's treasury secretary, Ogden L. Mills—signed a public letter that rejected the endorsement. The letter argued, bizarrely, that endorsing a candidate based on Prohibition repeal politicized the issue and the organization. Dozens of Republican women eventually left the WONPR, though that had little impact on a group that now counted more than 1.5 million members.[14]

Still, Hoover's tack to step away from full support of Prohibition followed the national mood. Political polling had yet to take root as a given in political campaigns, and it was left mostly to media outlets using mail-in responses. But statistician and Stanford alum J. David Houser had developed a system based on face-to-face interviews with large and weighted samples of consumers that had proven useful for developing marketing strategies for commercial clients. Houser thought the technique could also be useful to politicians.

From his offices at the corner of Lexington Avenue and East Forty-Second Street in Manhattan, in June 1931, Houser began making overtures through intermediaries to the White House. He argued that his technique could help Hoover assess which political issues mattered the most to potential voters, and craft policies accordingly. He put it in terms of cost and benefit. "It would seem apparent that the possibilities of the most effective expenditure of time and money in a political campaign, if one knew the actual weight of the issues which were operating at the time, would be enormous."[15]

Initially he received no response, so in March 1932, Houser got Lewis Strauss, a close Hoover advisor, to press his case, which Strauss did in a letter to Lawrence Richey, one of Hoover's top aides, touting Houser's work for Macy's and other businesses. He included a brief overview from Houser on his approach eliciting information from consumers themselves, not experts reading tea leaves. "It cannot be too strongly emphasized that all of this material would have an ultimate authority—the authority of the public itself," Houser wrote. "It would be no one's opinion, no one's pronouncements. It could not be called 'propaganda.'"[16]

Edgar Rickard, Hoover's friend and private business manager, also wrote to Hoover on March 9, suggesting Houser's methods could elicit useful information about how the public viewed Hoover's Reconstruction Finance Corporation. The White House agreed on March 10 to a meeting, but, for unspecified reasons, insisted that Strauss set it up.

Strauss worked fast. Two days later, Houser arrived at the White House for a half-hour meeting with Hoover on Saturday morning, March 12, where he made his pitch. Houser expected no pay for his effort and would not release the findings publicly; he planned to use the survey to help the president get a better understanding of the mood of the nation.

For a president who thrived on facts, data, and commissions issuing reports, Houser's approach had appeal. No records detail their discussion, but after Houser left, he began preparing what would become the first significant national political survey of voters' attitudes. And his interviewers would not only be asking about the RFC, but also about whom—the government, Wall Street, business, or the American people—voters held responsible for the depression, who could make it better, whether the government should speed up the veterans' bonus payment, how they felt about tariffs on imported goods, and, most significantly, where they stood on repeal of Prohibition.[17]

IN LATE AUGUST, Hoover went to the Commerce Building to deliver opening remarks at a three-day conference of committees of the twelve regional Federal Reserve offices. The topics were limited. First, the banking industry had somewhat stabilized, according to June economic data, but there were regional disparities. Hoover wanted the committees to come up with national strategies for making access to loans more even. Second, Hoover wanted suggestions for expanding employment, including possibly limiting work hours for existing employees so companies could add more people to the rolls.[18]

In his speech Hoover told the economists that he believed "we have overcome the major financial crisis—a crisis in severity unparalleled in the history of the world—and that with its relaxation confidence and hope have reappeared in the world." Next up, he said, must be "further steps in solution of the industrial and agricultural problems with which we are still confronted." He offered a brief history of the economic collapse, putting a healthy amount of blame on financial instability in the European banking systems that became further stressed by political revolutions in Spain and South America, and Japan's invasion of Manchuria, that had stalled some loan repayments.

To try to stabilize its own economy, England delinked its currency from the gold standard, in part to stop a panicked public from turning in their cash for gold, which had significantly depleted the Bank of England's gold holdings. In Hoover's view the global economy then spun out of control and led to the withdrawal of $2.4 billion in U.S. gold and currency by foreign nations and investors, and another $1.6 billion withdrawn by American depositors.

But that had ended, Hoover proudly reported to the group, in large part through the work of the Reconstruction Finance Corporation in funneling money to banks. "Confidence is returning," Hoover said, adding that foreign investments had changed course and money had begun flowing back into the United States, and requests from American banks for help from the RFC had decreased. More work needed to be done, of course, but that would fall to industry and labor leaders, and the American people—not the government.

"What I wish is that banking and industry and business generally should in this new setting assume further initiative and responsibility and they should cooperate with agriculture and labor and the government agencies" to keep the recovery moving. Invoking the Great War, Hoover said the nation had survived the economic version of the Battle of Château-Thierry, the first significant Allied victory after U.S. troops arrived in Europe. "That attack on our line has been stopped, but I warn you that the war is not over. We must now reform our forces for the Battle of Soissons"—another Allied victory that changed the tide of the war.

News coverage of the speech trumpeted Hoover's optimism: HOOVER DECLARES CRISIS IS OVER, the *Evening Star* screamed in a banner page-one headline. HOOVER SEES MAJOR CRISIS OVERCOME, *The New York Times* told its readers. HOOVER SAYS CRISIS OVER, reported the *Des Moines Register*. But it was all a chimera. One in four workers remained off the job; credit was hard to find; farmers continued to lose their farms; and while bank closures had stabilized, they would soon fall off a cliff.

CHAPTER 16

Roosevelt Goes West

OUT OF DEFERENCE TO USUALLY harsh weather and difficult travel conditions in November, the state of Maine routinely held its state elections in September (they would return to the polls in November for the presidential election). In this election year the sitting Republican governor had declined to run again, which meant the top state office was open. Voters going to the polls on September 12 also were choosing who would fill three seats in Congress, down from four after redistricting from the 1930 Census, and all of the seats in the state legislature. Much like early voting skirmishes in the national conventions, how Maine voters acted in September would be perceived as a harbinger for November. "Some sinister fellow had coined that irritating phrase, 'as Maine goes, so goes the nation,'" James Farley noted.[1]

Given the national political climate, the Maine election drew unusual attention from national party leaders, including Farley, who had sent an emissary to the state and had flooded his contacts with letters and telegrams. Listening to his ears on the ground and to a state delegation sent to meet with him in New York, Farley bought into the potential for a Democratic upset and "directed the treasurer's office to give them a substantial sum of money" to help with the effort. Louis Howe "snorted in disgust" at Farley's decision, and Roosevelt ribbed Farley "intimating that a few shrewd gentlemen from the sticks had put one over on a city slicker."

But Farley was right. The state Democrats focused on Prohibition repeal as the key issue, and voters, already dissatisfied with Hoover and the Republicans, responded by electing the state's first Democratic governor since before the Great War and ousting two of the three Republican members of Congress, though the Republicans managed to hang on to control of the state legislature.

News of the upset ricocheted through the political world, including the White House. "Well, Maine has done its worst," Theodore Joslin noted in his diary. Party leaders tried to chalk it up to elections dominated by local issues, but that challenged credulity. The Republican losses in Maine coincided with dispatches to the White House from Hoover supporters in the Midwest—editors of newspapers in Des Moines and Minneapolis—warning that "all of the Middle West, from the Mississippi to the Rockies, was lost." Hoover felt "discouraged, yet he is carrying on with all the determination of his being," Joslin noted. Hoover took the loss as a wake-up call for the party.[2]

"[I]t imposes need for renewed and stronger effort that the people may fully understand the issues at stake," Hoover wrote in reply to a letter from the head of the Republican National Committee that party leaders still expected Hoover to carry Maine in November. "We have known all along that, owing to the ravages of the world depression, our fight is a hard one. But we have a strong case and a right cause. Our task is to acquaint every man and woman in the country with the facts and issues which confront the nation."

In other words, if voters only knew the facts, as Hoover saw them, then they would back him. The strategy hardly commanded the moment, but the steep hill ahead did force Hoover to make a significant change in how he intended to win reelection.

He had long believed that it was undignified for a sitting president to actively campaign, instead letting surrogates do the heavy lifting and barnstorming. He felt confident in his response to the depression and did not consider Franklin Roosevelt to be his political equal. The weeks since the Democratic National Convention had not shown Hoover anything to change his perception that of all the potential Democratic contenders, the party had served him up the weakest.

As Hoover viewed the political landscape, he believed that he had strong support in the eastern states, a belief belied by Maine. But he knew he faced deep trouble in the traditionally conservative and Republican Midwest—even though his campaign maintained a satellite headquarters in Chicago—and the Western states primarily because of anger and frustration coursing through farming-dependent regions. So Hoover decided, after Joslin informed him that William Howard Taft and Woodrow Wilson had both personally campaigned for reelection, that he would hit the trail himself to deliver three speeches. He would begin with a trip to the Midwest, focusing on his hometown of West Branch in eastern Iowa, and then Des Moines, in the heart of the farmers' rebellion.

But even as Hoover made his travel plans, he was already trailing Roosevelt on that front as well.[3]

MAINE ELECTION OFFICIALS were still counting the day's votes when Roosevelt left the governor's mansion in Albany late in the evening for a planned 8,900-mile, twenty-four-day, twenty-state trip to the West Coast and back in a six-car "Roosevelt Special" train. While he planned to deliver four long speeches and scores of short, mostly ad-libbed talks from the back of his train, Roosevelt carefully framed the trip less as a campaign whistle-stop tour than as a chance to meet voters across the country and "to listen and to learn." Roosevelt never traveled alone, and on this trip he would be accompanied by his son James and daughter-in-law

Betsey, and his daughter Anna Dall (Eleanor would join in Arizona); Raymond Moley, who would be coordinating the final versions of a series of speeches Roosevelt had planned; Joseph P. Kennedy and an aide; and five other advisors, eventually to include James Farley after the first days of the trip. And, of course, three cars' worth of reporters and photographers.[4]

The Roosevelt Special was smaller and less decked-out than the one Al Smith used during his train tour four years earlier, and Governor Roosevelt intentionally had a smaller entourage than Smith. But it wasn't all for image. The 1928 campaign had more money during those heady pre-crash days than the Roosevelt campaign could bring in.

Roosevelt's itinerary would take him through Cleveland and St. Louis, then across the Great Plains to Denver, north to Cheyenne, Wyoming, before veering west again through the Rockies to Ogden and Salt Lake City, Utah. From there he would head for Tacoma, Washington, before turning south through California's Central Valley to Sacramento, then to the coast for stops in San Francisco and Los Angeles. From there the return trip would take Roosevelt through Arizona and into New Mexico. At Albuquerque, the train would head north back to Denver, then northeast through Nebraska and Iowa, followed by a jog north into Wisconsin, then back through northern Illinois, another jog north to Detroit, and on home to Albany.

It was an ambitious trip, which Democratic Party leaders hadn't wanted Roosevelt to undertake. Even Howe preferred that the governor remain in Albany, limit his speeches to radio addresses, and run as risk-free a campaign as possible. As it stood, Hoover had little chance of winning, and it made no sense for Roosevelt to risk inadvertently giving the president some breathing space by slipping and falling in public, which would raise questions about his physical ability and stamina, or committing a gaffe during unscripted comments. Ultimately, though, it was Roosevelt's call, and he genuinely enjoyed campaigning. He intended to ramp up his criticism of Hoover and Republican policies in a series of speeches.[5]

Hoover, on the other hand, did not like campaigning, or many of the other personal efforts normally required to succeed in politics. He had won the presidency four years earlier in a romp, riding public support of Republicans during a strong economy and benefiting from the vile efforts of the Klan and other anti-Catholics to defeat Al Smith because of his faith. While the 1932 election cycle differed significantly, Hoover's game plan did not, much to Roosevelt's surprise.

The president, so far, had delivered no significant campaign speeches beyond his acceptance of the Republican nomination. When Roosevelt criticized the president and his administration on a range of issues, centering on the response to the Great Depression, Hoover did not respond. Rather, he had Joslin and others on his staff work up rebuttals and dispense them to cabinet secretaries and supporters in Congress to defend Hoover in his staff's words, but their own voices. So Roosevelt generated heat in the headlines while the nonpresidential Republican reactions barely registered. A more direct response from Hoover likely would have helped; without it the nation perceived a one-sided campaign. Hoover also suffered from the delusion that Roosevelt was such a lightweight political figure without a guiding political philosophy that voters would naturally gravitate to someone of Hoover's record and stature.[6]

Roosevelt initially was hurt by reports of Hoover's lack of regard for him as a political equal, but personal offense quickly transformed into anger and fueled Roosevelt's drive to take his campaign deep into the heart of traditionally Republican territory. Roosevelt wanted to fundamentally change how government operates and how it interacts with the economy and with its own citizens. That would require a quantum shift in Congress and among the attitudes of American citizens accustomed to celebrating the individual over the overall health of society.

Roosevelt remained a believer in free markets and individual free-doms, but also in the need for a more expansive and activist government. His belief was anathema not only to Republicans, but to more conservative members of his own party's leadership, most of whom were drawn from the elite sections of the economy and society. To achieve his goals, Roosevelt needed to make the November election not a Democratic victory, but a Roosevelt tsunami, which would give him the political and public support to overcome the conservative wing of his own party.[7]

Roosevelt made the first major speech of the train trip from the steps of the State Capitol Building in Topeka, Kansas, a sea of ten thousand faces standing before him, and countless others nationwide tuning in by radio. Speaking under fair skies and temperatures in the mid-eighties, Roosevelt cited his own background as the owner of farms in New York and Georgia (never mind that he did no actual farm work himself) in helping him understand the nature and scope of the multifaceted problems facing rural Americans.

As governor, he said, he pushed policies to reduce taxation in farm areas, changed a formula for distributing state road funds to send more money to rural areas and less to urban centers, and expanded the amount of state money available to rural governments for bridge and railroad crossing maintenance. He also pushed state funding for rural health programs and schools, a statewide soil survey, and backed efforts to extend telephone and electrical service to remote areas. None of those steps improved the markets for commodities, but they did improve the quality of life for New York's farmers and rural residents. "The great lesson of it all is that there is no single cure-all," Roosevelt said, "but that progress comes from a comprehension of many factors and a sincere attempt to move forward on many lines at the same time."[8]

Roosevelt reminded the farmers—as if they needed it—that nationally they received little support from Republican-led Washington, D.C., and what solutions that had emerged over the previous three years were either off the mark or inadequate to the task. Some 22 percent of the nation lived on farms, Roosevelt said, but they only received about 7 percent of the national income, down from 15 percent in 1920 on the eve of the postwar agriculture depression, and from 9 percent when Hoover took office. "Our economic life today is a seamless web," Roosevelt said, spotlighting the interdependence of the nation's different economies and regions. He blamed three successive Republican administrations—the current one led by Hoover and its two predecessors, in which Hoover served as a cabinet secretary—for failing "utterly to understand the farm problem as a national whole, or to plan for its relief."

Drawing on reports from his Brain Trust, Governor Roosevelt sketched out a six-point proposal that included reorganizing the Agriculture Department, with an eye toward national planning but decentralized decision-making; expanding soil testing to determine which lands were best suited for agriculture and which should be retired; changes in tax laws, along the lines of those in New York; and a thinning and redirection of tariffs that had not only failed to raise commodity prices, but had increased the farmers' cost of living and stunted international trade. Roosevelt offered few specifics, but promised a cooperative approach to devise new programs. In fact, Republicans immediately denounced the speech as filled with "glittering generalities."[9]

Yet, Roosevelt didn't intend to use specific proposals to win over the farmers. He was selling himself as a president who would be unafraid to try new ideas, and one without crippling, rigid loyalty to political and economic theories. He blasted Hoover's "cruel" acceptance of bankruptcies and foreclosures as a natural corrective to surplus production in a free-market economy, and without offering relief for those most harmed. Roosevelt ended his speech by declaring his "unbounded faith" in resurrecting agriculture and offered hope that "those of us who intend a solution and decline the defeatist attitude [will] join tirelessly in the work of advancing a better-ordered economic life."

In Salt Lake City, Roosevelt addressed another persistent economic problem: the shaky financial condition of the nation's railroad companies. Amid explosive nineteenth-century Western settlement and economic growth, individual rail lines in the new and often-cutthroat business frequently built redundant tracks and systems and fought to bankrupt or buy out competitors. Amid the business slowdown of the Great Depression, the railroads suffered reduced demand, augmenting the stresses they faced from the 1920s rise in personal ownership of automobiles and use of trucks to move goods. In 1932, some twenty thousand miles of rail lines owned by fifty mostly small rail companies were operating under receivership as they moved into bankruptcy, an expensive process that often took years to resolve. Overall, nearly 2 million people worked for railroad companies, and Roosevelt thought preserving those jobs would be crucial to turning around the economy, given that rail remained the prime conduit in the nation's supply chain, and for moving products from factories and farms to distant markets.[10]

Roosevelt believed the railroads, like the nation's agricultural sector, could benefit from government-led national planning. So Roosevelt laid out another six-point plan. This one centered on discarding the traditional capitalist theory of open competition and bankruptcies to weed out the weakest businesses. Instead, he argued, the government should drop some of its anti-monopolist policies and allow collaboration among rail lines (they often didn't even operate out of the same stations); streamline and speed up the receivership process; safeguard the reliability of the rail network from managerial malfeasance and profiteering; and focus on shoring up the financial health of individual railroads. "The railroad mesh is the warp upon which our economic web is largely fashioned," Roosevelt said. "It has made a continent into a nation."

In Seattle, Roosevelt laid out his argument for dropping most tariffs and reconfiguring others in such a way that would protect American businesses and jobs without sparking retaliation by other nations, preferably through nation-to-nation reciprocal agreements on specific tariffs and products. In Portland, Roosevelt turned to hydroelectric power and the need for federal regulation and possible public ownership to ensure that the benefits of electricity are extended as widely as possible, not just where privately or investor-owned utilities thought it would be profitable to operate them.

At each of his stops throngs of people greeted Roosevelt, from a few hundred as he spoke briefly from the back of the train at small-town stations to crowds of eight to ten thousand in cities. From the train Roosevelt bantered with audience members and exuded an easy confidence, reciting the names of local leading Democrats as he steadied himself at the rail with one hand, a sign obscuring his legs, and waved to the crowd with the other.

In many of the small towns, Roosevelt became a local event. For instance, the Roosevelt Special planned to stop at the station in Redding, California, for two minutes at 11:09 A.M. on September 22. The local schools let classes out early at 10:30 A.M. so students could attend, and most businesses in the village of 4,100 people shut their doors for a half hour around Roosevelt's scheduled arrival. Some 2,500 people crowded around the station and tracks, many traveling in from the countryside, and the size of the crowd slowed the train's departure. In the end Roosevelt stayed in Redding for ten minutes.[11]

Roosevelt's reception in San Francisco was of another magnitude. The candidate and his entourage detrained at the Sixteenth Street Station in Oakland, then boarded open-top cars that rode a ferry across the bay to the San Francisco Ferry Building at the foot of Market Street. They were greeted there by the Republican mayor, Angelo J. Rossi, a handful of local Democratic leaders, a brass band, and a throng of some one hundred thousand people jammed along the three-quarters of a mile route to the posh Palace Hotel.[12]

The next day in a speech at the Commonwealth Club, Roosevelt laid out his views of the proper relationship between government and business, invoking Thomas Jefferson, his distant cousin Teddy Roosevelt, and Woodrow Wilson. Roosevelt argued that government had been crucial to helping American industries rise, including targeted tariffs to protect specific parts of the economy against foreign competition; financial subsidies and land grants to ease construction of railroads; mail contracts to funnel revenues to steamship lines; and other efforts. He scoffed at Republican demands that government leave the business world alone. "The same man who tells you that he does not want to see the Government interfere in business . . . is the first to go to Washington and ask the Government for a prohibitory tariff on his product" or, when economic conditions threaten businesses, "he will go with equal speed to the United States Government and ask for a loan."[13]

Meanwhile, Roosevelt said, growth and consolidation among corporations meant that about six hundred firms controlled two-thirds of American businesses, leaving the thinner slice to be divided up among 10 million small business owners.

"If the process of concentration goes on at the same rate, at the end of another century we shall have all American industry controlled by a dozen corporations, and run by perhaps a hundred men," Roosevelt said with remarkable prescience. "Put plainly, we are steering a steady course toward economic oligarchy, if we are not there already." Under "a re-appraisal of values," he argued, it fell to government to ensure the nation's wealth and economic power would be more evenly distributed, and to protect average Americans from the excesses of unscrupulous profit- and power-driven corporate titans.

The *Los Angeles Times* reporter covering the speech said Roosevelt "advocated a doctrine which, to many of his hearers, seemed like a page from a thesis on socialism." But to Roosevelt, it was the embrace of calm pragmatism. Without the government acting as protector of the "forgotten man" from the concentrated wealth and power of the economic elites, the American traditions of individual liberty and reaping the rewards of personal initiative were in peril. And one only had to look to the spread of communism and fascism in Europe to see where political instability and social upheaval might lead.[14]

HOOVER HAD ALREADY decided to make his own Western trip, but Roosevelt's agriculture speech in Kansas, coming on the heels of the Maine election upset, added some urgency to his planning. Hoover initially wanted to go to West Branch, his birthplace, but a few days later changed his mind and opted instead for the state capital, Des Moines. His advisors tried to talk him into delivering the speech in Kansas City, in part because they feared confrontations if Hoover appeared in the heart of the Farmers' Holiday rebellion. But Hoover held his ground, "saying it was the capital of the State in which he was born, and he wanted to go back there." They set the date for October 4, coincidentally the day after Roosevelt arrived back in Albany after his Western swing.[15]

Unlike Roosevelt, who relied on Sam Rosenman and his Brain Trust to do the heavy lifting on speechwriting, Hoover insisted on dictating his own speeches, which he then would share with Joslin and other aides and advisors for their feedback. Hoover worked slowly; Joslin once noted that "writing a speech to him is as great an ordeal as childbirth to a woman." Hoover also lacked the gift of oratory. The president believed in facts and his own analysis of them, and rarely incorporated any notable or memorable rhetorical flourishes in his speeches (with the notable exception of once describing Roosevelt as a "chameleon on the Scotch plaid").[16]

The speech on agriculture, which would branch off to other topics as well, became especially challenging for Hoover as he recognized how much trouble his reelection was in. Roosevelt and the Democrats had spent four years building a national staff, while also, under Farley and Howe, establishing a decentralized, state-by-state network of local leaders and supporters. Roosevelt's circle of advisors had assumed he would win the nomination and so had been developing a national strategy to launch as soon as the party gave him the mantle. They sent small samples of campaign literature, with an offer to send more to everyone on their massive list of precinct captains, which broke with the tradition of simply sending boxes of material to county party offices, where it often sat untouched and undistributed. A secondary benefit of the direct contacts: Precinct captains felt like they were an integral part of the campaign, seemingly getting requests and advice directly from the top levels of the campaign, making each "feel that he has a new standing in the home community." The Democrats also established a separate office targeting women voters, with Eleanor Roosevelt playing a prominent role. And they still had Charley Michelson, "that wise old fox" who continued to bedevil Hoover and the Republicans with his publicity machine.[17]

Hoover had neither a Farley nor a Howe, let alone a Michelson. In fact, the Republican National Committee was in such disarray—not to mention demoralized over the fall prognosis—that Hoover found himself with a thin and tattered support network. In mid-September, as Roosevelt generated headlines, the Republican National Committee hardly seemed to be breathing, infuriating Hoover. As Roosevelt began heading back east from California, the Republican leadership had barely reacted to the challenger's speeches. "The President is being compelled to direct every move in his behalf," Joslin noted. "There is not a single self-starter in either headquarters" in Washington, D.C., or Chicago. "It is pitiable."[18]

The president's rupture with the progressive wing of the party also had cost him the campaign support of Senator William Borah, of Idaho, who had been a key advocate for Hoover four years earlier, and James J. Couzens, the former Ford Motor Company executive and current senator from Michigan. Unable to budge Borah through party intermediaries, Hoover sent his friend Mark Sullivan, the syndicated columnist, to Idaho in a vain effort to persuade the senator to help the campaign. From Michigan, Couzens wouldn't even respond to the president's overtures. "Evidently the President must go along on his own," Joslin noted in his diary. "He is chafing under the onslaughts and [untruths] of Roosevelt. The blasts of the opposition and the puny efforts of our workers make our position positively pathetic."

Yet, Hoover did get some assistance. Treasury Secretary Ogden L. Mills delivered speeches on his behalf, including a sharp-edged rebuttal in Los Angeles dismissing Roosevelt's Western tour as disseminating a "philosophy of despair," and argued that with Election Day nearing, the nation still had no idea what solutions Roosevelt proposed. Elsewhere, Calvin Coolidge issued a couple of statements from his retirement refuge in Northampton urging Hoover's reelection. And on October 3, the day Hoover left Washington by train for Iowa, the party launched a weeknight series of fifteen-minute radio programs aired over the NBC network featuring well-known Republican supporters discussing the campaign and the state of the nation. First up would be Edward F. Hutton, co-founder of the E. F. Hutton & Co. stock brokerage firm, interviewed by publicist and ad man Bruce Barton. Kansas newspaper editor and Hoover supporter William Allen White would join for part of the program.[19]

Hoover's staff and Secret Service detachment began the Midwestern trip with trepidation over reports of planned "demonstrations by hostile farmers, 'egging,' heckling and much worse," Joslin noted. "Mrs. Hoover revealed her apprehensions, talking with me at dinner tonight about her deep sorrow when McKinley was assassinated."

Hoover's trip looped through Chicago, then on to Iowa, though Hoover made no statements or whistle-stops until the train reached Rock Island, Illinois, on the eastern bank of the Mississippi, then stopped at Davenport, Iowa, and West Liberty—about eight miles southwest of West Branch—where one of Hoover's elementary school teachers boarded for a greeting and photo opportunity. From there the train stopped briefly in Iowa City and Newtown before steaming into Des Moines, where the Hoovers had dinner with Governor Daniel Turner and his wife before heading to the Coliseum for his speech.

As Hoover's train neared Des Moines, the farmers did hold a demonstration, with some two thousand people—including Milo Reno—parading through downtown Des Moines, ironically passing beneath IOWA WELCOMES YOU banners bearing oversized photographs of Hoover. Cars and trucks carried signs reading IN HOOVER WE TRUSTED, NOW WE ARE BUSTED, and WE DON'T WANT LOANS—THEY MEAN MORE DEBT. But the parade started at noon, ended well before Hoover arrived, and the feared confrontation never materialized.[20]

Hoover had his supporters. Tens of thousands of people were on the streets as he arrived, and some 8,500 jammed into the Coliseum on the bank of the Des Moines River, with several thousand more listening in by speakers placed outside and in a nearby Shrine Temple building. Hoover reminisced about his childhood, spoke of his experiences in Europe, and defended his administration's effort to counter the depression. He also heaped scorn on Democrats in Congress, under Speaker Garner, for expensive "pork barrel" legislation and in backing the early bonus payment to Great War veterans—steps that undermined public confidence in the government, Hoover said, and were a distraction and impediment to Republican solutions.

It's unclear whether he did it intentionally, but Hoover offered a twelve-point program—double what Roosevelt laid out—for addressing the agricultural crisis. It included maintaining high tariffs against imported goods; a reassessment of agricultural land "to divert land from unprofitable use to profitable use" (similar to Roosevelt's soil survey); coordinating efforts among governments at all levels to streamline and reduce rural taxes (again similar to Roosevelt's proposal); some relief for drought-stricken farmers unable to repay feed and seed loans; unspecified farm mortgage relief; and expansion of credit for farmers.

It took the president about ten thousand words to make his case, running some two hours, and while the audience was receptive, and at times enthusiastic, newspaper accounts suggest the energy levels much lower than at Roosevelt speeches. The *Des Moines Register* noted a full house and said that "the audience was quiet and the president, without raising his voice, was making himself heard plainly through the amplifying system."

Joslin, though, generously declared the speech "a great success," in line with the rest of the trip, where thousands of people had gathered at rail stations to see and cheer the president on the way to Des Moines, and on the return trip. Some one hundred telegrams reached Hoover's train before it left Des Moines, and he read them during down moments. "The reception and the telegrams made him warm up" and "were a fine tonic for the President." But Joslin also knew that cheering crowds do not necessarily mean votes. "The enthusiasm was such that it was hard to believe the President was in . . . danger of defeat," Joslin wrote in his diary. "Yet I know that every state we passed through is likely to go Democratic. I cannot reconcile the two opposites."

In fact, the day before Hoover arrived, the *Des Moines Register* reported that seventy-five thousand Iowans had returned ballots in a straw poll it conducted. Just over 60 percent of them were for the Democratic governor from New York over the Republican president born in Iowa, a state "which ordinarily casts a 60 percent Republican vote."[21]

CHAPTER 17

The Final Push

BEAUTIFUL EARLY-AUTUMN WEATHER GRACED the nation's capital on October 10, with a light breeze, scattered clouds, and temperatures reaching the mid-seventies. It was, in fact, lovely weather for a demonstration, and authorities braced for one. The United States Supreme Court had set that day to hear oral arguments in the Scottsboro Boys' appeals of their Alabama death sentences, and for weeks there had been growing street demonstrations in the United States and Europe demanding justice. Thousands of postcards arrived at the Supreme Court urging freedom for the young men, and now there were rumors that the Reds planned an argument-day rally outside the Capitol Building, the *Evening Star* reported.[1]

In preparation of this on-site D.C. demonstration, more than two dozen extra police officers—some of whom had been involved in trying to remove the Bonus Army in July—were redeployed from around the District of Columbia to augment the Capitol police force. A contingent of officers watched over the hallways and in the Old Senate Chamber, where the nine justices were to convene. (Three days later, Chief Justice Charles Evans Hughes would lay the cornerstone for the court's new home across the street.) Scores more were positioned outside the building, some enforcing a temporary ban on motor vehicles from the eastside plaza.

The fears of unrest, though, went unmet. Some seventy-five people showed up to march outside and chant a bit while carrying signs, but otherwise they maintained a low-key presence. Inside, the gallery was comprised of mostly Black attendees, but the crowd also included the white, Irish-born Mary Mooney, mother of West Coast radical Tom Mooney, serving a life sentence after perjured testimony led to his conviction on charges that he set a bomb that killed ten people during San Francisco's 1916 Preparedness Day Parade. Mother Mooney was on a months-long tour on behalf of International Labor Defense to raise money and publicity for the "Free Tom Mooney" movement and the Scottsboro Boys' legal defense. "I'm interested in seeing that other mothers' sons get justice," she told a reporter before she entered the building. "I know what injustice means to them."[2]

The ILD had hired Walter Pollak, a New York City lawyer with a long history of defending political radicals, to handle the Scottsboro Boys' appeal. In addition to George Chamlee, the lawyer from Chattanooga, Pollak was joined by a half-dozen other prominent civil liberties lawyers, including Joseph Brodsky, head of the ILD. Alabama attorney general Thomas E. Knight Jr., whose father wrote the state supreme court opinion upholding the convictions the son had defended before the state court, sat at the other table.

Pollak spoke for the appellants, arguing that the defendants had inadequate access to legal counsel before and during a trial that moved at indefensible speed as thousands of white people clamored outside the courthouse for the jury, drawn from an all-white pool, to convict the defendants. Those factors, Pollak said, meant the accused had been denied their Sixth Amendment right to legal representation and their Fourteenth Amendment right to due process.

Knight then stood and denied any rights had been violated. He said the defendants had lawyers, defended the speed with which the trials were conducted, disputed that the mob outside had any influence on the outcome, and argued disingenuously that just because only whites were on the jury didn't mean Black people weren't in the pool of names from which the jury was drawn (though it appears none were). No justices asked questions of the lawyers, and the court announced that it would be a month or so before they issued a ruling, which a Black newspaper noted meant the decision would conveniently come after the November election, though it's unclear whether any decision would have an influence on voters.[3]

With that, the gallery emptied, and the demonstrators outside slowly drifted away.

THE SCOTTSBORO BOYS oral arguments coincided with a break in Hoover and Roosevelt's campaign trips. The president had returned from Iowa to the White House four days before the Supreme Court hearing, and Roosevelt had ended his West Coast trip a few days before that. But there were many more miles to travel before the November 8 election. In fact, five days after the oral arguments, Hoover headed to Cleveland, the first of four two-day campaign trips that would include, in order, Detroit, Indianapolis, and New York City.

On the way to Cleveland, Hoover talked up the protective tariff at several of ten whistle-stops, including in Cumberland, Maryland, where he cited the state's history of embracing tariffs dating back to "the first session of the first Congress. Indeed, it was the first petition filed with the Congress." Most of his stops had less substance, though: a greeting by a local Republican leader, some bands playing music, bouquets presented by young girls to the first lady, and a couple hundred words thanking people for turning out.[4]

In Cleveland, the marquee stop on the trip, Hoover dove deeply into the economic history of war in Europe to explain why the United States bore little responsibility for its own economic calamity, and that the Democrats and Roosevelt were misrepresenting facts to attack his administration. It was a long and stultifying speech crammed full of statistics accented by the occasional pounding of the podium. It's easy to imagine some of the attendees softly muttering "thank you" when Hoover said, "I will not review for you the German moratorium which prevented the total collapse of the German people or the standstill agreement or a half dozen other measures in this direction."

Hoover also condemned the smear campaigns accusing him of importing low-wage Chinese laborers to South African mines three decades earlier and tried to use the accusations against him as an indictment of the Democratic National Committee. "Such contemptible statements in a political campaign would be ignored—should be ignored—were it not issued by the authority of the Democratic National Committee as a part of this campaign," Hoover said. "And it would be of no interest to the American people except that it is proposed that a political party shall be placed in power over one hundred twenty million people on the basis of votes secured in that manner."

So even an affronted Hoover was a stilted Hoover. "It was the speech of a man fighting on the defensive" delivered with "what was for him an unaccustomed warmth of indignation," *The New York Times* noted in an editorial. While it credited Hoover with working hard to counter the economic depression—with the help of Democratic legislators—the editorial dismissed his "unwinking defense" of tariffs and his efforts to blame Europe for America's woes as a "thesis . . . open to grave dispute."[5]

A week later, Hoover hit the road again to West Virginia, Ohio, and Michigan, in which he continued to defend the tariff, but also affirmed his support for limited immigration as part of a protectionist vision. "It is just as important to protect the American workman from the movement of people into the United States to take over his job as to protect him from a flow of goods from abroad which would take away his job," he said in Columbus, Ohio.

The main event was a speech in Detroit, where the economic collapse had a devastating effect. "The city was in an ugly mood," which made Edmund W. Starling, head of Hoover's Secret Service protective detail, very nervous. Fear of assassination lurked in Hoover's mind. Theodore Joslin reported the president had spoken several times during the year about the possibility of someone shooting and killing him, as had happened in May to French president Paul Doumer.[6]

Hoover's speech was scheduled for the city's five-year-old Olympia Arena, home to the Detroit Red Wings hockey team. That meant Hoover would have to be driven about four miles from the train station. Starling selected a route along wide boulevards with few turns, ordered buildings along the way checked out, and planned to load up the motorcade inside the station, then speed away to the arena.

As they left the shadows of the station, Starling saw a large waiting crowd, which began cheering at the sight of the motorcade. "There were also other sounds. For the first time in my long experience on the detail I heard the president of the United States booed." Starling saw signs, too, with such messages as DOWN WITH HOOVER and BALONEY AND APPLESAUCE, contemporary slang for nonsense. "The president looked bewildered and stricken."

The arena held a more welcoming crowd, and Hoover's hour-long speech aired over national radio. He once again defended his administration's handling of the Great Depression and argued that recent data indicated the economy was climbing back out of the economic hole. But progress would be lost if the Democrats took over and acted on their proposals to increase government spending.

Hoover took the rare step, for him, of attacking Roosevelt by name over a letter in which the governor said he believed "in the inherent right of every citizen to employment at a living wage" and pledged "to provide employment for all surplus labor at all times." Such a position, Hoover declared, was a promise that "no government on Earth can fulfill. It is utterly wrong to delude suffering men and women with such assurances."

ROOSEVELT, FOR HIS part, also focused on parts of the Midwest and the South, the latter where his support was already strong. He began an eight-day, seventeen-state, three-thousand-mile tour on October 18, with appearances in Syracuse, Rochester, and Buffalo, supporting his lieutenant governor, Herbert H. Lehman, to succeed him as governor. He planned major speeches in Pittsburgh, St. Louis, and Baltimore, but also scheduled dozens of whistle-stops in small cities and crossroads throughout the region. The regimen would have been exhausting for most people, but it seemed to energize Roosevelt. It also, combined with radio addresses, offered people a chance to measure the stark differences in personality and bearing between the reserved and dour-seeming president and the New York governor who, despite his physical disability, exuded warmth, vigor, and empathy.

Roosevelt also began making a notable shift. While in the early stages of the campaign, he focused on the need for a radical change in the relationship between the people and their government, on this trip he focused more on balancing budgets and restraining government spending. Incredulously, he accused the Hoover administration—which he had routinely attacked for an anemic response to the economic crisis—of overspending and running a deficit.

The change in tone and focus frustrated the more liberal members of the Brain Trust, but the switch displayed yet again Roosevelt's shrewd political sense. He was making the case to the business class that it need not fear him as an economic loose cannon. He sought to portray himself as a politician untethered to a fixed economic worldview and willing to find solutions wherever he could, landing somewhere between recognizing the need for more government involvement in economic planning—especially industrial and agricultural capacity—and the centralized economies in regimes that had taken root in Europe. He was putting himself forward as the answer to the crisis of the moment.[7]

Roosevelt was doing it with a dogged determination, but also a warm smile. Raymond Moley, the de facto head of the Brain Trust, noted in his memoir that between September 12 and Election Day, Roosevelt traveled thirteen thousand miles, delivered sixteen major speeches, sixty-seven "second-string speeches," and made countless appearances at whistle-stops with extemporaneous comments from the back railing of a train car. "He never wearied or lost his good humor," Moley wrote. "Campaigning, for him, was unadulterated joy."[8]

But Roosevelt also used his time on the train to nurture his network of supporters, picking up local Democratic leaders and officials at one stop, chatting with them, then dropping them off at a later stop. Moley estimated hundreds of people hopped on and off the trains, including "governors, senators, mayors, obscure county politicians, farmers, miners, mine owners, tradespeople, local bankers, newspaper owners, reporters, manufacturers, welfare workers." Roosevelt "never stopped having a wonderful time."

AFTER THE ROUTING of the Bonus Army in July, Walter W. Waters, the man who started it all, effectively disappeared from public view. Waters traveled with his wife to Miami, Florida, and began working on his memoir of the march. He sent a letter to an October 4 national convention of the remnants of the Bonus Expeditionary Force in Uniontown, Pennsylvania, southeast of Pittsburgh, that he would not attend. He was ill, he said.

The convention was called to recast the Bonus Expeditionary Force as a permanent, more political organization, with an agenda of relief measures it would lobby for in Washington. It's unclear whether Waters approved of the convention, or of the new direction. He had adamantly opposed involving the group in any political activity beyond demanding early payment of the bonuses, at which it had failed. Regardless, he remained a force even in his absence, and after some internal drama, Waters was elected commander by a voice vote to which he responded with a letter of resignation, which the BEF refused to accept. In the end Waters won out, but internal divisions left the BEF disorganized.

Still, the veterans pressed for relief for veterans, and early payment of the promised bonus. But national interest faded; a veterans' convention did not carry the dramatic heft of a march and a Capitol Hill showdown. Newspapers carried brief reports on the tumultuous Uniontown meeting, a separate gathering in Washington between Hoke Smith, the de facto head of the group after Waters's departure, and members of Congress, and the resignations of three top officials angry that Smith had positioned himself as speaking for the group. And there was a little sordidness added in when a sheriff in Georgia issued an arrest warrant for Smith after his wife filed a complaint that he had abandoned her and their new baby. Disarray was an understatement.[9]

Waters might have stepped away from the BEF, but he remained a vocal force. He gave speeches to veterans' groups in the Miami area and wrote a letter to the editor of the *Miami Herald* defending the BEF against the charge that it consisted mainly of criminals and communists, which the *Herald* raised in an article about the local arrest of a BEF member. Waters pointed out that the man had only been arrested, not convicted, and was but one member of a very large group. The *Herald*, Waters wrote, carried stories about local crimes. "Am I to infer that this means that all the people of this fine community should be placed in the same category as those accused of crimes? Ridiculous!"[10]

Otherwise, Waters effectively dropped out of public view until publication of his memoirs in April 1933.

———————

ON THE DAY Roosevelt began his second campaign swing, and a day before his planned speech in Pittsburgh, Father James R. Cox summoned local reporters to the rectory at Old St. Patrick's for an announcement. He had suspended campaigning five days earlier because the Jobless Party was out of cash. Now he was withdrawing from the race entirely, though his name would still appear on ballots in some states.

Cox's campaign had begun as an effort to organize the jobless into a political movement, in part to take the issue away from communist organizers, but also to pressure the government to do more for those in desperate straits. Despite the heat of his words, Cox never gained much traction. The one and only Jobless Party national convention in St. Louis failed to spark the mass movement Cox expected and it dissolved in acrimony as he and the leader of a fringe political movement, the Liberty Party, broke off merger negotiations when they couldn't agree on who ought to be the candidate of the masses.

A subsequent Western campaign trip by Cox sputtered. His speeches rarely drew more than one thousand people, and often barely reached one hundred. Cox insisted on flying back and forth between Pittsburgh and campaign appearances to raise money (never mind that the flights burned through cash), while his retinue of six campaign aides drove a donated "trailer"—a bus or small truck converted into a rolling campaign stand—between appearances, trailing a two-man advance team in a car. They often stayed in cheap hotels, but sometimes had to pull into campgrounds, according to a travelogue pieced together by Andrew Krupnick, Cox's aide, treasurer, and logistics coordinator.[11]

In Elk City, Oklahoma, they met up with Cox's running mate, Victor C. Tisdal, a local medical doctor and part owner of a hospital, who delivered his formal acceptance speech. Then the entourage continued westward through Amarillo, Texas; Tucumcari and Santa Fe, New Mexico; then Flagstaff, Arizona, where they ran out of cash and had to wait for Father Cox, who had returned temporarily to Pittsburgh, to wire them money so they could pay their Flagstaff hotel bill and food, gas, and room rents as they headed for the California coast.

After a hastily arranged and poorly advertised speech on September 30 at the plaza outside San Francisco City Hall, Cox flew home and his entourage began the long drive back to Pittsburgh. They made overnight stops until they reached Terre Haute, Indiana, after which they drove nonstop to Pittsburgh, arriving at three o'clock in the afternoon on October 9, the forty-second day of the trip, after more than a half-dozen flat tires, without a car they sold to raise cash, short on patience with each other, and utterly broke.

All told, they drove 7,800 miles, Cox delivered thirty-three speeches to crowds that ranged from sixty, at a banquet in his honor at Elk City, to six thousand, at stops in Ohio and Indiana. He also performed thirteen masses at Catholic churches. The campaign raised $479.88 by passing the hat at Cox's appearances, but spent $1,731.04, according to Krupnick's meticulous record-keeping, including $356.07 on airplane tickets. Cox and one of his supporters and financiers, Sara Voit, of Grafton, West Virginia, who had traveled as part of his campaign staff, covered the deficit. At its end Cox declared that he had gained 250,000 supporters, a risible claim given that the experience apparently persuaded him to quit the race.[12]

After the reporters gathered in his rectory, Cox made his withdrawal announcement, but also continued to pummel Hoover as the protector "of a few who have amassed swollen fortunes and who desire to dominate the country and its government for their own selfish gain," and for the "barbarous" rousting of the Bonus Army. "America must reject Herbert Hoover and all that he represents if she means to continue as a democracy," Cox said.[13]

But Cox dropped his previous harsh condemnations of both major parties as acting primarily in the interests of Wall Street and the wealthy. Roosevelt, he told the reporters, "has pledged himself to look out for the interests of this country as a whole," as well as seeking the repeal of Prohibition. And so, he said, his supporters could vote for him in good conscience.

In fact, Cox said, he had done his own duty to the poor by mounting a campaign to bring attention to their plight. "Your duty remains to be done," he said. "It will be your duty as well as mine to vote for Franklin Delano Roosevelt."

AS THE CANDIDATES were campaigning, interviewers and analysts for Houser Associates, statistician J. David Houser's polling firm, were quietly completing their work. They had met with and asked questions of some five thousand rural and urban residents—twice as many men as women—from in and around fourteen cities, including Seattle, Los Angeles, New Orleans, Tulsa, Cleveland, New York, and Boston. With less than three weeks to go until Election Day, Houser sent along his summary of the findings to Lewis Strauss, Hoover's longtime friend in Manhattan, to pass on to Hoover. Had the Republicans received the results earlier in the campaign, they might have been able to tweak some of Hoover's messaging to address the issues spotlighted in the survey, but it probably wouldn't have done much good.[14]

Houser's people asked interviewees for whom they had voted in 1928, whom they planned to back in the current race, and about "their attitudes on certain critical matters such as the tariff, the soldiers' bonus, the government's part in the Depression, responsibility for the Depression, war debts, etc." Houser then zeroed in on Republican voters from 1928 who were leaning toward the Democratic ticket in the current race, reasoning that "if enough people can be reclaimed to Republican loyalty, the Republican ticket can be elected."

Somewhat surprisingly, the survey found that most of the drifting away from Hoover wasn't over the economy. Of the five thousand people interviewed, 670 said they voted for Hoover in

1928, but were abandoning him in 1932. While about half of Hoover's loyal supporters backed repeal, 84 percent of those switching to Roosevelt agreed with the statement that repeal "would be good for the country," and that repeal was inevitable. Many believed that it would be good for the economy and for the government, presumably by putting people to work in producing and distributing alcoholic beverages and taxing production and sales. "Faith that there is a greater probability of the Democrats bringing this about is a most powerful cause of lost votes to the Republican Party," Houser concluded.

Similarly, most of those switching to Roosevelt believed that tariffs needed to be reduced, and while 58 percent believed "the government was at least somewhat responsible for the Depression," most felt the government had taken steps "to make the Depression less severe" and mostly blamed Wall Street and Big Business for the crisis. The survey didn't ask people to rank the issues in order of importance to them, but it's notable that among those who were switching parties, 62 percent believed that business was picking up and 82 percent believed "there will be more employment a year from now." In other words, people leaving Hoover generally had a positive view of the economy's direction.

But the survey also didn't pick up on regional and class distinctions. For many, the national conventions had taken the steam out of Prohibition as an issue, and in places like the rural Midwest, journalists reported that Prohibition had fallen away under the weight of the economic crisis, where countless farmers and owners of businesses catering to them feared failure, bankruptcy, and eviction. In early October, Pauline Sabin toured the Midwest, trying to rally support for local and regional candidates who supported repeal, but received little more than polite notice.

Roland M. Jones, an editorial writer for the *Omaha World-Herald* and regular contributor to *The New York Times,* noted that "the chief reason for this apathy is because the question has been shouldered out of the way by the economic problem." Hoover's

Des Moines speech on October 4 may have energized his supporters, Jones wrote, but over the next few days, farm prices
dropped yet lower, accenting the failure of the federal government to meaningfully address the crisis. Corn farmers, he
predicted, would hang on to their crops rather than harvest and
transport to markets at a loss. Instead, they would burn it as a
cheaper alternative to buying coal. "It is estimated that about ten
acres will comfortably heat the average farm home."[15]

FATHER COX MAY have abandoned his quixotic bid for the White
House, but other fringe candidates forged ahead. The Communist Party had nominated William Z. Foster, a former labor
organizer, as its candidate for the presidency. Foster, a Stalinist,
had been a member of the Industrial Workers of the World—the
Wobblies—before moving to the American Federation of Labor
(AFL). A 1921 trip to Moscow for an international meeting of radical trade unionists stretched out for three months as Foster
studied communism among the Bolsheviks while they cemented
their control in the aftermath of the Russian civil war. "As a result of my intense observations and reading I declared myself a
Communist," Foster wrote later.[16]

Back in the United States, Foster focused on trying to bring
a more radical slant to the AFL. Foster's activism led to numerous arrests, including in March 1932. Foster had delivered a
speech in Detroit the night before the hunger march on the Ford
Rouge plant, where the shooting deaths of four demonstrators
would occur. Police issued a warrant for Foster's arrest, even
though he had returned to New York City before the violence
broke out. Foster spent several days in jail before the charges
were eventually dropped.[17]

The Communist Party had previously nominated Foster as
its presidential candidate in 1924 and 1928 and, despite embarrassing showings in those two elections, nominated him again
during the May 1932 national convention, also selecting James

Ford, a Black union activist and Chicago postal employee, to run as vice president.

Foster, who had a history of heart trouble, mapped out a series of campaign trips that, beginning in early June, would cover thirty thousand miles and include at least 105 speeches, a pace that almost immediately began taxing his health. He also wound up getting arrested several more times. In Los Angeles, Foster managed to utter "ten mumbled words" as he exited a car to address a rally at the Plaza, near the Union Station train depot, before police arrested him on a charge of criminal syndicalism, using alleged criminal acts to foment political change. As police began arresting other speakers, a melee broke out with swung sticks, thrown rocks, and a dense fog of tear gas.[18]

In early July, Foster began feeling overwhelmed physically by the demands of traveling and speaking, while also tending to party business during often contentious meetings among rival factions, all while facing steady harassment and fear of arrest. He told a doctor that he had begun to develop recurring pains in the left side of his chest as he made public speeches. It all caught up with him on September 8 in Moline, Illinois, when he collapsed after a speech. Doctors diagnosed angina pectoris, often caused by insufficient blood flow to the heart—a form of heart disease. With that, Foster's third long-shot campaign for the presidency effectively ended. Foster spent the next two months mostly on bed rest, sheltered from party business, international news, and the election itself, save for a telephoned address to a rally at Madison Square Garden in Manhattan, just before the election.[19]

The political left also was represented by Norman Thomas, running on the Socialist Party line for the second time. Four years earlier, he had picked up only 268,000 votes nationwide, less than 1 percent of the total, a much worse showing than the previous Socialist Party quadrennial candidate, Eugene V. Debs, who over five races had peaked at 6 percent of the vote in 1912 (won by Woodrow Wilson after Teddy Roosevelt split the Republican vote by running as a Progressive, or the Bull Moose Party).

In 1932, Thomas was just emerging from an internecine war between rival factions for control of the Socialist Party, still trying to recover from the federal anti-radical clampdown that saw its membership drop from a peak of 113,000 in 1912 to just fourteen thousand. Thomas was a respected pacifist, entertaining public speaker, and an unrelenting critic of both Hoover and Roosevelt. But since he was fighting Roosevelt for the anti-Hoover vote, he targeted the New York governor as part of a political system that existed to support capitalists, not the people. Like the other fringe candidates, Thomas attracted core supporters, but didn't resonate much farther than the sound of his own voice. The Prohibition Party, which had endorsed Hoover in 1928, nominated former Georgia representative William David Upshaw, a Klan supporter and leader of the Southern Baptist Convention, who also failed to gain much traction, even though his cause lay at the center of a raging national debate.

That none of the more radical candidates could tap into the nation's deep rivers of dissatisfaction and, in many cases, desperation to build a political base of any breadth affirmed a key aspect of the American body politic. They wanted resolutions to their problems from within the established political order.

NEWSREEL IV

October to December, 1932

The Dow Jones Industrial Average closes on October 1 at 72.2 points, recovering nearly most of its losses from the start of the year—but down from its peak of 79.9 points reached in early September... The musical revue Americana opens on Broadway. It fizzles and closes a few weeks later, but not before it introduces the nation to a new song, "Brother, Can You Spare a Dime?"... The Soviet Union's Communist Party expels twenty people, including allies of Leon Trotsky, living in exile in Turkey. Despite being a mass producer of grain, Russia reportedly seeks to buy tons of it on international markets amid reports of famine conditions in the Volga region. Josef Stalin ends the first Five-Year Plan a year early, as the Soviet Union claims large gains in industrial production and capacity but doesn't mention the collapsed agriculture sector. Critics who do are rounded up... Italian premier Benito Mussolini once again condemns the peace treaties drawn up at the end of the Great War as born of politics, not peace, and warns they cannot be considered eternal... The New York Yankees sweep the Chicago Cubs for the team's fourth World Series championship; stepping to the plate, slugger Babe Ruth points to where he will hit a home run, then does so... New York City's Palace Theater, longtime home to vaudeville, converts into a movie house, part of a broad transition... Radio City Music Hall also opens in New York.

CHAPTER 18

Final Days

THE FINAL WEEK OR SO of the campaign carried an aura of inevitability. President Hoover tried to seem confident, and a few loyalists reassured him that his speeches and campaign trips were having an effect, but it was a hard illusion to maintain. "The news is about as bad as it could be, with every newspaper analysis giving the election to Roosevelt by anywhere from a comfortable margin to a landslide," Theodore Joslin noted in his diary.[1]

The campaign had been taking its toll on Hoover as well. In the days before he left the White House for a final campaign trip to the West Coast, where he planned to vote then await the election results at his family home in Palo Alto, the president worked himself to exhaustion. He was often awake until two o'clock in the morning, then was back at it around 6 A.M. "The President was more fatigued today than I have seen him at any time," Joslin noted in his diary after seeing Hoover the first thing one October morning. "His eyes were blood shot, and he was groggy."

The president had planned a final East Coast speech for October 31, in New York City, where he drew so many people to Madison Square Garden that fire marshals ordered the doors closed as a safety measure, causing a small riot. *The New York*

Times estimated thirty thousand people remained outside the Garden (an estimate that invites skepticism), forcing the New York City Police Department to deploy about three hundred officers, including many on horseback, to separate the crowd from the doors. Officers locked arms, side by side, in a human wall and tried to push back at the surging crowd as the mounted officers moved back and forth behind them. Fists and curses flew, and several people and police officers suffered minor injuries. The showdown lasted more than an hour before the crowd began dissipating; those who remained were able to hear Hoover's speech over loudspeakers.[2]

After all that, the speech, Joslin reported, "did not ring a bell." Hoover went on for about an hour with the now-familiar recitation of his administration's accomplishments and warned that if the Democrats managed to enact their plans to cut tariffs, "the grass will grow in streets of a hundred cities, a thousand towns; the weeds will overrun the fields of millions of farms." He painted a picture of a nation impoverished by a larger, more expansive, and centralized government that would "enslave" taxpayers with two months of every twelve months' income diverted to taxes across all levels of government. "It was the speech of a statesman," Joslin wrote in his diary, "and what the crowd wanted to hear was the speech of a politician" with "a lot of fight in it."[3]

Hoover didn't seem to have much fight left. The president planned to leave Washington, D.C., at 4:20 P.M. on November 3 for the trip West. Joel Boone, the White House doctor, went early to Union Station to be on the train before the Hoovers arrived. The first couple ran about twenty minutes late, unusual for them. When they finally boarded, Lou Hoover pulled Boone aside and told him they were late because the president continued polishing speeches inside the White House as she sat in the motorcade. "When he finally came out of the White House front door and got into the car beside me, he slumped into his seat, looking very pale and wan," she said. The president then told his wife, "I do not know whether I will be able to weather this trip. I have reason to doubt that I will live through it," a rare admission of weakness. She arranged to have Boone sleep in a compartment in the president's car during the trip and asked the doctor to stay as close to Hoover as he could.[4]

After a couple of whistle-stops in Maryland and West Virginia, the president's train sped through the night to Indiana, where the whistle-stops resumed in the morning. He delivered speeches in Springfield, Illinois, and St. Louis, Missouri, then a brief talk in Madison, Wisconsin, before a planned nationally aired speech from St. Paul, Minnesota, on November 5, about fifty-two hours after he left Washington.

By the time Hoover reached the Minnesota capital city, he could barely function. The campaign hoped the speech would help Hoover regain support in a state he had won four years earlier with 57 percent of the vote. Joslin, who spoke with Hoover by phone and listened to the speech over the radio, described his boss as "absolutely punch drunk ... The delivery of his speech was terrible. The address itself was good, but his voice was worn out and so were his eyes for he spoke haltingly and frequently lost his place."[5]

At one point the president stopped talking completely. His longtime friend Edgar Rickard, listening in Manhattan, noted that he was "shocked at the very tired voice" and Hoover's inability to keep his place in the speech. "I was stunned by the delivery and feared he might collapse." So did Dr. Boone, who, assigned a seat behind Hoover on the stage, deftly slid a chair forward in case the president lost his balance. Hoover later told the doctor that he paused during the speech because "there was something wrong with me. I reached a point where I couldn't see the damned print at all and I was short of breath." Yet, after the speech Hoover told reporters he felt strong—except for his voice.[6]

It didn't help Hoover's election chances any when, responding to a Democratic statement that a Republican victory would lead to mobs in the streets, Hoover strayed from his prepared remarks to say, "Thank God, we still have some officials in Washington that can hold out against a mob," immediately conjuring images of the U.S. Army rousting the veterans just three months earlier. "A ripple went through the audience," recalled Edmund Starling, the head of the Secret Service protective detail. At the speech's end, Starling said, a local Republican leader asked him, "[W]hy don't they make him quit? He's not doing himself or the party any good. It's turning into a farce."[7]

Where President Hoover, on his heels politically, was waging a defensive campaign, Governor Roosevelt knew it was his election to lose and campaigned like a front-runner, careful to avoid errors, while heaping blame for the depression on the Republicans. He remained highly visible and, as ever, exuded a sense of vitality. In late October, Roosevelt undertook a three-day trip to all six New England states, including stopping by the Groton School in northeast Massachusetts, to visit two of his sons studying there. Roosevelt himself was an alum, as were a handful of other Roosevelts. From there he drove through the working-class cities of Lowell, Lawrence, and Haverhill, Massachusetts, "in each of which idle factories furnished mute evidence of the extent of the depression." Thousands of people lined the motorcade route and cheered as Roosevelt passed through the heart of the traditionally Republican region.[8]

Roosevelt continued through southeastern New Hampshire to South Berwick, Maine, to meet with the new Democratic governor, Louis J. Brann, whose surprise September victory was read as a harbinger for the Democrats in the national election. From there Roosevelt passed through Biddeford and Saco en route to Portland, Maine, where he delivered a midday speech to an overflow crowd of more than five thousand of "my old friends and neighbors" in a City Hall auditorium. Roosevelt told the crowd he had first visited Maine as an infant and had sailed the entire coastline, so he knew the state well.[9]

He avoided policies and positions, again selling himself. He congratulated the normally Republican state for supporting Democrats in September and urged them to do so again. "Maine has pointed the way" for the rest of the country, he said, noting that it took partisan cooperation for the state to elect Democrats. He tried to differentiate between Republican voters and the party hierarchy: "That bears out what we have been doing all this year," seeking to rally "members of both parties against Republican leadership."

The strategy seemed to be working.

IN EARLY NOVEMBER, the International Labor Defense and several other leftist groups began organizing a rally on the plaza outside the United States Capitol Building after word came that the court would announce its decision in the Scottsboro Boys case on the Monday morning before Election Day. For the members of the ILD, the decision would either be cause for celebration or outrage.

District and Capitol police forces, which had denied a permit for the demonstration, girded for a showdown, and they got one. As the unpermitted rally came together at 10 A.M., the police ordered demonstrators marching to the plaza to stop. They continued. Police confronted them and the plaza "resounded with the whacking of nightsticks on communist heads," followed by tear gas that drove off most of the protesters; fourteen were arrested. The *Evening Star* reported that two police officers were injured in the melee but didn't see fit to count injured protesters.[10]

The midmorning breeze had barely cleared away the tear gas when the Supreme Court announced in its packed courtroom that it had overturned the Scottsboro convictions and ordered a new trial. By a vote of seven to two, the justices agreed with the defendants' legal team that the teens and young men had been denied access to effective legal counsel before and during their rushed convictions, which meant they had not received a fair trial.

The decision was narrow in its impact. Alabama already required the state to appoint defense counsel for defendants in capital cases who couldn't afford a lawyer on their own, which is what the trial judge did. But the appointed counsel in this case was so ineffective, and came into the case so late, that the defendants did not receive adequate counsel, the court said. Conservative justice George Sutherland wrote in the majority opinion that "the right to the aid of counsel is of . . . fundamental character" under the concept of due process. The court didn't address any of the other issues raised in the appeal, including the racial composition of the jury or whether the presence of a howling mob outside the courthouse also denied the defendants justice. But the due process argument was enough to win new trials.[11]

The decision hit the front pages of many newspapers, often appearing next to stories about the final day of the campaign. The *Atlanta Constitution*, one of the largest newspapers in the South, ran adjacent news articles, but ignored the decision in its editorials over the next few days, focusing instead on the election and its results (exuberantly pro-Roosevelt). The *Chattanooga News*, a Tennessee newspaper published about fifty miles northeast of Scottsboro, editorialized that the decision was "the only one which could have been reached," and pushed back against talk that it would provide the ILD "rich ground for fertilization of its subversive doctrines among the Negroes of the South."[12]

The New York Times approved, too, noting that the court said nothing about guilt or innocence, but defended due process. "However people may feel about the case itself, there will be, we believe, general approval of the lofty position taken by the majority of the court," the editorial board wrote, adding that the court is "mindful of human rights" and affirmed that class does not affect the right to justice. "It ought to abate some of the rancor of extreme radicals, while confirming the faith of the American people in the soundness of their institutions and especially in the integrity of their courts."[13]

The *Daily Worker*, the Communist Party newspaper, had a different take, arguing the decision validated the party's strategy of using mass protests to bend the system, while undercutting the Socialist Party and the "treacherous leaders" of the NAACP and had "brought the issue of Negro liberation and self-determination to the forefront." Yet, the paper also condemned the decision as a "brazen and far-reaching maneuver" to shore up public faith in the judiciary in the face of protests. It also denounced the Supreme Court for resting the case on a legal point—which, of course, is what the Supreme Court is supposed to do.

But the paper also was prescient about the minimal influence the decision would have on Black Americans. "It leaves the Scottsboro boys in the hands of the same authorities who framed them," the editorial said. "It does more than that. It warns the Alabama lynchers that in using the legal machinery against the Negroes, they must be more careful to avoid infractions of the code, and it tells them how to do it."[14]

So the Black defendants won the moment, but the press reaction focused less on racism, ill treatment, and use of the justice system to repress Blacks than on the opportunity the court victory might afford communist organizers.

HOOVER AND ROOSEVELT wound up on opposite coasts on Election Day, a fitting metaphor for the distances between them politically.

After his fumbled speech in St. Paul, Hoover meandered through Minnesota, then Iowa, and across the Missouri River to Omaha, Nebraska, then across the Great Plains to Denver. There the route jogged north into Wyoming, then west again to Salt Lake City, southwest through Nevada to Sparks, before climbing the Sierra Nevada to reach Roseville and Sacramento, then on to the Pacific Ocean. When it reached San Francisco, the train would be abandoned in favor of a motorcade for the final thirty miles of the trip to Palo Alto.[15]

Most of the stops were brief, as were Hoover's remarks, although during a half-hour stop in Denver on Sunday, he delivered a longer speech, avoiding an overtly political message because "it would not be proper for me on this Sabbath Day." From a platform erected in front of Union Station, before an estimated crowd of twenty-five thousand people, Hoover spoke in broad terms about the nation and about programs to help children. He delivered a full campaign speech the next day in the Mormon Tabernacle in Salt Lake City, hitting on his familiar themes and defenses, then later that evening sat down for a fifteen-minute nationally broadcast speech from the train, a rarity if not a first, in hopes of making one last connection with the nation on the eve of the election. In fact, polls would be opening in some states on the East Coast seven hours after Hoover's speech ended.

Hoover reached San Francisco around noon on Election Day, and after a brief parade to City Hall, where he took part in an equally brief reception, Hoover rode to Stanford University, where he and Lou met briefly with old friends and some of Hoover's former instructors, before casting their ballots. Then they went home for the first time in four years.

A couple of blackboards stood in a hallway in the Palo Alto house waiting to keep track of the vote results as they came in, but back east a strong sense of foreboding pervaded the White House, where Joslin had remained behind. "Mark Sullivan called me up" from New York around 5 P.M. "and said it looked mighty bleak." They discussed the wording of the concession telegram for Hoover to send to Roosevelt after the race had been called. Then Joslin called the president's house. "It fell to my lot to tell the president the chances were none too good. He took it without flinching. Then I dictated the message Mark and I had agreed upon."[16]

The Hoovers sat down to a dinner with about sixteen close friends and family members, then later entertained neighbors. Eventually Hoover, receiving a note from his steward, excused himself and left the dining room. When he didn't return, the others went in search and found him alone in his study. Slowly the numbers began trickling in, as did telegrams and phone calls. Hoover shared the information in the note his steward had passed him: New York, which Hoover had won four years earlier over Smith, had gone for Roosevelt.[17]

ELEANOR AND FRANKLIN Roosevelt started Election Day in two different cities; Franklin in the family home in Hyde Park, and Eleanor at the Sixty-Fifth Street town house in Manhattan, which adjoined a town house owned and inhabited by Franklin's mother, Sara. Eleanor kept her morning commitment to teach a class at the Todhunter School, an academy for girls, then met her husband at the Hyde Park Town Hall to cast their ballots and pose for the news cameras. Afterward they traveled by motorcade to Manhattan for a buffet they were hosting for family and friends at the town house.[18]

The real party, which they soon joined, was at the Biltmore Hotel, about twenty blocks south of the town house and across the street from where Louis Howe, James Farley, and the rest of the core staff had spent the campaign. Howe had arranged to have wire service reports sent to his office, and he holed up there for the evening while the bulk of the staff went to the Biltmore, where the campaign had its own suite adjacent to the larger Democratic Party election night headquarters on the hotel's first floor.

Roosevelt spent most of the evening at a large table in one of the suite's rooms. Twenty operators handled a bank of phones bringing in results from Roosevelt's massive network of supporters and local party officials. Roosevelt took some of the calls himself, chatting briefly with leading Democrats around the country. Meanwhile, hundreds of people roamed the hallways and drifted in and out of the grand ballroom, where Roosevelt would speak once the results were in. The mood was jubilant, a celebration awaiting confirmation of the reason for it. "There was really no feeling of tension at all," Farley recalled. Roosevelt eventually gave up tracking the returns "to enjoy a few hours of fun and frolic with his friends."[19]

Roosevelt intended to wait for Hoover to concede before saying anything himself, though the president, still clinging to hope, waited until 9:30 P.M., Pacific time, to send his telegram to Roosevelt, who, by then, had gone to bed. "I congratulate you on the opportunity that has come to you to be of service to the country and I wish for you a most successful administration," the president wrote. "In the common purpose of all of us I shall dedicate myself to every possible helpful effort."

Hoover retired about 11 P.M., but a few minutes later, a choir of Stanford students gathered outside the house and began serenading the soon-to-be former president. Hoover emerged on a second-floor balcony, listened for a bit, thanked the students in a halting voice, then went back in. Moments later, the house went dark.[20]

PRESIDENT-ELECT ROOSEVELT'S victory was stunning in its scope. Where Al Smith had won only eight states four years earlier, with Hoover dominating everywhere but in Massachusetts and the Deep South, Roosevelt won every state in the nation except four of the New England states and Pennsylvania. Connecticut and Pennsylvania could have gone for Roosevelt had Norman Thomas not siphoned away more than 3 percent of the vote in each. And Hoover barely prevailed in New Hampshire; conversely, Ohio was the only state Roosevelt carried by a narrow margin. In the end Roosevelt won 7 million more votes nationwide than Hoover and took the electoral college, 472 to 59.

The loss extended far beyond Hoover's presidential bid. Democrats won control of both the House and the Senate, an overwhelming repudiation of the party that had dominated national politics for decades. Many Dry incumbents lost, too, which meant Wets were now in charge. The Constitution required two-thirds majorities in each chamber to pass an amendment. *The New York Times* counted one hundred Drys losing their seats, giving more than two-thirds of the House seats and three seats short of that threshold in the Senate to the repeal forces. But some of the surviving Drys had signed on to the notion of resubmitting the issue to the states, which indicated "sufficient Wet strength in the new Congress to put through a resolution for repeal." At the same time eleven states had repeal-related issues on their ballots, and the results were overwhelmingly for repeal. Some talk surfaced that in the face of the national mood, the lame-duck Congress could even take up resubmission.[21]

The election results would mean profound changes for both the Hoovers and the Roosevelts. The Hoovers were nominally Californians; Lou had designed and overseen construction of their home on the grounds of Stanford University. But they had spent most of their lives together elsewhere: China, where Herbert was living when they married in 1899, then London before the Great War, and finally to New York and Washington, D.C., as Hoover pursued his careers in mining and business, and then in public service. Now the couple faced a decision: What would they do?

Lou had always seen the Stanford house as the family's home, never mind that the whole family was rarely in it at the same time. Though she had been born in Waterloo, Iowa, about eighty miles northwest of Herbert's birthplace in West Branch, Lou's parents had moved to Monterey, California, when she was sixteen. News reporters asked Hoover the morning after the election whether he planned to stay in Washington, D.C. No, he said. "I will come back to California, I am sure." But to do what? "I haven't given consideration to anything of that sort," Hoover said. "I will probably have to earn something of a living. I have been in public service now ever since 1914, and it is a long drain on one's resources."

For Franklin and Eleanor Roosevelt, the change would be less disruptive. They lived in both Hyde Park and Manhattan, but also in the governor's mansion in Albany. Roosevelt's new job would change the government address, but they would still have the New York roots relatively close by. But the presidency would mean a change in the scale of Roosevelt's work as the chief executive of a much larger, more sprawling and complicated government than he handled as governor.

The bigger change would fall on Eleanor, who had developed her own career and life in New York. She had a political presence, first as her husband's stand-in at events as he recovered from polio, but also in her own stead. As part of the Women's Trade Union League, she advocated for a range of policies, including the abolition of child labor and a shorter workweek. She co-owned the Todhunter School, where she taught history courses; with friends she had founded the Val-Kill Industries at Hyde Park, hoping to provide extra work to local farmers; and she helped publish the *Women's Democratic News,* a monthly news-letter. Becoming the first lady, she feared, meant an end to much of that hard-fought life.

Eleanor felt happy for her husband, "but for myself I was deeply troubled. As I saw it, this meant the end of any personal life of my own."[22]

DIARIES V

Tuesday, November 8

WILLIAM E. WARFIELD, FORT WAYNE, INDIANA

On my way home this morning I voted a straight Republican ticket. The colored voters are divided between the two major parties this time more so than ever before, but I am still voting for the source of my freedom and my franchise and for what I consider the best interest of the country. My son is working in this election. He is driving a Republican car taking people to the polls who prefer to ride. He will be paid about $5.00 or more for using his car. My wife is ready to go and vote.

FAY WEBB GARDNER, RALEIGH, NORTH CAROLINA

At 3:30 we went to Mamie Mahler's to Tea and Topics Book Club, Sadie Connor of Chapel Hill lecturing on her England trip. An interesting social half-hour afterward and then home. After the [illegible] left, Madge and I to movies and back to hear the radio election news. The trend for Roosevelt for Pres. overwhelming early in evening.

Wednesday, November 9

JAMES BALL, HELENA, MONTANA

It snowed about four inches of wet heavy snow last night again and is warmer today and cloudy. Plume went to the timber after *green firewood. (Illegible word) Taft came up from Avon on foot. He said it was rumored that Roosevelt was elected President of the United States.*

NELLIE COWLEY, GLENDORA, CALIFORNIA

Roosevelt is elected by a landslide and the House and Senate are both Democratic.

WILLIAM E. WARFIELD, FORT WAYNE, INDIANA

Roosevelt has carried 42 of our 48 states. Hoover is beaten more decisively than he beat Al Smith four years ago. I voted for Hoover but many millions voted against him. I spent much time today reading accounts of the landslide to the Democrats. The entire country (almost) is Democratic. There are not more than four Republican governors out [of] the 48. This long Depression had made the people long for change and willing to risk anything to get one.

Thursday, November 10

NELLIE COWLEY, GLENDORA, CALIFORNIA

Harry writes that on election night at Douglas [Arizona] they were carrying banners saying, "We now have a real true blue American for our President." I don't know why they are so bitter against Hoover. I think that in course of time he will be recognized as one of our great Presidents.

FAY WEBB GARDNER, RALEIGH, NORTH CAROLINA

Now for definite election news! Roosevelt tide swept the nation and Democratic victory becomes more impressive as returns from isolated areas are added. 42 states put their electoral votes in Roosevelt's column. This victory won by Gov. Roosevelt without parallel in century of American history ... Roosevelt interprets great landslide as an expression of liberal thought and a national mandate transcending party lines.

Saturday, December 31

EMILY A. C. RICH, OGDEN, UTAH

The close of another year. We have much to be thankful for though it has been the poorest year for doctor's business in many years. We have lost heavily in a financial way but the greatest blessing health we have enjoyed. We have had some worry and sorrow, but we too have had many blessings. We have never known such depression as exists everywhere in our married life.[1]

CHAPTER 19

Transition

THE CONSTITUTION HAD YET TO catch up with modern communications and transportation, but it was coming close. In the late eighteenth century it could take weeks for people, letters, and newspapers to travel even middling distances. Individual states' selections of presidential electors spanned several weeks, not just one day, so it made sense for the Founding Fathers to look to early March as the day to inaugurate a new president. That also happened to come after the worst of winter weather had passed.

But that was then. By 1932, communication could be done instantly over the telephone, and modern transportation—planes, trains, automobiles—meant people could travel from place to place in hours or days. In recognition of these changes and advancements, on March 2, Congress passed an amendment changing the start of a presidential term to January 20 after a presidential election. But at the time of the November 1932 election, the required number of states had yet to ratify the Twentieth Amendment, leaving Hoover and Congress with four more months of service and very little political will or power to do anything.

A lot needed tending to. In mid-1931, the largest bank in Austria, Creditanstalt—sometimes styled as Credit-Anstalt—failed and threatened to collapse the nation's economic system and spread to Germany. Both countries were drowning in reparations debt from the Great War. The United States was loaning money to Germany and Austria so they could meet their debt payments to France and Great Britain, which then used that money to repay their $10 billion in debts to the United States (several other nations owed debts to the United States, too, including Poland and Czechoslovakia).

Getting out from under those debts would give the European economies breathing room and a chance to stabilize and grow. But the fresh banking crisis accelerated the movement of money and gold out of Germany and Austria and into perceived safer harbors, such as American gold. Henry Stimson, Hoover's secretary of state, later wrote that "unless something was done quickly, Germany would once more slide down the inclined plane of inflation to financial ruin." And that, he believed, would undermine political stability in a region still trying to get its postwar bearings.[1]

A default on the debts would also exacerbate the global financial crisis. For the United States to cancel the debts would be the most expedient resolution, but Americans had little appetite for that. This was in part because the nation had become isolationist after the war and, struggling with its own financial crisis, wasn't particularly interested in forgiving billions of dollars owed by the Europeans. In Europe, the war debts were becoming a political issue as well, and fed nationalist movements, particularly Hitler's Nazi Party. Fearing a resurgence of animosities, European nations were rearming to the tune of $5 billion annually, a 70 percent increase from what they invested before the Great War.[2]

Hoover hit upon a possible compromise: a yearlong moratorium on the debt payments, with the possibility of adding a second year if circumstances warranted. It took a lot of diplomacy abroad and at home, but Hoover persuaded Congress to approve a yearlong moratorium, which he signed on December 23, 1931. Unfortunately, as the December 15, 1932, expiration date neared, economic conditions had only worsened, as had European political instability: Hitler was on the verge of taking over Germany, which, with Mussolini's Fascists controlling Italy, made for a formidable axis in the heart of Europe. Also, Hoover was now a lame-duck president without a mandate, and without a cooperative Congress.[3]

Hoover invited Roosevelt to the White House to discuss the war debt issue, as well as an international disarmament conference in Geneva and a world economic conference in London that would carry over into Roosevelt's administration. Roosevelt had no intention of joining Hoover's approach to the war debts, writing Hoover that the responsibility for dealing with the deadline "rests upon those now vested with executive and legislative authority." But Roosevelt said he would go to Washington, D.C., and suggested they "make this meeting wholly informal and personal. You and I can go over the entire situation."

Roosevelt took Raymond Moley with him, and they met with Hoover and Treasury Secretary Ogden Mills in the Red Room of the White House, where Hoover spent an hour laying out the international debt crisis. "It was clear that we were in the presence of the best-informed individual in the country on the question of the debts," Moley later wrote. "His story showed a mastery of detail and a clarity of arrangement that compelled admiration." Hoover finished by urging Roosevelt to join him in announcing a debt commission to begin negotiations that would transcend both of their administrations.[4]

But Roosevelt and Hoover had radically different assessments of the root of the depression, and of the solution. A couple of days later, Roosevelt told reporters he opposed creating a debt commission and said existing diplomatic channels would be sufficient to handle negotiations between the United States and individual debtor nations. In truth, Roosevelt preferred to let Hoover and the present Congress do whatever they thought best as he continued piecing together his own legislative

plan while assembling the cabinet he would need to turn the policies into action.[5]

THE ORGANIZED FARMERS held a deep disdain for Hoover, reflected
in the overwhelming support the traditionally Republican-voting
bloc had given Roosevelt. Hoover had won his native Iowa with
62 percent of the vote in 1928; in 1932, he barely reached 40 percent. In Kansas, Nebraska, and Minnesota, the swing was even
wider. Milo Reno and the other organizers had decided to stand
back during the election to see what would happen, but also during their September gathering in Sioux City, they had set in
motion a December 7 through 10 Farmers' National Relief Conference in Washington, D.C. It would overlap with yet another
small but energetic hunger march organized by communists. It
was, in a sense, both a reprise and a continuation of the demonstration a year earlier that compelled Father Cox, of Pittsburgh, to
organize his own march and shorted-out presidential campaign.[6]

The farmers were described as "picturesque," arriving as they
did in farm clothes, most of them driving themselves alone or
with allies. They met in a typographical union hall and dispatched small delegations of two or three to deliver petitions to
Vice President Charles Curtis and House Speaker, and Vice President–elect, John Nance Garner. At the conference some three
hundred farmers from across the country debated demands, and
finally adopted resolutions calling for $500 million in direct relief
for farmers; a moratorium on farm debts, taxes, and evictions; a
commission to set price floors; diplomatic recognition of the Soviet Union to enable export of agricultural products; and, among
other planks, a federal fund to buy farm products to distribute
to unemployed people in cities.[7]

The leaders of the Farmers' Holiday Association, including
Reno, had agreed shortly after the election to suspend their
strike activities until they saw what the incoming administration
might do for the agricultural economy. Still, the "penny sales"

and other actions continued through the winter. One such "save" involved Hoover's cousin, farmer Arthur E. Hoover, who had approached the Farmers' Holiday Association for help staving off the foreclosure of his farm in Grand Meadow, Minnesota. Reno took the opportunity to tweak the president, writing in a letter to the White House that he had written several times before seeking Hoover's help for farmers, to no avail. Now the association, he noted, had persuaded the cousin's mortgage holder to back down, saving the farm.[8]

"It has occurred to me that since you have been unable to accomplish anything during the past four years except to bring this cousin and other farmers nearer bankruptcy," Reno wrote, "that you would gladly make a contribution to the Minnesota and National Farmers' Holiday Associations, in order that they may give real and militant protection to a greater number of real, 'dirt farmer' Hoovers."

There's no indication that Hoover's secretary passed the letter on to the president or whether the White House responded. And while Reno and the others took a wait-and-see attitude toward Roosevelt, they continued to organize. Letters flew between Reno and farmers around the country sharing advice on building or expanding local chapters, with Reno sending out boilerplate arguments and transcripts of his radio addresses on how the federal government had failed to look out for the interests of the farmers. The government, he argued, was aligned with the banks and the wealthy. The farmers had to organize and stand for themselves.[9]

THREE DAYS BEFORE Christmas, Hoover and his wife left Washington, D.C., for a ten-day vacation to Georgia and Florida for saltwater fishing. Since Hoover remained a sitting president, a simple vacation became a significant production. Hoover, his wife, and entourage left Washington, D.C., by train on December 23, reaching Savannah, Georgia, on the afternoon of Christmas Eve, then almost immediately boarded a boat to reach the 116-foot *Sequoia*, a ship maintained by the Department of Commerce, which had become the presidential yacht. They would be accompanied by a similar-sized lighthouse tender, the *Kilkenny*; two seventy-five-foot U.S. Coast Guard boats carrying Secret Service agents; and two other boats exceeding one hundred feet each.[10]

The president had a good trip, largely disconnected from pressing matters. Hoover caught nothing during the first week of fishing, but then hit a couple of days of luck off Palm Beach. He landed three sailfish, including one exceeding seven feet, on December 30, followed by two more catches the next day, one again measuring more than seven feet. Back ashore on January 2, Hoover boarded a train for the return trip to Washington, D.C.[11]

Roosevelt planned his own warm-water trip, setting sail from Jacksonville on February 4, 1933, aboard the *Nourmahal*, a 263-foot steamship custom-built four years earlier for Vincent Astor by the Krupps Shipyard in Germany (a major supplier of U-boats during the Great War). Roosevelt hoped the trip would give him a chance to relax and rest up before assuming the presidency, but he still had a cabinet to assemble. So he spent much of his time at sea reviewing names for different cabinet positions and lower-level offices. Yet, he also managed to rest, get some fishing in, and spend time with Astor, a friend and distant relative who owned a house near Roosevelt's in Hyde Park. Kermit Roosevelt, one of Theodore's sons, was also aboard, as were three friends from the president-elect's Harvard days—two of whom were Republicans.[12]

Roosevelt came back ashore on February 15, a little after 9 P.M., at Pier One of Miami's Municipal Docks, off North Bayshore Drive, then took a short motorcade trip to Bayfront Park, where some fifteen thousand people awaited him at the amphitheater. Roosevelt's driver steered the car to a cleared space between the band shell and the waving, cheering crowd. Local dignitaries had their say and then introduced the president-elect, who pulled himself up to sit on the top of the back seat. A local radio announcer handed the president-elect a portable microphone. Roosevelt, speaking easily and breezily, claimed to have gained ten pounds while aboard the yacht, and waved toward Chicago mayor Anton J. Cermak (and noted Al Smith supporter during the Democratic National Convention), seated on the platform, to join him at the car.[13]

When Roosevelt finished speaking, Cermak came down, shook the president-elect's hand, and "talked with him for nearly a minute" before Cermak turned away. "I heard what I thought was a firecracker, then several more," Roosevelt later told reporters. The radio announcer retrieving the microphone noticed flashes in the crowd and immediately thought they were from photographers.

They were gunshots—five of them. None of the bullets hit Roosevelt, the assassin's intended target, but Cermak wobbled, then collapsed to the ground, wounded in the abdomen. Another bullet hit the upper torso of Mabel Gill, who had been standing on the bandstand stage; she collapsed as she tried to descend the stairs. Three other people also suffered relatively minor wounds.[14]

The gunman was Giuseppe Zangara, a five-foot-tall Italian bricklayer, who told police he suffered from postsurgical pain, hated "all the rich and powerful," wanted to kill Hoover, but decided to shoot Roosevelt—whom he liked—after reading that the president-elect would be in Miami. Because of his short stature, Zangara had to stand on a chair to see Roosevelt, and when the moment came, he pulled out a long-barreled .32-caliber handgun, aimed it over the shoulder of a woman standing in front of him, and began firing. The woman reacted by swatting at Zangara's hand and arm with her purse, throwing off his aim, and other audience members and police quickly disarmed him and wrestled him to the ground.

Roosevelt ordered Cermak be loaded into his car, since it would be the first and fastest car to leave. Police placed him in the back seat next to Roosevelt, who wrapped an arm around Cermak's shoulders. "He was alive, but I didn't think he was going to last." One of the victims suffering from a head wound was bundled into the second car, which held Mosley and Astor. Surprisingly, police tossed Zangara onto the luggage rack at the back of the second car and, standing on running boards, held him in place as the cars sped off to Jackson Memorial Hospital, where Cermak underwent emergency surgery, but died of peritonitis nineteen days later. Zangara pleaded guilty and was executed on March 10.[15]

The assassination attempt rattled Hoover, who had feared a similar attack on himself. In fact, Joslin noted that in the previous year the Secret Service had handled about one hundred threats or perceived threats against Hoover. During the train trip to Palo Alto, a watchman near Elko, Nevada, stumbled across men trying to wire a bridge with dynamite before Hoover's train had crossed it. Joslin wrote in his diary that during the Bonus Army March, the Secret Service intercepted a man who had wrapped himself in dynamite. The morning after the assassination attempt on Roosevelt, Hoover sent a telegram to his successor-in-waiting: "Together with every citizen I rejoice that you have not been injured. I shall be grateful to you for news of Mayor Cermak's condition."[16]

Much to Moley's surprise, Roosevelt had no reaction upon his return to the ship for the night with his friends and close staff. Moley said Roosevelt had discussed the chance of assassination during the campaign, "but it is one thing to talk philosophically about assassination, and another to face it. And I confess that I have never in my life seen anything more magnificent than Roosevelt's calm that night."

IN BETWEEN THE presidential vacations, nineteen-year-old Angelo Herndon had his day in an Atlanta court. Herndon had been indicted the previous July under the Reconstruction-era Georgia anti-insurrection law, though his only action was to help organize demonstrations and possess leftist literature. A conviction carried the potential of a death sentence, and Herndon had been jailed since his arrest, often in solitary confinement for days at a time, until early December, when his two lawyers persuaded a judge to release him on a $2,500 bond.

The lawyers were partners Benjamin J. Davis Jr. and John H. Geer, both Black and natives of the South. Davis was born in Dawson, a small town in southwest Georgia, the son of a politically active businessman who had moved the family to Atlanta when Benjamin was young. Benjamin's father founded the *Atlanta Independent,* one of the city's earliest Black newspapers (it closed in 1928). Benjamin attended a high school operated by Morehouse College, then Morehouse itself, before moving to study at Amherst College in Massachusetts. From there he went to Harvard Law School, then worked in publishing for a couple of years before returning to Atlanta.

Geer grew up in Greenville, South Carolina, about one hundred miles northwest of Columbia. Geer had little formal legal training; he took correspondence courses and then was accepted into the Georgia bar in 1928. The two met in Atlanta and decided to set up practice together.

Herndon's arrest and detention outraged Davis, who was offended that police would target a Black activist while turning a blind eye to routine acts of intimidation and violence by Klan members. He and Geer went to the Fulton County jail to persuade Herndon to let them represent him. Herndon agreed, and the partners got to work. By the time the trial started on January 16, 1933, they had a strategy. On the first day of the trial, they attacked the Fulton County jury system for excluding Black residents. They subpoenaed educated, successful Blacks, who testified that they had never been called for jury service. The defense also subpoenaed the white officials in charge of the system, who struggled to defend their practices. But Herndon lost the argument before a hostile judge, who then led the two sides in selecting a trial jury from the all-white pool.[17]

As Davis and Geer left the courtroom at the end of the first day, a group of white men closed in on them near the elevators. "Watch yourself or we'll string you up," one said; another openly carried a knife; a third said, "Leave the Klan out of this." The two lawyers kept walking, trying to ignore the intimidation.

Reverend J. A. Martin, a muscular Black man weighing about 220 pounds, and three other similar-sized Black men moved in next to Davis and Geer, and the white men filtered away. Reverend Martin, who was a friend of Davis's, and his companions escorted the lawyers back to their offices, and the reverend announced that the lawyers would have similar escorts for the duration of the trial.

But the racist harassment did not end there. A four-foot-tall white cross greeted Davis as he stepped out of his house the next morning. A note read, "The Klan Rides again. Get out of the Herndon case. This is a white man's country." Davis, startled, pulled up the cross from his lawn and tucked it inside his door, then continued to court.

The jury was seated on the second day, and the prosecution began its case with one of the police officers who had arrested Herndon at the post office. He described the nature of the books and other reading material they had confiscated from the mailbox and Herndon's apartment. Then the prosecution read to the jury lengthy excerpts they contended proved that Herndon was bent on insurrection. Noticeably absent was any evidence that Herndon himself was organizing an insurrection, let alone violence of any sort. In fact, none of the witnesses could say they had seen Herndon even distributing the literature. But there was plenty of racism on display, with Davis hopping up regularly to object to the prosecutor and his witness referring to Herndon by racial epithets. The judge finally persuaded them just to refer to Herndon as "the defendant."

Herndon himself was the heart of the defense. Under Georgia court proceedings at the time, the defendant was allowed to make a statement from the witness stand, but could not be questioned by his lawyer or the prosecution. Herndon spoke for twenty minutes in a somewhat rambling but incendiary review of his involvement in the Unemployed Council, of the searing needs of the impoverished in Atlanta, and about his efforts to get poor white and Black Atlantans to work together. "Both are starving, and the capitalistic class will continue to play on this tune of segregation" to maintain power.

Herndon talked about his arrest and his detention, including being locked in a cell with a dead inmate. It was emotional, but at the end Herndon brought the topic back to the political. "The present system under which we are living today is on the verge of collapse," Herndon told the jurors, likening it to an overfilled balloon that will burst if more air is blown into it. "I don't know if that" popped balloon "is insurrection or not," he concluded, letting the point hang.[18]

Closing arguments brought more of the same from the prosecution. For the defense Geer offered a subdued recital of the failure of the state to make its case; then Davis, clearly out of patience with the judge and the system itself, described the case as "not one of prosecution, it is one of persecution." He attacked the prosecutor for pursuing a young man organizing the poor to seek relief for themselves, while not going after "the Ku Kluxers who are allowed to roam the land of this state burning innocent Black people at the stake in defiance of every law of justice, humanity, and right." He asked the jury whether they "want to see a man burn in the electric chair because he had the courage to fight for the Negroes and whites who are without bread or jobs."[19]

The jury began its deliberations just after lunch on January 18 and announced to the judge around 6 P.M. that it had reached a verdict. Guilty, they said, but recommended leniency: eighteen to twenty years on a chain gang—not death. The audience erupted, and after it quieted down, the bailiff led Herndon away.

Unknown to the public, on the last day of the trial, Davis, dis-gusted with the blatant racism in the courtroom and in the criminal justice system, quietly joined the Communist Party.[20]

No one expected Congress to do anything important after the elec-tion. The power was shifting; the sitting Congress would end March 3 and the incoming Congress was not scheduled to meet until the fall, unless called in for a special session (which was likely). But there were some flickers of life. On December 5, the House had brought to a vote a new amendment to repeal Prohibition, driven in part by Speaker—and Vice President–elect—Garner. Re-markably, it fell only six votes short of the two-thirds threshold required for passage. And the "no" votes included eighty-five members who had lost reelection bids, stoking faith that the new Congress would approve it.[21]

But other forces were at work as well. Pauline Sabin and her Women's Organization for National Prohibition Reform were sending small delegations to meet with nearly every senator, and John Raskob's group, the Association Against the Prohibition Amendment, was leaning on its contacts, too. The pressure worked, augmented by the reality that if Congress didn't act soon, then state legislatures (most were part-time) would adjourn be-fore they could take up ratification, adding months, if not years, to the prospects of repeal.

On January 9, the Senate Judiciary Committee approved a bill by Senator John J. Blaine, of Wisconsin, a Wet Republican who lost his seat in November, that roughly tracked with the Republi-can platform of letting the states reconsider Prohibition, while promising federal support for protecting Dry states from the liq-uor trade. And it left ratification up to the state legislatures, where Sabin, Raskob, and other prominent Wets insisted that it be left to state conventions, fearing sufficient Dry-dominated legislatures would derail repeal. The measure dangled in the wind until Senate Majority Leader Joseph T. Robinson—who was Dry—moved to amend the Blaine bill, stripping out the federal role in enforcement and putting ratification in the hands of state conventions—essentially, the Democratic Party platform.

The bill progressed with remarkable speed. The amended measure passed the Senate on February 16 and cleared the House on February 20, sending the amendment out for ratification by at least thirty-six of the forty-eight states. The amendment's passage angered many Drys, who claimed betrayal by some of the elected officials they had supported. They vowed to stymie the repeal effort at the state level. The Wets were pleased, but acknowledged, in the words of Pauline Sabin, that "the fight is only half won."

While many people weighing in figured it would take two, three, or maybe more years for the question to be answered by the states, the dominoes began falling almost immediately as state legislatures considered bills repealing state prohibition laws and scheduled conventions for ratification votes on the federal measure. In the end, on December 5, 1933, Utah would become the thirty-sixth state to ratify the Twenty-First Amendment, ten months after Congress set the wheels in motion.[22]

OVER THE WINTER there had been a steady drain of depositors' cash from two major consortiums in Detroit—the Detroit Bankers Company Group and the Union Guardian Group, also known as the Ford Group because of its links to Henry Ford. Both groups owned several different banks in Detroit and elsewhere in Michigan, and they were nearing the breaking point. In January 1933 alone, depositors withdrew $2.5 million to $3 million a week, leading the Guardian Group to seek another loan from the Reconstruction Finance Corporation, which agreed but required first that Henry Ford move back in the line of the bank's creditors in favor of the new RFC loans. Ford refused.[23]

The fear was that if Guardian failed, it would start a massive bank run that could imperil the nation's banking system. Hoover had been monitoring the crisis from D.C. and feared that the

Michigan crisis, along with smaller but similar problems with the Hibernian bank in New Orleans, and elsewhere, could be a fresh financial disaster. "I don't know whether a [national] panic can be avoided," Hoover told Joslin in his office. Hoover persuaded Ford to meet on February 13, a Monday, with Roy Chapin, secretary of commerce, and Arthur A. Ballantine, undersecretary of the treasury, but it did no good. Ford would not budge and, in fact, told Chapin and Ballantine that if the Guardian bank didn't open on Tuesday, he would withdraw some $25 million in deposits at the First National Bank, which would force the bank to close and likely spark a wildfire engulfing the entire state's financial institutions.[24]

Ford, who somehow perceived that unidentifiable enemies were conspiring against him, held his ground. In his view such a crash would be cleansing from an economic standpoint. The weak institutions would die and the strong would carry on. Michigan governor William A. Comstock trumped Ford early the next morning by declaring an eight-day statewide banking holiday, which precluded Ford from making the withdrawal, and froze the entire system; depositors could not access their money.

The impact was immediate. Ford laid off half of his already slashed workforce, and other auto companies suspended spending on such things as advertising. Businesses desperate for cash to cover operating costs began withdrawing their deposits in banks in neighboring Ohio, Indiana, and Illinois. Ten days later, Maryland, its system teetering, declared a bank holiday, too, followed by suspensions in sixteen more states by March 3, the eve of the inauguration. Foreigners holding dollar reserves redeemed them for gold, leading to a massive and sudden drain of gold from the United States as well.[25]

The nation, in dire straits when Roosevelt had started his campaign a year before, was in even worse shape now on the eve of his inauguration. And spiraling ever downward.

CHAPTER 20

The Dawn of a New America

HOOVER BEGAN MARCH 3, HIS last full day in the White House, with yet another breakfast with his close friend Mark Sullivan, the syndicated newspaper columnist. Then came a steady parade of top officials and well-wishers; a final informal gathering with the Washington press corps; and strategy sessions with a handful of incoming Republican members of Congress, several of whom would become steadfast opponents of Roosevelt's New Deal.

But the banking crisis weighed heavily on Hoover, and he spent part of his day in meetings and on telephone calls with governors and bank presidents, as well as with Roosevelt and some of his top aides. Hoover desperately wanted the president-elect to join him in either of two options: a proclamation suspending operations of the nation's banks to end the runs on money and gold, or—Hoover's preferred step—dusting off the 1917 Trading with the Enemy Act to freeze unnecessary domestic withdrawals and those by foreign governments and investors. Never mind that the act gave the president that authority during war, not peace.

Hoover believed that reducing the outflow of cash and gold from a torrent to a relative dribble would keep the banks open and solvent. And the public's faith in the financial system—banks in particular—would be buoyed if the incoming president pledged to limit spending, raise taxes to balance the federal budget, and not interfere with currency policies. Hoover had first broached the idea of a joint public statement with Roosevelt in a private letter hand-delivered February 18 by a Secret Service agent, who tracked Roosevelt down at a banquet at New York City's Waldorf-Astoria.

"It is obvious that as you will shortly be in position to make whatever policies you wish effective, you are the only one who can give these assurances," Hoover wrote. "I am taking the liberty of addressing you because both of my anxiety over the situation and my confidence from four years of experience that such tides as are now running can be moderated and the processes of regeneration which are always running can be released."[1]

Hoover wanted Roosevelt to link his first steps as president to Hoover's strategy to propel the country out of the economic depression. But Roosevelt and the Democrats had swept the Republicans from power by persuading voters that the financial crisis had been exacerbated by Hoover and the Republicans. Hoover still believed that encouraging business growth, and keeping government at a remove from the economy, was the only constitutional way forward, and he wanted Roosevelt to commit to staying that part of the course. Roosevelt refused.[2]

"The final consensus was that there was no need for joint action or approval by Roosevelt to make either proposal effective," Raymond Moley, one of the economic advisors in the Brain Trust who had been working on the bank crisis, later wrote. "President Hoover was free to proceed as he thought best."[3]

Hoover didn't see that he had much room to maneuver. After lunch on March 3, the day before Roosevelt's inauguration, the White House began receiving reports of increased bank withdrawals around the country. Hoover, despite the ticking clock, felt obliged to address the problem. The Federal Reserve had rejected his proposal that it guarantee all bank deposits, which Hoover felt "would have kept all banks open and functioning." Without a joint statement with Roosevelt on closing banks temporarily, or invoking the Trading with the Enemy Act, Hoover feared any actions he took would disappear with the end of his presidency and do nothing to assuage the fears in the financial sector or on Main Street. The banking crisis would spiral out of control.[4]

THE ROOSEVELTS ARRIVED in Washington, D.C., on the evening of March 2 and checked into the Mayflower Hotel, about four blocks up Connecticut Avenue from the White House. The hotel teemed with out-of-town visitors, part of a horde that descended on the city to witness the inauguration. Despite requests by city officials that attendees arrive by train to avoid overwhelming city streets, tens of thousands of cars with out-of-state plates drove around the heart of the capital, a rolling party of sightseeing revelers that, at times, made Pennsylvania Avenue and the streets around the National Mall all but impassable.

Tradition called for the departing president and his wife to invite the incoming first couple to tea on the afternoon before the inauguration. But Hoover on the sly sought to make it a working tea. By the time the Roosevelts arrived at four o'clock, accompanied by their son James and his wife, Betsey, Hoover had arranged to have Treasury Secretary Ogden Mills and Eugene Meyer, chairman of the Federal Reserve Board, walk in after the social event started to further pressure Roosevelt on the bank crisis. Hoover continued to misread Roosevelt's character, seeing him as a pliable opportunist without a guiding political vision who did not recognize the severity of the bank crisis, and who could be talked around to Hoover's position. Hoover thought a direct, unannounced appeal by the top economic officials could do the trick.[5]

But the surprise was ruined. For reasons that remain unclear—perhaps he was just trying to be a neutral and graceful host—Irwin

"Ike" Hood Hoover, the White House chief usher (and no relation to the president), greeted the Roosevelts when their car arrived, and quietly informed the president-elect that the other men would be joining the tea. Roosevelt, smelling trouble, summoned Moley, who rushed from the Mayflower Hotel to the White House, arriving just as Mills and Meyer joined the gathering.

It was a tense and ultimately fruitless meeting. Hoover, Mills, and Meyer pressed Roosevelt again for a joint proclamation declaring the bank closures, but Roosevelt demurred. As the tea ended, Roosevelt, trying to be solicitous of Hoover, told the president that "as you know, it is rather difficult for me to move in a hurry . . . I know how busy you must be. So please don't wait for me."

Hoover had no intention of waiting.

"Mr. Roosevelt, after you have been president for a while, you will learn that the President of the United States waits for no one." Then Hoover left.[6]

The Roosevelts and Moley returned to the Mayflower, but the day was nowhere near an end. Roosevelt juggled telephone calls and meetings with House leaders into the evening as aides and advisors rushed in and out of the rooms. Over at the Treasury Building, officials from both administrations struggled to hit the right approach to stop, or at least mitigate, the banking crisis, which would become Roosevelt's responsibility in a matter of hours.

"The hours after that, until one o'clock the next morning, were a blur of talk in the Roosevelt suite," Moley wrote later. "The telephone rang constantly. Party leaders were calling to check up on the situation and tender advice. Thomas W. Lamont [a partner in J. P. Morgan] called from New York to recommend that no action be taken: it was thought by the leading bankers there that the banks could pull through to the next noon and possibly, then, with Roosevelt in office, a sweeping change in psychology would take place before Monday."

Hoover also called Roosevelt to relay that bankers in New York and Chicago were now telling him the same thing: They preferred no action be taken and that it would be best to wait until the transition to the new administration. "Still the talk went on," Moley wrote. "We were all, by then, indescribably tense—even Roosevelt."

In a final phone call, just after 1 A.M., Roosevelt suggested to Hoover that both men go to bed and rang off. "We are at the end of our rope," Hoover told Theodore Joslin. "There is nothing more we can do." In a few hours the problem would be Roosevelt's alone to solve, and history would be left to assign blame or credit for whatever unfolded.

DESPITE RETIRING AT such a late hour, Hoover arose before 7 A.M., shaved, dressed, and walked to his private study. Hoover's usual morning exercise session with his medicine ball cabinet, which had helped him lose weight during his presidency, fell victim to the pressing calendar of the day. Instead, Hoover read over telegrams and other communications that had come through during the night, then flipped through the morning papers as he waited for Lou and their sons and families to join him for a final breakfast in the residence. Afterward, he moved to the private Executive Office for more telephone calls about the banking crisis, a brief meeting with Harvey Crouch, a director of the Reconstruction Finance Corporation, and to review last-minute bills passed by Congress for his signature or veto.

All occupancies of the White House are temporary, and the pomp and excitement of inaugurations obscure the logistics of changing who is in the seat of power. Lou Hoover had spent the previous few weeks overseeing the packing up of the family belongings, in the process donating a small library of her husband's presidentially acquired books to friends as keepsakes. Government employees did the actual boxing up and toted the Hoovers' possessions to Union Station to be shipped to the Hoovers' Palo

Alto home. So by the morning of Inauguration Day, most of the evidence of the Hoovers' four years in the White House had disappeared. Some of the Roosevelts' personal belongings had already arrived and would be moved into the residence as soon as the Hoovers departed for the swearing-in ceremony. More possessions from the Roosevelts' homes in Hyde Park and New York City had already been loaded onto U.S. Army transport trucks and would arrive over the next few days.[7]

As Hoover tended to final business inside the White House, thousands of people anxious to play a small role in a historical moment milled outside on the grounds. "Shortly before 9 o'clock, the hour set for closing the grounds, the walkways and roadways were thronged with sightseers," a local reporter noted. "In the vicinity of the portico over the front doorway there was a congested group of people waiting expectantly for a glimpse of the President or some member of his household." They were disappointed: The Hoovers stayed hidden from view.

The Roosevelts left the Mayflower a little after ten o'clock to attend a brief church service at St. John's Episcopal Church—"A private citizen is going to say his prayers before undertaking a great office," said Reverend Robert John, the church rector—then arrived at the White House gate at eleven o'clock, to the boisterous cheers of people lining Pennsylvania Avenue.

Roosevelt's mobility issues forced a change in routine for Inauguration Day. Rather than entering the White House for a private moment with the outgoing president, Roosevelt remained in the open-top car and the Hoovers, who had been waiting inside for about twenty-five minutes, emerged from the building. Lou Hoover joined Eleanor Roosevelt in the second car of the procession as Hoover himself strode to the open back door of the first car and extended his hand to Roosevelt as he sat down. The two men exchanged a few words in a noticeably icy engagement between rivals forced by tradition to endure each other's company for a little bit longer. The two men shared a blanket over their laps to protect against the raw weather, and as the seven-car motorcade left the White House grounds and slowly cruised down Pennsylvania Avenue to the Capitol, tens of thousands of well-wishers cheered and waved. Roosevelt, beaming, waved back. Hoover sat impassively as the blocks dragged past.

On Capitol Hill, Roosevelt's son James offered his arm to help the president-elect make his way inside. Late-winter gray skies began clearing, making a brisk breeze and temperatures just above freezing a bit more tolerable for the 150,000 or so people awaiting the swearing-in ceremony on the east steps of the Capitol Building.

After joining Roosevelt in the Senate chamber to witness John Garner taking his oath as vice president, which preceded the main event, Hoover sequestered himself in an office set aside in the Capitol for the president's use and worked his way through a stack of legislative bills. As one o'clock neared, Hoover and his wife made their way to their seats a few feet from the podium. After a brief delay Roosevelt emerged on the arm of his son and slowly made his way from the building to the dais as the crowd cheered.

The oath itself, as dictated by Article II, Section I of the Constitution, was brief. Roosevelt provided a family Bible brought to America in the 1650s by his Dutch ancestor Claes van Rosenvelt—the same Bible on which he took two oaths as governor of New York—and swore to Chief Justice Charles Evans Hughes that he would "to the best of my ability, preserve, protect and defend the Constitution of the United States." The crowd erupted into extended cheers as Roosevelt remained on his feet waiting for the clamor to die down before beginning his inaugural address.[8]

"I am certain that my fellow Americans expect that on my induction into the Presidency I will address them with a candor and a decision which the present situation of our Nation impels," he began, his words amplified across the throng of people backing up past the Library of Congress and the under-construction Supreme Court building and onto the side streets of Capitol Hill, and carried by radio coast-to-coast. "This is preeminently the time to speak the truth, the whole truth, frankly and boldly. Nor need we shrink from honestly facing conditions in our country today. This great Nation will endure as it has endured, will revive and will prosper. So, first of all, let me assert my firm belief that the only thing we have to fear is fear itself—nameless, unreasoning, unjustified terror which paralyzes needed efforts to convert retreat into advance."

Roosevelt spoke for about twenty minutes. While he did not mention Hoover or anyone else by name, he offered a succinct indictment of government policies that put corporate profits and the interests of Wall Street ahead of the needs of the people. He blamed much of the nation's economic pain on "the rulers of the exchange of mankind's goods" who "through their own stubbornness and their own incompetence" failed the American people.

The nation's "greatest primary task is to put people to work," and he would use government to do it. Working people spend money; spending creates demand; demand creates production; production creates more jobs. "This is no unsolvable problem if we face it wisely and courageously," Roosevelt said, urging the nation to approach the economic revival as it would a war— through concerted, communal action using government to accomplish "greatly needed projects to stimulate and reorganize the use of our natural resources."

And he once again emphasized his belief in the need for collective action of the people for the benefit of the people.

"If I read the temper of our people correctly," the new president continued, "we now realize as we have never realized before our interdependence on each other; that we cannot merely take but we must give as well; that if we are to go forward, we must move as a trained and loyal army willing to sacrifice for the good of a common discipline, because without such discipline no progress is made, no leadership becomes effective. We are, I know, ready and willing to submit our lives and property to such disci-

pline" in response to an election in which the people "have registered a mandate that they want direct, vigorous action."

The crowd again erupted in cheers. Roosevelt looked out at
them and around the stage, seemingly uncertain about what his
next step ought to be. Hoover rose and moved toward the new
president. If the ex-president felt the sting of words from a man
he had come to loathe, or if he objected to Roosevelt's invocation
of the very fear Hoover believed Roosevelt had invoked in the campaign to defeat him, he gave no indication. The former president
removed his top hat and bobbed his head slightly as he extended
a hand to Roosevelt, who leaned his own head back. They exchanged a few words—it lasted about three seconds, no time for
more than a perfunctory "congratulations" and "thank you"—before Hoover turned, replaced his hat, and made his way back
toward the Capitol, leaving Roosevelt to bask in the moment.

The Hoovers, who no longer had a place to go in Washington,
D.C., were driven the four blocks to Union Station and a send-
off by supporters as they boarded a private railcar that would
take them to Philadelphia. From there Lou would head directly
to Palo Alto, while the former president carried on north to
spend a few days in New York City before joining her on the
West Coast.

Inaugural parties, of course, are for the victors. The Roosevelts made the return trip to the White House and a luncheon for
family and close friends and supporters, then ascended a reviewing stand outside on Pennsylvania Avenue to watch the inaugural
parade. It was a massive undertaking, stretching six miles. General Douglas MacArthur served as grand marshal (retired
General John J. Pershing had been Roosevelt's first choice, but
he was ailing), and he joined Roosevelt for nearly three hours reviewing the passing parade of marching bands and delegations
representing all forty-eight states.

As dusk settled in, Roosevelt retreated into the White House
to oversee the swearing-in of ten members of his cabinet in a sin-

gle ceremony, greet thirteen disabled youths invited from the Warm Springs spa, and share dinner with some six dozen friends and members of the extended Roosevelt family in the State Dining Room. Afterward, Eleanor Roosevelt led a caravan of family and friends to a massive charity ball at the six-thousand-capacity Washington Auditorium a few blocks west of the White House, where the evening began with opera star Rosa Ponselle singing the national anthem, backed by the National Symphony Orchestra. "Bands played, brilliant military uniforms mingled with the more somber garb of guests, and the flags of many States made a scene unsurpassed in interest," one reporter noted.[9]

Roosevelt stayed behind. As the others went off to celebrate, he settled into the Lincoln Study with Louis Howe, the strategist who had made it his life mission to get Roosevelt elected president; then the new president retired around 10:30 P.M. It had been a long and physically taxing day. Roosevelt would need his rest for the morning, when he would fully confront the daunting challenge of pulling the nation out of a deep abyss and restoring America's faith in itself.

DIARIES VI

Saturday, March 4, 1933

DOROTHY SIMONSON, ISLE ROYALE, MICHIGAN

Up early to get all work done before inauguration ceremonies began. We listened to everything and were much impressed by it all. Just as Mr. Garner was being inaugurated, Togo (her pet dog) scared up a moose right outside the store, and we all rushed over, and out on to the dock, cameras in hand. Got some dandy shots of him, a "calf"— if only they turn out well. We were thrilled at President Roosevelt's address—the feeling of assurance and confident leadership which he brought should do much to encourage us all.

WILLIAM E. WARFIELD, FORT WAYNE, INDIANA

Chilly and gloomy today. All thoughts and eyes have been directed toward Washington where the nation is inducting into office a new chief who promises a New Deal. I heard him take the oath of office and also heard his address over the radio. I think he is capable and very anxious to bring this country out of its worst Depression. I did not vote for him but I think he will make a good president.

Tuesday, March 7, and Wednesday, March 8

NELLIE COWLEY, TUCSON, ARIZONA (IN TUCSON WITH HARRY, HER HUSBAND)

Cermak died yesterday afternoon. The Nazis were victorious in

275

Sunday's election in Germany. This will make Hitler virtually dicta-
tor. He is in favor of breaking the Versailles Treaty so it may mean
another war. Roosevelt has called Congress to begin a special session
at noon Thursday. "Men's hearts failing them for fear." I felt tired all
day. Set a [printing] job for the P.D. stores, did some mending, then
rested. I have been doing a good deal of studying and work, but I
think worry is at the base of it. I wonder if I could get a fruit stand or
something of the sort to run next winter.

AUTHOR'S NOTE

I FIRST BEGAN THINKING ABOUT this project during the last part of Donald Trump's presidency, and quickly realized there were some parallels. Herbert Hoover won in 1928 in large part due to conservative Protestant animosity toward Democrat Al Smith's Roman Catholic faith, with the nativist Ku Klux Klan exerting considerable influence. Trump was elected in 2016 in part by fanning anti-Muslim prejudices among a new generation of nativist conservative Christians. Ninety years ago, Prohibition divided the nation with the anti-alcohol movement driven primarily by Christian conservatives, mostly in the South and Midwest, while primarily urban liberals in the Northeast fought for repeal of Prohibition. In our current times similar forces array against each other over abortion.

Another similarity: Hoover and Trump were businessmen who won presidential elections in their first serious tries for elective office, and both were initially opposed by their party's traditionalists. And while Hoover was a capable administrator—as a former cabinet secretary he also knew how the government worked—both he and Trump were woefully ill-equipped to handle the crises that befell them as presidents, the Great Depression in Hoover's case and the COVID pandemic in Trump's.

But this is not a work of comparisons. Rather, it's an attempt to mesh several story lines from the pivotal year 1932. Many books have been written on the presidential election, on the history of Prohibition, and on radical movements seeking traction in the depths of American capitalism's biggest failed moment. But I was intrigued with the idea of trying to create a synchronous replay of the year, and the forces at play across the nation. Limiting the scope to 1932 proved to be difficult. The Great Depression, for instance, began in 1929, so some explanation was needed. One also can't understand the 1932 election without understanding the 1928 election, and Hoover and Roosevelt required drawing in some biographical material for context, and, well, portions of this book strayed outside the lines I set for myself. But I hope not too far.

This is my seventh book, and it was the most difficult of them, thanks to lengthy COVID-19 closures of archives and libraries, which also forced me to break my usual approach of researching then writing the book from first chapter to last. I wound up having to write chapters out of sequence based on material in hand while waiting for the reopening of archives and libraries necessary for other parts of the book. That made it more challenging to ensure I included everything I wanted, or felt I needed, while not repeating material. I still have a headache from that.

I should note that the short sections of diaries and newsreels were inspired by devices John Dos Passos used in his magisterial *U.S.A.* trilogy (the novels *The 42nd Parallel, 1919,* and *The Big Money*) about the early part of the twentieth century. The diary entries, which have been cleaned up from the originals for clarity but still retain the individual personalities and quirks of their authors, are intended to broaden the reader's sense of life among average Americans without intruding on the main narratives. Similarly, the newsreel segments present a broader sense of the state of the world as the United States wrestled with its specific problems.

Thanks are due to several people. Paul Dickson, co-author of the deeply researched and well-told *The Bonus Army: An American Epic*, generously shared his files with me while the archives remained shuttered, and Cynthia Kullberg, Walter Waters's great-niece, patiently walked me through the family history.

Librarians and archivists are the unsung heroes of nonfiction research, and I was greatly aided by their professionalism and spirit of cooperation during what proved to be a trying time for them as well. Spencer Howard and Craig Wright at the Herbert Hoover Presidential Library and Museum, in West Branch, Iowa, were exceptionally helpful in running down loose threads for me from afar and, during my visit to the archives, in streamlining my research and directing me to overlooked potential sources. Their zeal and deep knowledge of the contents of the library's holdings are admirable.

Similarly, Virginia Lewick at the Franklin D. Roosevelt Presidential Library and Museum, in Hyde Park, New York, was gracious, informative, and helpful even as I kept hitting dry holes, which was expected. As a presidential repository the vast bulk of the library's enormous holdings began primarily where my book ended, with Roosevelt's first inauguration.

Dennis P. Wodzinski, director of the Archives & Records Center for the Catholic Diocese of Pittsburgh, and Kathleen Washy, archivist for the Sisters of St. Joseph of Baden, in Baden, Pennsylvania, offered help and guidance running down details on Father James R. Cox. Thanks and appreciation are also due to staff members and officials at the Library of Congress, the National Archives, the State Historical Society of Iowa, the Hoover Institution Library & Archives at Stanford University, and the Historical Association for Isle Royale, Michigan.

Deep appreciation is owed to Adam Hochschild, who has been a generous sounding board on several of these projects, and my wife, Margaret. They had similar reactions to my initial data-heavy opening chapter and urged me to change it to something less dense and more relatable. Readers don't know what they saved you from. Thanks, too, to editor Denise Silvestro and her colleagues at Citadel Press for taking on this project, and to copy editor Stephanie Finnegan, who saved me from several small embarrassments. As usual, any errors that may have crept into the final manuscript belong to me alone.

And, as always, special thanks to my agent, Jane Dystel, and her colleagues at Dystel, Goderich & Bourret, whose support over nearly two decades and seven books has been unflagging, reassuring, uplifting, and deeply appreciated.

SOURCES

Archives and Libraries Visited

Franklin D. Roosevelt Presidential Library and Museum, Hyde Park, New York
Herbert Hoover Presidential Library and Museum, West Branch, Iowa
Hoover Institution Library & Archives at Stanford University near Palo Alto,
    California
Library of Congress Manuscript Division, Washington, D.C.
State Historical Society of Iowa, Iowa City, Iowa
University of Iowa Libraries, Iowa City, Iowa

Selected Bibliography

NEWSPAPERS, NEWS AGENCIES, AND NEWSWIRES

Associated Press
Atlanta Constitution
Baltimore (MD) Sun
B.E.F. News
Black Dispatch (Oklahoma City, OK)
Charlotte (NC) News
Chattanooga (TN) News
Chicago (IL) Tribune
Cumberland (MD) Evening Times
Daily Times (Davenport, IA)
Daily Worker (New York City)
Des Moines (IA) Register
Detroit (MI) Free Press
Evening Star (Washington, D.C.)

Los Angeles (CA) Times
Marysville (OH) Journal Tribune
Miami (FL) Herald
Miami (FL) News
Nebraska State Journal (Lincoln)
New York Daily News
New York Times
Newcastle (PA) News
Omaha (NE) World-Herald
Oregonian (Portland)
Pittsburgh (PA) Catholic
Pittsburgh (PA) Post-Gazette
Pittsburgh (PA) Press
Pittsburgh (PA) Sun-Telegraph
Portland (ME) Evening Express
Sacramento (CA) Bee
San Francisco (CA) Examiner
Sioux City (IA) Journal
St. Louis (MO) Globe-Democrat
Tampa (FL) Daily Times
Times (Shreveport, LA)
United Press

Books

Balderrama, Francisco E. and Rodriguez, Raymond. *Decade of Betrayal: Mexican Repatriation in the 1930s.* Albuquerque: University of New Mexico Press, 1995.

Barber, Lucy G. *Marching on Washington: The Forging of an American Political Tradition.* Berkeley: University of California Press, 2004.

Berle, Adolf. *Navigating the Rapids, 1918–1971.* New York: Harcourt Brace Jovanovich, 1973.

Brands, H. W. *Traitor to His Class: The Privileged Life and Radical Presidency of Franklin Delano Roosevelt.* New York: Anchor Books, 2009.

Burns, James MacGregor. *Roosevelt: The Lion and the Fox.* New York: Harcourt, Brace and Company, 1956.

Caro, Robert A. *The Power Broker: Robert Moses and the Fall of New York.* New York: Vintage Books, 1975.

Carter, Dan T. *Scottsboro: A Tragedy of the American South.* New York: Oxford University Press, 1969.

Cornwell, Elmer. *Presidential Leadership of Public Opinion.* Bloomington: Indiana University Press, 1965.

Dallek, Robert. *Franklin D. Roosevelt: A Political Life.* New York: Viking, 2017.

Davis, Kenneth S. *FDR: The New York Years, 1928–1933.* New York: Random House, 1985.

Dickson, Paul and Allen, Thomas B. *The Bonus Army: An American Epic.* New York: Walker & Co., 2004.

Douglas, Jack. *Veterans on the March.* New York: Workers Library, 1934.

Dyson, Lowell K. *Farmers' Organizations.* Westport, CT: Greenwood Press, 1986.

Eichengreen, Barry. *Hall of Mirrors: The Great Depression, the Great Recession, and the Uses—and Misuses—of History.* New York: Oxford University Press, 2015.

Eig, Jonathan. *Get Capone: The Secret Plot That Captured America's Most Wanted Gangster.* New York: Simon & Schuster, 2010.

Eisinger, Robert M. *The Evolution of Presidential Polling.* New York: Cambridge University Press, 2003.

Farber, David. *Everybody Ought to be Rich: The Life and Times of John J. Raskob, Capitalist.* New York: Oxford University Press, 2013.

Farley, James A. *Behind the Ballots: The Personal History of a Politician.* New York: Harcourt, Brace and Company, 1938.

Fenster, Julie M. *FDR's Shadow: Louis Howe, The Force That Shaped Franklin and Eleanor Roosevelt.* New York: Palgrave Macmillan, 2009.

Ferrell, Robert H. *American Diplomacy in the Great Depression.* New Haven, CT: Yale University Press, 1957.

Foster, William Z. *From Bryan to Stalin.* New York: International Publishers, 1937.

Freidel, Frank. *Franklin D. Roosevelt: The Triumph.* Boston, MA: Little, Brown and Company, 1952.

Gazarik, Richard. *The Mayor of Shantytown: The Life of Father James Renshaw Cox.* Jefferson, NC: McFarland & Company, Inc., 2019.

Goodman, James. *Stories of Scottsboro.* New York: Random House, 1994.

Greenberg, David. *Republic of Spin: An Inside History of the American Presidency.* New York: W.W. Norton & Company, 2016.

Haskell, John. *Fundamentally Flawed: Understanding and Reforming Presidential Primaries.* Lanham, MD: Rowman & Littlefield Publishers, 1996.

Heineman, Kenneth J. *A Catholic New Deal: Religion and Reform in Depression Pittsburgh.* University Park: Pennsylvania State University Press, 1999.

Henderson, Caroline. *Letters from the Dust Bowl.* Norman: University of Oklahoma Press, 2003.

Hoffman, Abraham. *Unwanted Mexican Americans in the Great Depression: Repatriation Pressures, 1929-1939.* Tucson: University of Arizona Press, 1974.

Hoover, Herbert. *The Memoirs of Herbert Hoover: The Cabinet and the Presidency, 1920–1933* (Volume 2). New York: Macmillan Company, 1952.

Hoover, Herbert. *The Memoirs of Herbert Hoover: The Great Depression, 1929–1941* (Volume 3). New York: MacMillan Company, 1952.

Hoover, Herbert. *Public Papers of the Presidents of the United States: Herbert Hoover, 1932–1933.* Washington, D.C.: U.S. Government Printing Office, 1977.

Hoover, Irwin Hood. *Forty-two Years in the White House.* Boston, MA: Houghton Mifflin Company, 1934.

Hull, Cordell. *The Memoirs of Cordell Hull.* New York: Macmillan Company, 1948.

Hurt, R. Douglas. *The Dust Bowl: An Agricultural and Social History.* Chicago, IL: Nelson-Hall Publishers, 1984.

Janken, Kenneth Robert. *White: The Biography of Walter White, Mr. NAACP.* New York: The New Press, 2003.

Johanningsmeier, Edward P. *Forging American Communism: The Life of William Z. Foster.* Princeton, NJ: Princeton University Press, 1994.

Joslin, Theodore. *Hoover Off the Record.* Garden City, NY: Doubleday, Doran & Company, 1934.

Kramer, Dale. *The Wild Jackasses: The American Farmer in Revolt.* New York: Hastings House, 1956.

Kyvig, David E. *Repealing National Prohibition,* second edition. Kent, OH: Kent State University Press, 2000.

Laurie, Clayton D., and Cole, Ronald H. *The Role of Federal Military Forces in Domestic Disorders, 1877–1945.* Washington, D.C.: Center of Military History, 1997.

Liggett, Walter W. *The Rise of Herbert Hoover.* New York: The H.K. Fly Company, 1932.

Lindley, Ernest K. *The Roosevelt Revolution: First Phase.* New York: Viking Press, 1933.

Lisio, Donald J. *The President and Protest: Hoover, Conspiracy, and the Bonus Riot.* Columbia: University of Missouri Press, 1974.

Lloyd, Craig. *Aggressive Introvert: Herbert Hoover and Public Relations Management, 1912–1931.* Columbus: Ohio State University Press, 1972.

Long, Huey P. *Every Man a King: The Autobiography of Huey P. Long.* New Orleans: National Book Co., 1933.

Martin, Charles H. *The Angelo Herndon Case and Southern Justice.* Baton Rouge: Louisiana State University Press, 1976.

McElvaine, Robert S. *Down & Out in the Great Depression : Letters from the Forgotten Man.* Chapel Hill: University of North Carolina Press, 1983.

McGillivray, Alice V. and Scammon, Richard M. *America at the Polls: 1920–1956 Harding to Eisenhower.* Washington, D.C.: Congressional Quarterly, 1994.

Michelson, Charles. *The Ghost Talks.* New York: G. P. Putnam's Sons, 1944.

Moley, Raymond. *After Seven Years.* New York: Harper & Brothers, 1939.

Morrison, Melanie S. *Murder on Shades Mountain: The Legal Lynching of Willie Peterson and the Struggle for Justice in Jim Crow Birmingham.* Durham, NC: Duke University Press Books, 2018.

Murray, Robert K. *The 103rd Ballot.* New York: Harper & Row, 1976.

Myers, William Starr, and Newton, Walter H. *The Hoover Administration: A Documented Narrative.* New York: Charles Scribner's Sons, 1936.

Nasaw, David. *The Chief: The Life of William Randolph Hearst.* New York: Houghton Mifflin, 2000.

Nasaw, David. *The Patriarch: The Remarkable Life and Turbulent Times of Joseph P. Kennedy.* New York: Penguin Press, 2012.

Okrent, Daniel. *Last Call: The Rise and Fall of Prohibition.* New York: Scribner, 2010.

Peel, Roy V. and Donnelly, Thomas C. *The 1932 Campaign: An Analysis.* New York: Farrar & Rinehart, 1935.

Powers, Elmer G. *Years of Struggle: The Farm Diary of Elmer G. Powers, 1931–1936.* Ames: Iowa State University Press, 1976.

Rappleye, Charles. *Herbert Hoover in the White House: The Ordeal of the Presidency.* New York: Simon & Schuster, 2016.

Ritchie, Donald A. *Electing FDR: The New Deal Campaign of 1932.* Lawrence: University Press of Kansas, 2007.

Rivera, Diego (with Gladys March). *My Art, My Life: An Autobiography,* revised edition. New York: Dover Publications, 1991.

Rollins Jr., Alfred B. *Roosevelt and Howe.* New York: Alfred A. Knopf, 1962.

Roosevelt, Eleanor. *The Autobiography of Eleanor Roosevelt.* New York: Harper & Brothers, 1961.

Roosevelt, James. *Affectionately, F.D.R.: A Son's Story of a Lonely Man.* New York: Harcourt, Brace and Company, 1959.

Roosevelt, Franklin D. *F.D.R.: His Personal Letters, 1928–1945* (Volume 3). New York: Duell, Sloan and Pearce, 1950.

Roosevelt, Franklin D. *Public Papers of Franklin D. Roosevelt, Forty-eighth Governor of the State of New York, 1932.* Albany, NY: J.B. Lyon, 1939.

Rose, Kenneth D. *American Women and the Repeal of Prohibition.* New York: New York University Press, 1996.

Rosenman, Samuel L. *Working with Roosevelt.* New York: Harper & Brothers, 1952.

Russell, Francis. *The President Makers: From Mark Hanna to Joseph P. Kennedy.* Boston: Little, Brown and Company, 1976.

Shover, John L. *Cornbelt Rebellion: The Farmers' Holiday Association.* Urbana: University of Illinois Press, 1965.

Simonson, Dorothy. *The Diary of an Isle Royale School Teacher.* Houghton, MI: Isle Royale Natural History Association, 1988.

Schlesinger Jr., Arthur M. *The Crisis of the Old Order: 1919–1933, the Age of Roosevelt, Volume I.* Boston: Houghton Mifflin, 1957.

Slayton, Robert A. *Empire Statesman: The Rise and Redemption of Al Smith.* New York: The Free Press, 2001.

Smith, Jean Edward. *FDR.* New York: Random House, 2007.

Starling, Edmund W. *Starling of the White House: The Story of the Man Whose Secret Service Detail Guarded Five Presidents From Woodrow Wilson to Franklin D. Roosevelt.* New York: Simon & Schuster, 1946.

Stiles, Lela Mae. *The Man Behind Roosevelt: The Story of Louis McHenry Howe.* Cleveland: World Pub. Co., 1954.

Stimson, Henry L. and Bundy, McGeorge. *On Active Service in Peace and War.* New York: Harper, 1948.

Sugar, Maurice. *The Ford Hunger March.* Berkeley, CA: Meiklejohn Civil Liberties Institute, 1980.

Sullivan, Mark. *The Education of an American.* New York: Doubleday, Doran & Co., 1938.

Svobida, Lawrence. *Farming the Dust Bowl: A First-Hand Account from Kansas.* Lawrence: University Press of Kansas, 1986.

Timmons, Bascom N. *Garner of Texas: A Personal History.* New York: Harper and Brothers, 1948.

Tugwell, Rexford G. *The Diary of Rexford G. Tugwell.* Westport, CT: Greenwood Press, 1992.

Vargas, Zaragosa. *Proletarians of the North: A History of Mexican Industrial Workers in Detroit and the Midwest, 1917-1933.* Berkeley: University of California Press, 1999.

Walch, Timothy, and Miller, Dwight M. *Herbert Hoover and Franklin D. Roosevelt: A Documentary History.* Westport, CT: Greenwood Press, 1998.

Waters, Walter W. and White, William C. *B.E.F.: The Whole Story of the Bonus Army.* New York: The John Day Company, 1933.

Wehle, Louis B. *Hidden Threads of History: Wilson Through Roosevelt.* New York: MacMillan Company, 1953.

White, Roland A. *Milo Reno, Farmers Union Pioneer: The Story of a Man and a Movement.* Iowa City, IA: Athens Press, 1941.

White, Walter. *A Man Called White.* Athens: University of Georgia Press, 1995.

Whyte, Kenneth. *Hoover: An Extraordinary Life in Extraordinary Times.* New York: Alfred A. Knopf, 2017.

Wicker, Elmus. *The Banking Panics of the Great Depression.* New York: Cambridge University Press, 1996.

Wirster, Donald. *Dust Bowl: The Southern Plains in the 1930s.* New York: Oxford University Press, 1979.

Zipser, Arthur. *Workingclass Giant: The Life of William Z. Foster.* New York: International Publishers, 1981.

ARTICLES AND DISSERTATIONS

Alston, Lee J. "Farm Foreclosures in the United States During the Interwar Period." *The Journal of Economic History,* Vol. 43, No. 4 (December 1983), pp. 885–903.

Awalt, Francis Gloyd. "Recollections of the Banking Crisis in 1933." *Business History Review,* Vol. 43, Issue 3 (Autumn 1969), pp. 347–371.

Barclay, Thomas S. "The Bureau of Publicity of the Democratic National Committee, 1930–32." *The American Political Science Review,* Vol. 27, No. 1 (February 1933), pp. 63–65.

Bernanke, Ben S. "Employment, Hours, and Earnings in the Depression: An Analysis of Eight Manufacturing Industries." *The American Economic Review,* Vol. 76, No. 1 (March 1986), pp. 82–109.

Bernanke, Ben S. "Non-Monetary Effects of The Financial Crisis In The Propagation Of The Great Depression." Working Paper 1085, National Bureau of Economic Research, January 1983.

Carcasson, Martin. "Herbert Hoover and the Presidential Campaign of 1932: The Failure of Apologia." *Presidential Studies Quarterly,* Vol. 28, No. 2 (Spring 1998), pp. 349–365.

Chase, Philip M. "William Gibbs McAdoo: The Last Progressive (1863–1941)." Doctoral Dissertation, University of Southern California, 2008.

Gilbert, Robert E. "Disability, Illness, and the Presidency: The Case Of Franklin D. Roosevelt." *Politics and the Life Sciences,* Vol. 7, No. 1 (August 1988), pp. 33–49.

Goodall, Alex. "The Battle of Detroit and Anti-Communism in the Depression Era." *The Historical Journal,* Vol. 51, No. 2 (June 2008), pp. 457–480.

Hausman, Joshua K.; Rhode, Paul W.; Wieland, Johannes F. "Farm Product Prices, Redistribution, and the Early U.S. Great Depression." Working Paper 28055, National Bureau of Economic Research, November 2020.

Hoyt, John C. "Droughts of 1930–1934." Water-Supply Paper 680, U.S. Geological Survey. Washington, D.C.: U.S. Government Printing Office, 1936.

Humphrey, Norman D. "Mexican Repatriation from Michigan Public Assistance in Historical Perspective." *Social Service Review,* Vol. 15, No. 3 (September 1941), pp. 497–513.

Karlsson, Jessica. "Herbert Hoover's Apologia of His Chinese Mining Career 1899–1912: Untangling the Refutation Campaign." Master's thesis, Harvard University, March 2018.

Killigrew, John W. "The Army and the Bonus Incident." *Military Affairs,* Vol. 26, No. 2 (Summer 1962), pp. 59–65.

Kollock, Will. "The Story of a Friendship: Mark Sullivan and Herbert Hoover." *The Pacific Historian: A Quarterly of Western History and Ideas,* Vol. 18, No. 1 (Spring 1974), pp. 31–48.

Margo, Robert A. "Employment and Unemployment in the 1930s." *Journal of Economic Perspectives,* Vol. 7, No. 2 (Spring 1993), pp. 41–59.

McIlroy, John and Campbell, Allan. "The Leadership of American Communism, 1924–1929: Sketches for a Prosopographical Portrait." *American Communist History* (November 2019).

McKee Jr., Oliver. "Publicity Chiefs." *The North American Review,* Vol. 230, No. 4 (October 1930), pp. 411–418.

Neumann, Caryn E. "The End of Gender Solidarity: The History of the Women's Organization for National Prohibition Reform in the United States, 1929–1933." *Journal of Women's History,* Vol. 9, No. 2 (Summer 1997), pp. 31–51.

Norpoth, Helmut. "The American Voter in 1932: Evidence from a Confidential Survey." *PS: Political Science & Politics,* Vol. 52, Issue 1 (January 2019), pp. 14–19.

Olson, James S. "Rehearsal for Disaster: Hoover, the R. F. C., and the Banking Crisis in Nevada, 1932–1933." *Western Historical Quarterly,* Vol. 6, No. 2 (April 1975), pp. 149–161.

Reid, Ira De Augustine and Hill, Thomas Arnold. "The Forgotten Tenth: An Analysis of Unemployment Among Negroes in the United States and Its Social Costs: 1932–1933." National Urban League, May 1933.

Rosenzweig, Roy. "Organizing the Unemployed: The Early Years of the Great Depression, 1929–1933." Chapter Eight in *Workers' Struggles, Past and Present: A "Radical America" Reader,* James Green, editor, (Philadelphia: Temple University Press, 1983).

Rosenzweig, Roy. "Radicals and the jobless: The Musteites and the Unemployed Leagues, 1932–1936." *Labor History,* Vol. 16, Issue 1, 1975.

Schuyler, Michael W. "The Hair-Splitters: Reno and Wallace, 1932–1933." *The Annals of Iowa,* Vol. 43, No. 6 (Fall 1976), pp. 403–429.

Sizer, Rosanne. "Herbert Hoover and the Smear Books, 1930–1932." *The Annals of Iowa,* Vol. 47, No. 4 (Spring 1984), pp. 343–361.

Slichter, Gertrude Almy. "Franklin D. Roosevelt and the Farm Problem, 1929–1932." *The Mississippi Valley Historical Review,* Vol. 43, No. 2 (September 1956), pp. 238–258.

Soffin, Stanley I. "How Seven Metropolitan Daily Newspapers in Michigan Reported and Interpreted the Hunger March on the Ford Motor Company in Dearborn on March 7, 1932." Master's thesis, Michigan State University, 1968.

U.S. Department of Labor, Bureau of Labor Statistics. "War and Postwar Wages, Prices, and Hours 1914–23 and 1939–44," Bulletin No. 852 (December 1945).

Valocchi, Steve. "The Unemployed Workers Movement of the 1930s: A Reexamination of the Piven and Cloward Thesis." *Social Problems,* Vol. 37, No. 2 (May 1990), pp. 191–205.

Vivian, James F. and Vivian, Jean H. "The Bonus March of 1932: The Role of General George Van Horn Moseley." *The Wisconsin Magazine of History,* Vol. 51, No. 1 (Autumn 1967), pp. 26–36.

Wall, Joseph Francis. "The Iowa Farmer in Crisis, 1920–1936," *The Annals of Iowa,* Vol. 47, No. 2 (Fall 1983), pp. 116–127.

Young, Dallas M. "Origin of the Progressive Mine Workers of America." *Journal of the Illinois State Historical Society,* Vol. 40, No. 3 (September 1947), pp. 313–330.

ENDNOTES

Preface

1. Details are drawn from "First in White House Line," *Evening Star,* January 1, 1932, and earlier newspaper accounts of Hunefeld's annual presence. Christina Hunefeld's Massachusetts death certificate dated February 25, 1908, was accessed via Ancestry.com.

2. *Eighteenth Annual Report of the Federal Reserve, Covering Operations for the Year 1931,* U.S. Government Printing Office, Washington, D.C., 1932, p. 125. Ben S. Bernanke, "Nonmonetary Effects of the Financial Crisis in the Propagation of the Great Depression," *The American Economic Review,* June 1983, Vol. 73, No. 3, pp. 257-276.

3. There are libraries' worth of books and papers on the causes and impacts of the Great Depression. A couple of useful windows can be found in Robert A. Margo, "Employment and Unemployment in the 1930s," *Journal of Economic Perspectives,* Vol. 7, No. 2 (Spring 1993), pages 41-59, and Milton Friedman and Anna J. Schwartz, *The Great Contraction* (Princeton University Press, Princeton, New Jersey, 2008 edition). Also see Roy Rosenzweig's "Chapter Eight: Organizing the Unemployed: The Early Years of the Great Depression 1929–1933" in *Workers' Struggles, Past and Present* (Philadelphia: Temple University Press, 1983), James Green, editor.

4. See "Chapter Five: Retrogression: Hoover," in Elmer E. Cornwell, Jr., *Presidential Leadership of Public Opinion* (Bloomington: Indiana University Press, 1965) for Hoover's ambiguous relationship with the media and subtle nurturing of his public image.

5. Bruce A. Lohoff, "Herbert Hoover's Mississippi Valley Land Reform Memorandum: A Document," *The Arkansas Historical Quarterly* Vol. 29, No. 2 (Summer, 1970), pp. 112-118. Kevin R. Kosar, "Disaster Response and Appointment of a Recovery Czar: The Executive Branch's Response to the Flood of 1927," Congressional Research Service, October 25, 2005. Hoover

also faced criticism for adhering to segregationist policies of the era, with white evacuees housed in buildings and Black evacuees forced into open-air camps often atop levees. Many were pressed by National Guard troops into unpaid labor unloading relief supplies. See Mike Swinford, "When the Levee Breaks: Race Relations and The Mississippi Flood of 1927," *Historia*, Vol. 16, 2007, pp. 151-163.

6. "Will Rogers Sees Hoover as Doctor for Sick States," *The New York Times*, August 19, 1927.

7. "Quick Victory for Hoover," *New York Times*, June 15, 1928.

8. *North Adams Transcript*, North Adams, Massachusetts, December 31, 1931.

9. "Arid New Year Contemplated," *Los Angeles Times*, December 31, 1931.

10. "Revelry Grips City; Welcome to a New Year," *Chicago Tribune*, January 1, 1932. "Revelry Acclaims New Year With Hope; Old Passes Unwept" and "Royal Box Club Shut by Sole Holiday Raid," *New York Times*, January 1, 1932.

11. See a roundup of city festivities in several articles in *The Washington Star*, January 1, 1932. Jean Edward Smith, *FDR* (New York: Random House, 2007), Chapter 13: Nomination.

12. "Washington Will Celebrate Brilliant Christmas Season and Help Unfortunate," *Washington Star*, December 20, 1931.

Diaries I

1. Fay Webb Gardner was married to Gov. Oliver Max Gardner, a Democrat and Roosevelt supporter. Gardner, F. W. (1932). Diary, 1929-1932, Fay Webb Gardner Collection, Gardner-Webb University Archives, John R. Dover Memorial Library, Boiling Springs, NC. Nellie Suydam Cowley papers (MS 158). She lived most of the time in Glendora, California, while her husband lived in Tucson, Arizona, where they owned a small printing business; they eventually divorced. Special Collections & University Archives, University of California, Riverside. Emily Almira C. Rich Diary, Special Collections Department, Stewart Library, Weber State University. William E. Warfield was a Black janitor and landlord who in 1932 owned six buildings, including a rooming house and a four-unit apartment building, in Fort Wayne, Indiana. William E. Warfield Diaries, 1932, Special Collections Division, Allen County Public Library, Fort Wayne, Indiana. Gardner, F. W. (1932). Diary, 1929-1932, Fay Webb Gardner Collection, Gardner-Webb University Archives, John R. Dover Memorial Library, Boiling Springs, NC. 1932 Emily Almira C. Rich Diary, Special Collections Department, Stewart Library, Weber State University, Utah. Nellie Suydam Cowley papers (MS 158). Special Collections & University Archives, University of California, Riverside.

Chapter One

1. While the Unemployed Councils had some local success in improving the lives of the poor and unemployed, mostly achieved through the work of grassroots campaigns, it did little for the CPUSA and never gelled as a broad movement. See Roy Rosenzweig, "Organizing the Unemployed: The Early Years of the Great Depression, 1929–1933," in *Workers' Struggles, Past and Present: A "Radical America" Reader*, edited by James Green (Philadelphia: Temple University Press, 2003). Chapter Eight.

2. Richard Gazarik, *The Mayor of Shantytown: The Life of Father James Renshaw Cox* (Jefferson, North Carolina: McFarland & Company, Inc., 2019), pp. 38-40.

3. Thomas H. Coode and John D. Petrarulo, "The Odyssey of Pittsburgh's Father Cox," *The Western Pennsylvania Historical Magazine*, July 1972, pp. 217-238. Reynold M. Wik, "The Radio in Rural America during the 1920s," *Agricultural History* (Volume 55, No. 4, October 1981), p. 346. "St. Patrick Radio Mass on WJAS 32 years," *Pittsburgh Catholic*, October 3, 1957. Other accounts put the start of broadcasts from St. Patrick's as early as 1921, but those appear to have been one-off programs, not a regular schedule.

4. "Church to Give Beds for 300," *The Pittsburgh Press*, November 30, 1930.

5. A few days after the march, Cox detailed his version of events in "Father Cox Reveals Drama of March to Washington in Own Exclusive Story," *Pittsburgh Press*, January 10, 1932.

6. "Father Cox Will Take Lead in Hunger March on Capitol," *Pittsburgh Post-Gazette*, December 11, 1931.

7. Details gleaned from numerous daily newspapers covering the march, including the *Pittsburgh Post-Gazette* and *The Washington Star*. Crowd estimates varied widely but the ones I use reflect those cited by the more reliable news accounts and, though of a healthy size, were far lower than the 25,000 participants that Cox had claimed.

8. "Jobless Army Stages March to Capitol to Ask Government Aid," *The Evening Star*, Washington, D.C. January 7, 1932. Charles Rappleye, *Herbert Hoover in the White House: The Ordeal of the Presidency* (New York: Simon & Schuster, 2016), pp. 345-346.

9. "Plea to Hoover Broadcast by Father Cox," *Pittsburgh Sun-Telegraph*, January 9, 1932.

10. "55,000 Rally to Demand U.S. Aid for Needy," *The Pittsburgh Press*, January 17, 1932.

11. Ramon Eduardo Ruiz, *Triumphs and Tragedy: A History of the Mexican People* (New York: W.W. Norton & Company, 1992), pp. 334-335. "President Gives the Order," *New York Times*, March 11, 1916. Max Boot, *The*

Savage Wars of Peace: Small Wars and the Rise of American Power, (New York: Basic Books, 2002), p. 204.

12. Waters's military records were accessed through Familysearch.org and Fold3.

13. *The Medical Department of The United States Army in The World War, Volume VIII, Field Operations* (Washington, D.C.: Government Printing Office, 1925), pp. 99-102.

14. Waters glides over his service in his memoir (written with William C. White), *BEF: The Whole Story of the Bonus Army* (New York: John Day Company, 1933), pp. 4-5. Service details are from an application for a military gravestone by his widow.

15. Lena Waters's death certificate lists her as divorced. Details on the daughters are drawn from a family history provided by Waters's great niece, Cynthia Kullberg, and letters sent by one of the daughters, Billie, to Paul Dickson and Thomas B. Allen after publication of their book, *The Bonus Army: An American Epic* (New York: Walker Publishing Company, 2004). My thanks to them for sharing.

16. Walter Waters and William C. White, *BEF: The Whole Story of the Bonus Army* (New York: John Day Company, 1933), p. 5. Details on meeting his second wife, which differ somewhat from his abbreviated version, are from an interview with Universal Services published in *The Oregonian* on July 4, 1932.

17. *United States Army Field Service Pocket Book* (Washington, D.C.: The War Department, 1917), pp.247-250. "War and Postwar Wages, Prices, and Hours, 1914-23 and 1939-44," *Bulletin No. 852 of the United States Bureau of Labor Statistics, Monthly Labor Review,* October and November 1945.

18. Paul Dickson and Thomas B. Allen, *The Bonus Army: An American Epic* (New York: Walker Publishing Company, 2004), pp. 28-30.

19. "Rethinking the Bonus March: Federal Bonus Policy, the Veterans of Foreign Wars, and the Origins of a Protest Movement," Chapter Eight, Stephen R. Ortiz, editor, *Veterans Policies, Veterans Politics: New Perspectives on Veterans in the Modern United States* (Gainesville: University Press of Florida, 2012), pp. 279-281.

20. President Hoover's veto message to Congress, February 26, 1931.

21. Walter Waters and William C. White, *BEF: The Whole Story of the Bonus Army* (New York: John Day Company, 1933), pp. 13-15.

Chapter Two

1. "Gov. Roosevelt Enters Race for the Presidency in North Dakota Primary," *New York Times,* January 24, 1932.

2.   Jean Edward Smith, *FDR* (New York: Random House, 2007), pp. 64-67.

3.   Julie M. Fenster, *FDR's Shadow: Louis Howe, the Force That Shaped Franklin and Eleanor Roosevelt* (New York: Palgrave Macmillan, 2009), pp. 93-96.

4.   Jean Edward Smith, *FDR* (New York: Random House, 2007), pp. 94-95.

5.   H.W. Brands, *Traitor to his Class: The Privileged Life and Radical Presidency of Franklin Delano Roosevelt* (New York: Doubleday, 2008), p. 83. Timothy Walch and Dwight M. Miller, editors, *Herbert Hoover and Franklin D. Roosevelt: A Documentary History* (Westport, Connecticut: Greenwood Press, 1998), "Chapter One: Comrades in Arms."

6.   Kenneth Whyte, *Hoover: An Extraordinary Life in Extraordinary Times* (New York: Vintage Books, 2017), p. 235. Jean Edward Smith, *FDR* (New York: Random House, 2007), p. 177. Roosevelt to Gibson, January 2, 1920, Franklin D. Roosevelt, Papers as Assistant Secretary of the Navy, 1913-1920, Series: Personal Files, Sub-series: Correspondence, Folder: Ga-Gl, FDRL, Hyde Park, New York.

7.   Louis B. Wehle, *Hidden Threads of History: Wilson Through Roosevelt* (New York: The MacMillan Company, 1953), p. 83. Herbert Hoover, *The Memoirs of Herbert Hoover: The Cabinet and the Presidency, 1920-1933* (New York: The MacMillan Company, 1952), p. 33. Jean Edward Smith, *FDR* (New York: Random House, 2007), p. 177.

8.   On ambitions, see Robert Dallek, *Franklin Roosevelt: A Political Life* (New York: Viking Penguin, 2017), p. 39. On drafting Hoover, see Jean Edward Smith, *FDR* (New York: Random House, 2007), pp.176-177. Hoover to Roosevelt, July 13, 1920, included in Timothy Walch and Dwight M. Miller, editors, *Herbert Hoover and Franklin D. Roosevelt: A Documentary History* (Westport, Connecticut: Greenwood Press, 1998), p. 8.

9.   Jean Edward Smith, *FDR* (New York: Random House, 2007), pp. 215-218.

10. Robert A. Slayton, *Empire Statesman: The Rise and Redemption of Al Smith* (New York: The Free Press, 2001), pp. 206-210. Jean Edward Smith, *FDR* (New York: Random House, 2007), p. 209.

11. Robert A. Slayton, *Empire Statesman: The Rise and Redemption of Al Smith* (New York: Free Press, 2001), pp. 11-12. James C. Prude, "William Gibbs McAdoo and the Democratic National Convention of 1924," *The Journal of Southern History*, Vol. 38, No. 4 (November 1972), pp. 621-628.

12. Farley kept a loose journal from which this quote is drawn, undated, James A. Farley papers, Box 37, Private File, 1918-1930, Library of Congress Manuscript Division. Also, James A. Farley, *Behind the Ballots: The Personal History of a Politician* (New York: Harcourt, Brace and Company, 1938), pp. 52-53, 79-80.

13. In 2003 a fresh analysis emerged that Roosevelt may have contracted Guillain-Barre Syndrome, sparking a debate among medical scholars. But it seems most likely that the initial diagnosis of polio was correct. See John

F. Ditunno, Jr., et. al., "Franklin Delano Roosevelt: The Diagnosis of Polio-myelitis Revisited," *PM&R*, September 2016, pp. 883-93.

14. Statement announcing state unemployment study commission, March 29, 1930, Public Papers of Franklin D. Roosevelt, Forty-Eighth Governor of the State of New York, 1930 (Albany: J.B. Lyon Company, 1931), pp. 505-508.

15. James A. Farley, *Behind the Ballots* (New York, Harcourt, Brace and Company, 1938), p. 63. Letter to Owen Winston, Nov. 15, 1930, Elliott Roosevelt, editor, *F.D.R.: His Personal Letters, 1928-1945* (New York: Duell, Sloan and Pierce, 1950), p. 152. Kenneth S. Davis, *FDR: The New York Years, 1928-1933* (New York: Random House, 1979), p. 189.

16. Jean Edward Smith, *FDR* (New York: Random House, 2007), p. 229. "Roosevelt Denies Seeking Presidency," *New York Times*, November 8, 1930.

17. Lela Mae Stiles, *The Man Behind Roosevelt: The Story of Louis McHenry Howe* (Cleveland: The World Publishing Company, 1954), pp. 160-161. For letters, see Elliott Roosevelt, editor, *FDR: His Personal Letters, 1928-1945* (New York: Duell, Sloan and Pearce, 1950). One example comes in a May 6, 1930, letter to Archibald McNeil, a Democratic national committee member from Connecticut: "Please get it out of your head that I am in any shape, manner or form, thinking about 1932 or anything like it." Also, six of the seven most recent presidents had been Republicans, and Democrat Woodrow Wilson likely wouldn't have won the 1912 election had Theodore Roosevelt not run as a third-party Bull Moose candidate, splitting the Republican vote and costing William Howard Taft a chance for re-election. Roosevelt and Taft together took just over 50 percent of the popular vote to Wilson's 42 percent, though Wilson won an overwhelming majority of the electoral votes.

18. "Plans Laid to Boom Roosevelt for 1932," *New York Times*, November 7, 1930.

19. Lela Stiles, *The Man Behind Roosevelt: The Story of Louis McHenry Howe* (New York: The World Publishing Company, 1954), pp. 135-136.

20. Roy V. Peel and Thomas C. Donnelly, *The 1932 Campaign: An Analysis* (New York: Da Capo Press, 1973), pp. 68-70.

21. James A. Farley, *Behind the Ballots: The Personal History of a Politician* (New York: Harcourt, Brace and Company, 1938), pp. 70-71 and p. 82. Jean Edward Smith, *FDR* (New York: Random House, 2007), p. 250. Box 50, Itineraries 1931-1938, James A. Farley Papers, Manuscript Division, Library of Congress, Washington, D.C. Elliott Roosevelt, ed., *F.D.R.: His Personal Letters, 1928-1945* (New York: Duell, Sloane and Pierce, 1950), pp. 198-201.

Chapter Three

1. "Wind High Here As Barometer Touches New Low Record Level," Havre Daily News, January 11, 1932.

2. Donald Worster, *Dust Bowl: The Southern Plains in the 1930s* (New York: Oxford University Press, 1979), p. 83.

3. Timothy Egan, *The Worst Hard Time: The Untold Story of Those Who Survived the Dust Bowl* (New York: Houghton Mifflin Company, 2006), p. 43. Kenneth Whyte, *Hoover: An Extraordinary Life in Extraordinary Times* (New York: Penguin Random House, 2017), pp. 198-199.

4. Giovanni Federico, "Not Guilty? Agriculture in the 1920s and the Great Depression," *The Journal of Economic History*, December 2005, Vol. 65, No. 4 , p. 966. "Farm Income Fell A Fourth in a Year," *New York Times*, January 1, 1932. *Statistical Abstract of the United States, 1933* (Washington D.C.: U.S. Government Printing Office, 1933), p. 535.

5. "Mineola Man is Victim of Tuesday's Dust Storm," *The Hutchinson News*, Hutchinson, Kansas, March 31, 1932. Earle G. Brown, Selma Gottlieb, Ross L. Laybourn, "Dust Storms and their Possible Effect in Health," *Public Health Reports*, October 4, 1935, Vol. 50, No. 40, pp. 1369-1383.

6. "Some Information About the Dust Storms and Wind Erosion on the Great Plains," Department of Agriculture. Soil Conservation Service, Office of the Deputy Administrator for Management, Information Division. 1968-1976; National Archives, RG 144, Box 2, A1 Entry 1041, Reference Materials Relating to the Great Plains Program, ca. 1935 - 1973.

7. Rocky Mountain locusts arose in massive swarms in the 1800s and ravaged crops from the West to Maine. For reasons that remain murky, they are believed to be extinct – likely an inadvertent result of farmers plowing up of the western river-bottom lands where they laid their eggs. "Looking Back at the Day of the Locust," *The New York Times*, April 23, 2002.

8. Mari Jo Buhle, Paul Buhle, and Dan Georgakas, eds., *The Encyclopedia of the American Left* (Urbana: University of Illinois Press, 1990), pp. 7-12. Lowell K. Dyson, *Farmers' Organizations* (Westport, Connecticut: Greenwood Press, 1986), pp. 214-231.

9. Joseph Frazier Wall, "The Iowa Farmer in Crisis, 1920-1936," *The Annals of Iowa 47* (1983), pp. 119-121. For a broader discussion of the economics of agriculture in the lead-up to the Great Depression, see John L. Shover, *Cornbelt Rebellion: The Farmers' Holiday Association* (Urbana: The University of Illinois Press, 1965), "Chapter One: An Audience for the Agitators."

10. Details from an autobiographical sketch by Reno, Milo Reno Papers, Box 1, Special Collections Department, University of Iowa Archives. Roland A. White, *Milo Reno: Farmers Union Pioneer, 1866-1936; A Memorial Volume* (Iowa City, Iowa: The Iowa Farmers Union, 1941), pp. 18-19. Bruce E. Field, *Harvest of Dissent: The National Farmers Union and the Early Cold War* (Lawrence: University Press of Kansas, 1998), p. 24.

11. Roland A. White, *Milo Reno: Farmers Union Pioneer, 1866-1936; A Memorial Volume* (Iowa City, Iowa: The Iowa Farmers Union, 1941), p. 40.

12. Reno autobiographical, Milo Reno Papers, Box 1, Special Collections Department, University of Iowa Archives. Lowell K. Dyson, *Farmers' Organizations* (Westport, Connecticut: Greenwood Press, 1986), pp. 220-221.

13. Reno autobiographical sketch, Milo Reno Papers, Box 1, Special Collections Department, University of Iowa Archives. Roland A. White, *Milo Reno: Farmers Union Pioneer, 1866-1936; A Memorial Volume* (Iowa City, Iowa: The Iowa Farmers Union, 1941), p. 149.

14. Blomme, Robert P. (1989) "'The Iowa Cow War' Revisited," *Iowa State University Veterinarian*: Vol. 51 : Iss. 1 , Article 5. "Mycobacterium bovis (Bovine Tuberculosis) in Humans," (2011), Centers for Disease Control, accessed at https://www.cdc.gov/tb/publications/factsheets/general/mbovis.pdf.

15. "Strike Proposal defeated," *Cedar Rapids Evening Gazette and Republican*, November 19, 1931. John L. Shover, *Cornbelt Rebellion: The Farmers' Holiday Association* (Urbana: The University of Illinois Press, 1965), pp. 34-35.

16. Thomas E. Howard testimony before the Senate Subcommittee on Agriculture and Forestry, February 3, 1932, 72nd Congress, First Session, on S. 1197 (Washington, D.C.: Government Printing Office, 1932), p. 60.

Chapter Four

1. For a detailed history of Hoover's involvement with the Commission for Relief in Belgium see Chapters Seven and Eight in Kenneth Whyte's *Hoover: An Extraordinary life in Extraordinary Times* (New York: Vintage Books, 2017).

2. Mollie Best, "Mr. and Mrs. Hoover," Washington *Evening Star*, December 19, 1915.

3. Kenneth Whyte, *Hoover: An Extraordinary Life in Extraordinary Times* (New York: Alfred A. Knopf, 2017), p. 195.

4. Ellis W. Hawley, "Herbert Hoover, the Commerce Secretariat, and the Vision of an 'Associative State,' 1921-1928," *The Journal of American History*, Vol. 61, No. 1 (June 1974), p. 116-140. Herbert Hoover, *The Memoirs of Herbert Hoover: The Cabinet and the Presidency, 1920-1933* (New York: MacMillan Company, 1952), pp. 120-121.

5. Elmer E. Cornwell, Jr., *Presidential Leadership of Public Opinion* (Bloomington: Indiana University Press, 1965), pp. 100-101.

6. Charles Michelson, *The Ghost Talks* (New York: G.P. Putnam's Sons, 1944), p. 5 and p. 15.

7. Donald A. Ritchie, *Electing FDR: The New Deal Campaign of 1932* (Lawrence: University Press of Kansas, 2007), p. 41.

8. Thomas S. Barclay, "The Bureau of Publicity for the Democratic National Committee, 1929-1932," *The American Political Science Review*, Vol. 27, No. 1, February 1933, pp. 63-65.

9. "Chicago Jobless Colonize," *New York Times*, November 12, 1930. David Greenberg, *Republic of Spin: An Inside History of the American Presidency* (New York: W.W. Norton, 2016), pp. 183-185.

10. Journal entry January 2, 1932, Box 2, James H. MacLafferty Papers, Hoover Institution Library & Archives, Palo Alto, California. Theodore G. Joslin, *Hoover Off the Record* (Garden City, New York: Doubleday, Doran & Company, Inc., 1934), p. 34. Oliver McKee, Jr., "Publicity Chiefs," *The North American Review*, Vol. 230, No. 4 (October 1930), pp. 411-418

11. For a succinct look at this oft-told tale, see Rosanne Sizer, "Herbert Hoover and the Smear Books, 1930-1932," *The Annals of Iowa* 47 (1984), pp. 343-361.

12. Diary entry for January 4, 1932, Theodore G. Joslin Papers, Box 10 (transcript provided), Herbert Hoover Presidential Library and Museum, West Branch, Iowa. Kenneth Whyte, *Hoover: An Extraordinary Life in Extraordinary Times* (New York: Alfred A. Knopf, 2017), pp. 474-475. Journal entry January 8, 1932, Box 2, James H. MacLafferty Papers, Hoover Institution Library & Archives, Palo Alto, California.

13. Rosanne Sizer, "Herbert Hoover and the Smear Books, 1930-1932," *The Annals of Iowa* 47 (1984), p. 360.

14. "At the White House at 7 a.m.," *New York Times*, November 29, 1931.

15. Diary entry for May 21, 1932, Box 31, Folder: HH Notes – JTB, 1930-33, 1959, through transition, Joel Thompson Boone Papers, Manuscript Division, Library of Congress, Washington, D.C. MacLafferty's diary observation is dated May 21, 1932, James H. MacLafferty Papers, Box 2, Hoover Institution Library and Archives, Stanford University.

16. Box 31, Folder: Hoover 1932-1937, Joel Thompson Boone Papers, Manuscript Division, Library of Congress, Washington, D.C.

17. Simon Kuznets, "National Income, 1929-1932," *National Bureau of Economic Research Bulletin 49*, June 7, 1934, p. 5. *Nineteenth Annual Report of the Federal Reserve Board Covering the Year 1932* (Washington, D.C.: Government Printing Office, 1933), p. 8 and p. 154. James S. Olson, "Rehearsal for Disaster: Hoover, the R. F. C., and the Banking Crisis in Nevada, 1932-1933, *Western Historical Quarterly*, Vol. 6, No. 2 (April 1975), pp. 149-161.

18. Hoover laid out his positions in a letter Herbert S. Crocker who, as president of the American Society of Civil Engineers, had written to Hoover seeking federal funds for large public-works projects to put people back to work. Letter dated May 12, 1932, Herbert Hoover Papers, 1913 – 1964; President's Subject Files, 1929 – 1935; Unemployment-Correspondence, 1932, Herbert Hoover Presidential Library, West Branch, Iowa. Accessed at https://catalog.archives.gov/id/26465637.

19. "Nation's Industrial Chiefs Confer with Hoover today," *New York Times*, November 21, 1929. *Public Papers of the Presidents of the United States: Herbert Hoover, 1929* (Washington, D.C. Government Printing Office, 1974), p. 384-385.

Chapter Five

1. Nelson Lichtenstein, *The Most Dangerous Man in Detroit: Walter Reuther and the Fate of American Labor* (New York: Basic Books, 1995), p. 26.

2. David Moore interview reprinted in *Detroit: A History of Struggle, a Vision of the Future* (Chicago; People's Tribune, 2010), p. 9.

3. Henry Ford III, "1932: A Year of Tragedy and Triumph," *Autoweek*, August 13, 2007.

4. Weather report from *Detroit Free Press*, March 6-7, 1932. David Moore interview reprinted in *Detroit: A History of Struggle, a Vision of the Future* (Chicago; People's Tribune, 2010), p. 8.

5. Edward P. Johanningsmeier, *Forging American Communism: The Life of William Z. Foster* (Princeton, New Jersey: Princeton University Press, 1994), pp. 58-68.

6. Maurice Sugar, *The Ford Hunger March* (Berkeley, California: Meiklejohn Civil Liberties Institute, 1980), pp. 31-32.

7. David Moore interview reprinted in *Detroit: A History of Struggle, a Vision of the Future* (Chicago; People's Tribune, 2010), p. 11.

8. This is the route David Moore detailed in *Detroit: A History of Struggle, a Vision of the Future* (Chicago; People's Tribune, 2010), p. 11. Contemporary newspaper accounts detailed a slightly different route.

9. The beatings may have been committed by the Black Legion, a violent secret society (and Ku Klux Klan offshoot) that had recently organized in the Detroit area, and included top elected and high-level police officials among its ranks. Members would go on to kill or beat Black men and union or political activists before one of its hitmen revealed details of its operations and crimes in 1936. See my *Detroit: A Biography* (Chicago: Chicago Review Press, 2012), Chapter Ten: The Black Legion.

10. Scott Martelle, *Detroit: A Biography* (Chicago: Chicago Review Press, 2012), pp. 122-125.

11. "4 Die in Riot at Ford Plant," *Detroit Free Press*, March 8, 1932. "U.S. Gets Plea to Apprehend Riot Leaders," *Detroit Free Press*, March 9, 1932.

12. "Red Propaganda Turns Hunger March into Riot," *Los Angeles Times*, January 4, 1932.

13. "1,000 Routed in Red Riot at City Hall," *New York Daily News*, January 16, 1932. "Tear Bombs Rout Red Rioters," *Pittsburgh Sun-Telegraph*, February 4, 1932. "Red Riot Breaks Loose," *The Times*, Munster, Indiana, April 22, 1932.

14. Roy Rosenzweig, "Radicals and the Jobless: The Musteites and the Unemployed Leagues, 1932–1936," *Labor History*, 16:1, p. 56.

15. "Mapping American Social Movements Project," University of Washington, accessed November 26, 2021. https://depts.washington.edu/moves/

CP_map-members.shtml. The protest tally was gleaned from coverage by the *The Daily Worker*, the CPUSA's newspaper. https://depts.washing ton.edu/moves/unemployed_map.shtml.

16. Roy Rosenzwieg, "Chapter Eight: Organizing the Unemployed: The Early Years of the Great Depression, 1929–1933," *Workers' Struggles, Past and Present: A "Radical America" Reader* (Philadelphia: Temple University Press, 1983), pp. 184-185.

17. "All Around Detroit," Associated Press reprinted in *The Daily News*, Ludington, Michigan, May 1, 1932. Diego River, *My Art, My Life: An Autobiography* (New York: Dover Publications, 1991, p. 111).

18. Alex Goodall, "The Battle of Detroit and Anti-Communism in the Depression Era," *The Historical Journal*, June 2008, Vol. 51, No. 2, p. 461.

19. Abraham Hoffman, *Unwanted Mexican Americans in the Great Depression: Repatriation Pressures 1929-1939* (Tucson: University of Arizona Press, 1974), pp. 148-178. Francisco E. Balderrama and Raymond Rodríguez, *Decade of Betrayal: Mexican Repatriation in the 1930s* (Albuquerque: University of New Mexico Press, 1995), pp. 100-101.

20. "Unions Want Doak in Hoover Cabinet," *New York Times*, January 8, 1929. William Z. Foster, *From Bryan to Stalin* (New York: International Publishers, 1937), p. 225.

21. Francisco E. Balderrama and Raymond Rodríguez, *Decade of Betrayal: Mexican Repatriation in the 1930s* (Albuquerque: University of New Mexico Press, 1995), p. 7 and 81. Brian Gratton and Emily Merchant, "Immigration, Repatriation, and Deportation: The Mexican-Origin Population in the United States, 1920–1950," *International Migration Review*, Volume 47 Number 4 (Winter 2013), pp. 944–975.

22. Francisco E. Balderrama and Raymond Rodríguez, *Decade of Betrayal: Mexican Repatriation in the 1930s* (Albuquerque: University of New Mexico Press, 1995), p. 114.

23. "Chinese in Sonora Run for Border," *Los Angeles Times*, February 27, 1932.

24. Zaragosa Vargas, *Proletarians of the North: A History of Mexican Industrial Workers in Detroit and the Midwest, 1917-1933* (Berkeley: University of California Press, 1993), pp. 178-186.

Chapter Six

1. Charles Michelson, *The Ghost Talks* (New York: G.P. Putnam's Sons, 1944), pp. 133-134.

2. Roosevelt's animosity toward Moses was a mix of personality clash and Roosevelt's belief (with good reason) that during the Smith governorship Moses had lied to him while sabotaging his efforts to create a parkway sys-

tem in the Hudson Valley. See Robert Caro, *The Power Broker: Robert Moses and the Fall of New York* (New York: Alfred A. Knopf, Inc. 1974), pp. 289-296. Kenneth S. Davis, *FDR: The New York Years 1928-1933* (New York: Random House, 1970), pp. 60-61. Robert A. Slayton, *Empire Statesman: The Rise and Redemption of Al Smith* (New York: The Free Press, 2001), pp. 360-362.

3. James A. Farley, *Behind the Ballots* (New York: Harcourt, Brace and Company, 1938), pp. 74-76. Jean Edward Smith, *FDR* (New York: Random House, 2007), pp. 252-254.

4. Cordell Hull, *The Memoirs of Cordell Hull, Volume One* (New York: The MacMillan Company, 1948), pp. 140-141.

5. Kenneth S. Davis, *FDR: The New York Years 1928-1933* (New York: Random House, 1970), pp. 244-245.

6. "Text of Ex-Governor Smith's Announcement of His Willingness To Be Democratic candidate," *New York Times*, February 8, 1932.

7. See multiple post-announcement stories in *The New York Times*, February 8, 1932.

8. David Farber, *Everybody Ought to be Rich: The Life and Times of John J. Raskob, Capitalist* (New York: Oxford University Press, 2013) pp. 220-221.

9. David Farber, *Everybody Ought to be Rich: The Life and Times of John J. Raskob, Capitalist* (New York: Oxford University Press, 2013) pp. 247-248.

10. Charles Michelson, *The Ghost Talks* (New York: G.P. Putnam's Sons, 1944), pp. 136.

11. James A. Farley, *Behind the Ballots* (New York: Harcourt, Brace and Company, 1938), pp. 69-85.

12. Homer Cummings to Louis Howe, February 14, 1932, General Correspondence, Box 1, James A. Farley Papers, Manuscript Division, Library of Congress.

13. James A. Farley, *Behind the Ballots* (New York: Harcourt, Brace and Company, 1938), p. 93. "Roosevelt Men Act to Thwart Raskob," *New York Times*, December 14, 1931.

14. Frank Friedel, *Franklin D. Roosevelt: The Triumph* (Boston: Little, Brown and Company, 1956), pp. 109-110, 194, 221.

15. Samuel I. Rosenman, *Working With Roosevelt* (New York: Harper & Brothers, 1952), pp. 56-59.

16. Moley, in his memoir, argued that Rosenman overstated the significance of that meeting. Moley described the convening of the Brain Trust as an inevitable evolution for Roosevelt, who as governor routinely consulted with academics as he tried to understand problems. Raymond Moley, *After Seven Years* (New York: Harper and Brothers Publishers, 1939), p. 6.

17. "The Lucky Strikes Program" of April 7, 1932, accessed at http://www.fdrlibrary.marist.edu/archives/collections/utterancesfdr.html.

Chapter Seven

1. "Dry Law is Scored by Women Leaders," *New York Times*, May 19, 1932.

2. "David E. Kyvig, *Repealing National Prohibition* (Chicago: University of Chicago Press, 1979), p. 123.

3. Helen Worden, *Round Manhattan's Rim* (Indianapolis: The Bobbs-Merrill Co., 1934), p. 108.

4. The statistics Sabin cited appear to have been drawn from reports by the Association Against the Prohibition Amendment, whose main players included John J. Raskob and Pierre S. DuPont, whose wife was the Delaware state leader of Sabin's group; Sabin's husband was treasurer of the AAPA. David E. Kyvig, *Repealing National Prohibition* (Kent, Ohio: Kent State University Press, 1979), pp. 106-107.

5. "End Prohibition and Save Billion, Urges Mrs. Sabin," *The Daily News*, May 20, 1932.

6. Milton MacKaye, "The New Crusade," *The New Yorker*, October 22, 1932, pp. 20-24. "Miss Pauline Morton's Debut," *New York Times*, December 18, 1904.

7. Pauline Morton Sabin, "I Change My Mind on Prohibition," *The Outlook*, June 13, 1928.

8. Grace C. Root, *Women and Repeal: The Story of the Women's Organization for National Prohibition Reform* (New York: Harper & Brothers, 1934), pp. 6-7.

9. Grace C. Root, *Women and Repeal: The Story of the Women's Organization for National Prohibition Reform* (New York: Harper & Brothers, 1934), pp. 10-11. "Women Organize to Fight Dry Laws," *New York Times*, May 29, 1929.

10. "Better Way," *The Tampa Times*, May 31, 1929.

11. Daniel Okrent, *Last Call: The Rise and Fall of Prohibition* (New York: Simon & Schuster, 2010), pp. 104-106.

12. K. Austin Kerr, "Organizing for Reform: The Anti-Saloon League and Innovation in Politics," *American Quarterly,* Vol. 32, No. 1 (Spring, 1980), pp. 37-53.

13. Daniel Okrent, *Last Call: The Rise and Fall of Prohibition* (New York: Simon & Schuster, 2010), p. 37. Ron Chernow, *Titan: The Life of John D. Rockefeller* (New York: Random House, 1998), pp. 310-311.

14. Margo J. Anderson, *The American Census: A Social History*, Second Edition (New Haven: Yale University Press, 2015), pp. 135-136.

15. "The Great Prohibition Poll's Final Report," *Literary Digest*, April 30, 1932, pp. 6-7.

16. See Report of Committee on Political Activities, April 12-13, 1932, Papers of the Association against the Prohibition Amendment and the Women's Organization for National Prohibition Reform.

Chapter Eight

1. "The Hullabaloo Over the $2,000,000,000 Bonus Plan," *Literary Digest*, April 9, 1932.

2. Hoover's March 29 statement and April 15 press conference are reprinted in *The Public Papers of the Presidents of the United States: Herbert Hoover, 1932-33* (Washington, D.C.: U.S. Government Printing Office, 1977), pp. 126 and 160.

3. Details of the start of the march are drawn mainly from Walter W. Waters and William C. White, *B.E.F.: The Whole Story of the Bonus Army* (New York: John Day Company, 1933), Jack Douglas, *Veterans on the March* (New York: Workers Library Publishers, 1934), and Paul Dickson and Thomas B. Allen, *The Bonus Army: An American Epic* (New York: Walker and Company, 2004). The Douglas book is the Communist Party's take on the events but includes first-person details by George Alman; it's unclear whether Alman was a communist.

4. Walter W. Waters and William C. White, *B.E.F.: The Whole Story of the Bonus Army* (New York: John Day Company, 1933), p. 22. Other details are gleaned from local news reports along the route, and from an informal memoir by John Steven Murray, who had been bouncing around the country when he met Waters in Portland and agreed to join the march. My thanks to Paul Dickson, who shared a photocopy of the Murray memoir obtained for his book, with Thomas B. Allen, *The Bonus Army: An American Epic* (New York: Walker & Company, 2004).

5. Murray memoir, p. 32.

6. "400 War Veterans Commandeer Train," *St. Louis Globe-Democrat*, May 20, 1932.

7. The number of times the news story was published is based on an analysis of the Newspapers.com database.

8. *Veterans on the March* (New York: Workers Library Publishers, 1934), the history by Jack Douglas (a pseudonym) and published by a Communist Party press, zeroed in on the analysis that Waters was trying to avoid arrest. That book repeatedly sought to cast Waters as more interested in power than in the best interests of the men he led. See pp. 32-35.

9. "Troops Mobilize Ten Miles from Marchers," *St. Louis Star and Times*, May 24, 1932.

10. Local newspapers carried updates on various organizing efforts. For example, see "Half Dozen 'Armies' of Vets Headed for Washington in Bonus Campaign," *The Morning Post*, Camden, New Jersey, May 27, 1932.

11. Details on MacArthur and his staff are drawn from Paul Dickson and Thomas B. Allen, *The Bonus Army: An American Epic* (New York: Walker and Company, 2004), pp. 73-76. Clayton D. Laurie and Ronald H. Cole,

The Role of Federal Military Force in Domestic Disorders, 1877-1945 (Washington, D.C.: Center of Military History, Department of Army, 1997), pp. 334-338.

12. The State, War and Navy Building is now the Eisenhower Executive Office Building. Fear of rising fascism drawn from Clayton D. Lurie and Ronald H. Cole, *The Role of Federal Military Forces in Domestic Disorders, 1877-1945* (Washington, D.C.: Center of Military History, United States Army, 1997), p. 367.

13. Walter W. Waters and William C. White, *B.E.F.: The Whole Story of the Bonus Army* (New York: John Day Company, 1933), p. 60.

14. Walter W. Waters and William C. White, *B.E.F.: The Whole Story of the Bonus Army* (New York: John Day Company, 1933), p. 61. Murray described the overnight facility as an auditorium.

Chapter Nine

1. Kenneth Whyte, *Hoover: An Extraordinary Life in Extraordinary Times* (New York: Random House, 2017), pp. 344, 402.

2. Janet Schmelzer, "Wright Patman and the Impeachment of Andrew Mellon," *East Texas Historical Journal*, Vol. 23, Issue 1, Article 8, p. 38. Charles Rappleye, *Herbert Hoover in the White House: The Ordeal of the Presidency* (New York: Simon & Schuster, 2016), p. 301.

3. November 30, 1931, diary entry, Theodore G. Joslin Papers, Herbert Hoover Presidential Library, West Branch, Iowa. Kenneth Whyte, *Hoover: An Extraordinary Life in Extraordinary Times* (New York: Vintage, 2017), p. 459. Hoover inaugural address delivered March 4, 1932.

4. February 24, 1932, diary entry, Theodore G. Joslin Papers, Herbert Hoover Presidential Library, West Branch, Iowa.

5. Kenneth Whyte, *Hoover: An Extraordinary Life in Extraordinary Times* (New York: Random House, 2017), pp. 377-380.

6. Ralph M. Goldman, *The National Party Chairmen and Committees: Factionalism at the Top* (Armonk, N.Y., M.E. Sharp, Inc., 1990), pp. 388-390. May 30, 1932, diary entry, Edgar Rickard Papers, Herbert Hoover Presidential Library, West Branch, Iowa. Veto tallies accessed at https://www.senate.gov/legislative/vetoes/vetoCounts.htm.

7. Joslin mentioned the meeting and Hoover's reaction in a memorandum included between April 30 and May 1 entries in his diary, Theodore G. Joslin Papers, Herbert Hoover Presidential Library, West Branch, Iowa. The meeting is mentioned in Mary Jane Matz, *The Many Lives of Otto Kahn* (New York: The McMillan Company, 1963), p. 263.

8. Claude M. Fuess, *Calvin Coolidge: The Man from Vermont* (Boston: Little, Brown and Company, 1940), p. 444. "Excerpt from Coolidge Article, Urging Party to Renominate Hoover," *New York Times*, September 30, 1931.

9. Claude M. Fuess, *Calvin Coolidge: The Man from Vermont* (Boston: Little, Brown and Company, 1940), pp. 446-447.

10. "Joseph I. France is Candidate for President," *The Baltimore Sun*, April 8, 1931.

11. "Roosevelt Defeats Smith in Primary of New Hampshire," *New York Times*, March 9, 1932.

12. "Hoover Enters G.O.P. Primary in Maryland," *The Baltimore Sun*, April 17, 1932. Donald A. Ritchie, *Electing FDR: The New Deal Campaign of 1932* (Lawrence: University Press of Kansas, 2007), pp. 96-97. "Headline Footnotes," *New York Times*, May 29, 1932.

13. Diary entry for February 7, 1932, Theodore G. Joslin Papers, and "Notes on Washington Visit," in February 28 diary entry, Edgar Rickard Papers, both collections in the Herbert Hoover Presidential Library, West Branch, Iowa.

14. Walter Lippmann syndicated Today and Tomorrow column, December 1, 1931.

15. Walter Lippmann, syndicated Today and Tomorrow column, January 8, 1932.

16. Farley to Roosevelt, November 10, 1931, Franklin D. Roosevelt, Letters as Governor, Series I, James A. Farley, Roosevelt Presidential Library, Hyde Park, New York. Kenneth S. Davis, *FDR: The New York Years 1928-1932: A History* (New York: Random House, 1985), pp. 252-253. Howe to Roosevelt, January 9, 1932, *F.D.R.: His Personal Letters, Vol. 3, 1928-1945*, (New York: Duell, Sloan, and Pearce, 1950), p. 252.

17. Bascom N. Timmons, *Garner of Texas: A Personal History* (New York: Harper & Brothers Publishers, 1948), p. 154.

18. David Nasaw, *The Chief: The Life of William Randolph Hearst* (Boston: Mariner Books, 2000), p. 452. William Randolph Hearst, "Who Will Be the Next President?" transcript printed in the *San Francisco Examiner*, January 3, 1932.

19. Russell M. Posner, "California's Role in the Nomination of Franklin D. Roosevelt," *California Historical Society Quarterly*, (Vol. 39, No. 2, June 1960), p. 124.

20. David Nasaw, *The Chief: The Life of William Randolph Hearst* (Boston: Mariner Books, 2000), pp. 444-445.

21. Russell M. Posner, "California's Role in the Nomination of Franklin D. Roosevelt," *California Historical Society Quarterly*, (Vol. 39, No. 2, June 1960), p. 125.

22. Arthur Krock, "A Week in American; a Roosevelt Setback," *New York Times*, May 1, 1932.

23. Roy V. Peel and Thomas C. Donnelly, *The 1932 Campaign: An Analysis* (New York: Farrar & Rinehart, 1935), p. 67.

24. May 4, 1932 entry, Theodore G. Joslin Diaries, Herbert Hoover Presidential Library, West Branch, Iowa.

25. "Farm Group for Month's Halt in Buying, Selling," *The Daily Times Union*, Davenport, Iowa, May 4, 1932. "Farmers Set Month Aside for Holiday," *Des Moines Register*, May 4, 1932.

26. Reno autobiographical sketch, Milo Reno Papers, Box 1, Special Collections Department, University of Iowa Archives.

Chapter Ten

1. Walter W. Waters and William C. White, *BEF: The Whole Story of the Bonus Army* (New York: John Day Company, 1933), pp. 62-64.

2. Details drawn from an interview with John Pace and Joseph Kornfeder, by then ex-communists, under oath on August 23, 1949, with Georgia Democratic Representative John S. Wood, chair of the House Committee on Un-American Activities (Washington D.C.: Government Printing Office, 1949).

3. Edmund W. Starling and Thomas Sugrue, *Starling of the White House* (New York: Simon & Schuster, 1946), p. 296.

4. "Edward J. Jeffries, Detroit Jurist, 75," *New York Times*, September 11, 1939.

5. "Scenes as Jobless of Akron Sought Relief," *Akron Beacon-Journal*, January 21, 1931.

6. "Police Battle War Veterans," *Marysville (Ohio) Journal Tribune*, June 4, 1932.

7. Entry for June 2, 1932, Theodore G. Joslin Diaries, National Archives, Herbert Hoover Presidential Library and Museum, West Branch, Iowa.

8. John Steven Murray, whose informal memoir chronicled the cross-country trip of the Oregon marchers, quit in early June after he "had a fall out" with the men he oversaw in Company F. He left D.C. at that point and after returning briefly eventually made his way South. The site strategy is in Donald J. Lisio, *The President and Protest: Hoover, Conspiracy, and the Bonus Riot* (Columbia: University of Missouri Press, 1974), p. 93.

9. "U.S. to Help Care for Bonus Army," *The Evening Star*, July 11, 1932. *The B.E.F. News*, July 9, 1932. "Home Lure Gets Many Bonus Men," *The Evening Star*, July 10, 1932.

10. John Steve Murray memoir. Also, news reporters for the Washington newspapers, as well as out of town papers, made regular visits to the encampment. These details are drawn from *The Evening Star*, June 9, 1932.

11. Walter W. Waters and William C. White, *BEF: The Whole Story of the Bonus Army* (New York: John Day Company, 1933), p. 107.

12. E. Francis Brown, "The Bonus Army Marches to Defeat," *Current History* (1916-1940), Vol. 36, No. 6 (September 1932), p. 685.

13. Hastings to Strother, July 18, 1932, World War Veterans-Bonus, Correspondence, July-August 1932, Presidential Papers-Subject File, Herbert Hoover Presidential Library, West Branch, Iowa.

14. Paul Dickson and Thomas B. Allen, The Bonus Army: An American Epic (New York: Walker and Company, 2004), p. 107. "Fowler Declares Camp Menace to City's Health," The Evening Star, June 9, 1932.

15. A copy of the telegram is in Correspondence 1927-1932, Milo Reno Papers, Box 1, Special Collections Department, University of Iowa Archives.

16. "D.C. Heads Move to Aid Bonus Camp," *The Evening Star*, June 14, 1932. "Knife Wounds Fatal to Colored Veteran," *The Evening Star*, July 9, 1932.

17. Walter W. Waters and William C. White, *BEF: The Whole Story of the Bonus Army* (New York: John Day Company, 1933), p. 81. "Police Guard Capitol," Associated Press reprinted in the *El Paso Herald-Post*, June 6, 1932.

18. "Sen. Lewis Tells Vets to go to Hell," *Cumberland* (Md.) *Evening Times*, June 7, 1932. Lewis would later apologize in person during a visit to Camp Marks.

19. "Rep. Patman Requires Total of 145 to Force House to Vote on Issue," *The North Adams (Mass.) Transcript*, May 25, 1932.

20. "Eslick Dies in House Pleading for Bonus," *The New York Times*, June 15, 1932.

21. "Bonus Bill Passes in House, 209-176," *The New York Times*, June 16, 1932.

22. Walter W. Waters and William C. White, *BEF: The Whole Story of the Bonus Army* (New York: John Day Company, 1933), pp. 150-153.

23. "Bonus Army Vows to Stay, Despite Defeat in the Senate," *The Evening Star*, June 18, 1932.

24. Walter W. Waters and William C. White, *BEF: The Whole Story of the Bonus Army* (New York: John Day Company, 1933), p. 111.

Chapter Eleven

1. "Negro Fired on in Dark, Is Not Wounded," *The Times* (Shreveport, Louisiana), July 26, 1932.

2. "Fifth Negro Pays With Life In Growing Race Trouble On Railroads," *Clarion-Ledger* (Jackson, Mississippi), March 24, 1932. "The Forgotten Tenth: An Analysis of Unemployment Among Negroes in the United States and its Social Costs, 1932-1933," report by the National Urban League, May 1933, p. 18.

3. "Four Texans Lynch Negro," *Pampa (Texas) Daily News*, April 3, 1932.

4. "What About This," *Charlotte News*, January 22, 1932. "Jacksonville Job Hunters in Riot," *Tampa Bay Times*, February 18, 1932. "The Forgotten

Tenth: An Analysis of Unemployment Among Negroes in the United States and its Social Costs, 1932-1933," report by the National Urban League, May 1933, p. 19.

5. Hollace Ransdall, a female investigator for the American Civil Liberties Union, traveled to Alabama and performed some of the basic work the defense lawyers failed to do, including uncovering the alleged victims' prostitution history. Report on the Scottsboro, Ala., Case, May 27, 1931, accessed at https://famous-trials.com/scottsboroboys/2344-firsttrial-2#report.

6. Kenneth Robert Janken, *White: The Biography of Walter White, Mr. NAACP* (New York: The New Press, 2003), pp. 148-151.

7. Melanie S. Morrison, *Murder on Shades Mountain: The Legal Lynching of Willie Peterson and the Struggle for Justice in Jim Crow Birmingham* (Durham, N.C.: Duke University Press, 2018), p. 17.

8. James Goodman, *Stories of Scottsboro* (New York: Pantheon Books, 1994), p. 84. In echoes of the Scottsboro Boys case, an unlikely suspect named Willie Peterson was identified by the survivor, despite not resembling the description she initially gave police, and after a deeply flawed trial he was convicted. He died in prison in 1940.

9. Dan T. Carter, *Scottsboro: A Tragedy of the American South* (Baton Rouge: Louisiana State University Press, 1969), pp. 54-55.

10. Angelo Herndon, *Let Me Live* (Ann Arbor: University of Michigan Press, 2007, reprinted from the 1937 original), p. 39.

11. Angelo Herndon, *Let Me Live* (Ann Arbor: University of Michigan Press, 2007, reprinted from the 1937 original), p. 44.

12. Angelo Herndon, *Let Me Live* (Ann Arbor: University of Michigan Press, 2007, reprinted from the 1937 original), Chapter Nine.

13. Angelo Herndon, *Let Me Live* (Ann Arbor: University of Michigan Press, 2007, reprinted from the 1937 original), Chapter Twelve.

14. "No Action Taken by County Board on Tax for Needy," *The Atlanta Constitution*, June 26, 1932.

15. "Labor Defense Group Flays Negro's Arrest," *The Constitution*, Atlanta, July 28, 1932.

Chapter Twelve

1. "Plan Political Pressure," *New York Times*, June 8, 1932.

2. David E. Kyvig, *Repealing National Prohibition, second edition* (Kent: Ohio State University Press, 2000), p. 153.

3. Folder 1023-54 Letters to Delegates, Papers of the Association against the Prohibition Amendment and the Women's Organization for National Prohibition Reform.

4. "Text of Rockefeller's Letter to Dr. Butler," *New York Times*, June 7, 1932.

5. "Drys are resentful, Wet Chiefs Jubilant," *New York Times*, June 7, 1932.

6. Charles Rappleye, *Herbert Hoover in the White House: The Ordeal of the Presidency* (New York: Simon & Schuster, 2016), pp. 356-357.

7. "Edgar Rickard, 77, Engineer, is Dead," *New York Times*, January 22, 1951. Rickard's diary entries for the year often mention the struggles facing his companies and the possible bankruptcy of the Pejobscot Paper business, Edgar Rickard Papers, Herbert Hoover Presidential Library, West Branch, Iowa.

8. Diary entries for June 7 and June 10, 1932, Edgar Rickard Papers, Herbert Hoover Presidential Library, West Branch, Iowa. Walter W. Liggett, *The Rise of Herbert Hoover* (New York: The H.K. Sly Company, 1932), p. 150.

9. Diary entry for June 11, 1932, Edgar Rickard Papers, Herbert Hoover Presidential Library, West Branch, Iowa.

10. Diary entry covering June 12-16, 1932, Edgar Rickard Papers, Herbert Hoover Presidential Library, West Branch, Iowa.

11. "Hoover Approves Dry-Wet Prohibition Plank," June 15, 1932, *New York Times*. H.L. Mencken, "G.O.P. Wet Revolt Amazing in Extent, Mencken Declares," June 17, 1932, *Baltimore Sun*.

12. "Again: Hoover and Curtis," *Chicago Daily Tribune*, June 17, 1932. "Police Roust France from Rostrum," *New York Times*, June 17, 1932.

13. Private File 1932, Box 37, The Papers of James A. Farley, Library of Congress Manuscripts Division. Edward J. Flynn, *You're the Boss: The Practice of American Politics* (New York: The Viking Press, 1947), p. 93.

14. James A. Farley, *Behind the Ballots* (New York: Harcourt, Brace and Company, 1938), pp. 108-109.

15. James A. Farley, *Behind the Ballots* (New York: Harcourt, Brace and Company, 1938), pp. 116-117.

16. Unless otherwise noted, details of the convention are drawn from daily news coverage, primarily the *Chicago Tribune*.

17. Roy V. Peel and Thomas C. Donnelly, *The 1932 Campaign: An Analysis* (New York: Da Capo Press, 1973), pp. 92-93.

18. James A. Farley, *Behind the Ballots* (New York: Harcourt, Brace and Company, 1938), pp. 123-124. Kenneth S. Davis, *FDR: The New York Years, 1928-1933* (New York: Random House, 1979), pp. 314-315. "Roosevelt in Peril of Upset," June 28, 1932, *Chicago Tribune*.

19. Edward J. Flynn, *You're the Boss: The Practice of American Politics* (New York: The Viking Press, 1947), p. 99.

20. David Nasaw, *The Patriarch: The Remarkable Life and Turbulent Times of Joseph P. Kennedy* (New York: Penguin Press, 2012), pp. 176-177. David Nasaw, *The Chief: The Life of William Randoph Hearst* (New York: Houghton Mifflin, 2000), pp. 456-457.

21. James A. Farley, *Behind the Ballots* (New York: Harcourt, Brace and Company, 1938), pp. 144-145.

22. Donald A. Ritchie, *Electing FDR: The New Deal Campaign of 1932* (Lawrence: The University Press of Kansas, 2007), pp. 106-108. David Nasaw, *The Chief: The Life of William Randolph Hearst* (New York: Houghton Mifflin, 2000), pp. 455-456.

23. "Roosevelt Vote is 945," *New York Times*, July 2, 1932.

24. "Boos Give Way to Victory Song as Tide Turns," *Chicago Tribune*, July 2, 1932.

25. James Roosevelt and Sidney Shalett, *Affectionally, F.D.R.* (New York, Harcourt, Brace & Company, 1959), pp. 225-226. Kenneth S. Davis, *FDR: The New York Years, 1928-1933* (New York: Random House, 1979), pp. 333-334.

Diaries III

1. Gardner, F. W. (1932). Diary, 1929-1932, Fay Webb Gardner Collection, Gardner-Webb University Archives, John R. Dover Memorial Library, Boiling Springs, NC. 1932 Emily Almira C. Rich Diary, Special Collections Department, Stewart Library, Weber State University. https://cdm.weber.edu/digital/collection/RICH/id/4870/rec/40.

Chapter Thirteen

1. "Victory in Defeat," *Evening Star*, June 28, 1932.

2. "Glassford Urges Veterans' Farms," *Evening Star*, June 17, 1932. "Proposes a Plan to Dispose of Bonus Army," *Evening Star*, June 19, 1932.

3. "Veterans Leaving City as Recruits are Being Sought," *Evening Star*, June 19, 1932. "Reds Urge Mutiny in the Bonus Army," *New York Times*, June 19, 1932. Statistics cited in Lucy G. Barber, *Marching on Washington: The Forging of an American Political Tradition* (Berkeley: University of California Press, 2002), p. 90. The July estimate is from "Veterans Barred from White House," *New York Times*, July 21, 1932.

4. Donald J. Lisio, *The President and Protest: Hoover, Conspiracy, and the Bonus Riot* (Columbia: The University of Missouri Press, 1974), pp.83-85.

5. "The B.E.F. News," *B.E.F. News*, June 25, 1932, p. 4.

6. Walter W. Waters and William C. White, *B.E.F.: The Whole Story of the Bonus Army* (New York: John Day Company, 1933), p. 138.

7. Walter W. Waters and William C. White, *B.E.F.: The Whole Story of the Bonus Army* (New York: John Day Company, 1933), p. 156. Jack Douglas, *Veterans on the March* (New York: Workers Library Publishers, 1934), p. 176.

8. "Crisis is Imminent in Ranks of B.E.F.," *The Evening Star*, June 26, 1932.

9. "B.E.F. Rift Stirs Departure Hopes," *The Evening Star*, June 25, 1932.

10. "Veterans Worry Over Next Meal and Leadership," *The Evening Star*, June 29, 1932. Walter W. Waters and William C. White, *B.E.F.: The Whole Story of the Bonus Army* (New York: John Day Company, 1933), p. 156. "Vets Hit Self-Appointment of Waters," *Daily Worker*, June 30, 1932. "United Veterans Face Disease and Shortage of Food," *The Evening Star*, June 30, 1932. "Waters Again Named by Vets as commander," *Brooklyn Citizen*, June 30, 1932.

11. John W. Killigrew, "The Army and the Bonus Incident," *Military Affairs*, Summer, 1962, Vol. 26, No. 2, pp. 59-60. Paul Dickson and Thomas B. Allen, *The Bonus Army: An American Epic* (New York: Walker and Company, 2004), p. 141.

12. Moseley, a white supremacist, would later become known for racist and anti-Semitic diatribes and tacit support for fascism, including the pro-Nazi German-American Bund. James F. Vivian and Jean H. Vivian, "The Bonus March of 1932: The Role of General George Van Horn Moseley," *The Wisconsin Magazine of History*, Autumn, 1967, Vol. 51, No. 1, pp. 26-36. The "White Plan" is quoted in John W. Killigrew, "The Army and the Bonus Incident," *Military Affairs*, Summer, 1962, Vol. 26, No. 2, p. 61. On the last-minute revisions see Clayton D. Laurie and Ronald H. Cole, *The Role of Federal Military Forces in Domestic Disorders, 1877-1945* (Washington, D.C.: Center of Military History, United States Army, 1997), pp. 374-376.

13. "Veterans Barred from White House," *New York Times*, July 21, 1932.

14. Walter W. Waters and William C. White, *B.E.F.: The Whole Story of the Bonus Army* (New York: John Day Company, 1933), pp. 181-185.

15. "Radical Veterans Clubbed by Police, Nine Arrested," *The Evening Star*, July 25, 1932.

16. For a deeply detailed description of the ouster of the veterans see Paul Dickson and Thomas B. Allen, *The Bonus Army: An American Epic* (New York: Walker and Company, 2004), Chapter Eight: "Tanks in the Street."

17. "Troops Rushed to Quell B.E.F. Outbreak," *The Evening Star*, July 18, 1932.

18. L.H. Reichelderfer for the Board of commissions to Hoover, July 28, 1932, reprinted as item 248, and entry 246, Statement About the Bonus Marchers, July 28, 1932, *Public Papers of The Presidents of The United States: Herbert Hoover, 1932-33*, (Washington, D.C.: United States Government Printing Office, 1977). Donald J. Lisio, *The President and Protest: Hoover, Conspiracy, and the Bonus Riot* (Columbia: University of Missouri Press, 1974), pp. 199-204.

19. Gen. Douglas MacArthur press conference on July 28, 1932, transcript in *Public Papers of The Presidents of The United States: Herbert Hoover, 1932-33*, entry 246, Statement About the Bonus Marchers, July 28, 1932 (Washington, D.C.: United States Government Printing Office, 1977).

20. Troop movements and time stamp from Brigadier General Perry L. Miles' "Report of Operations Against Bonus Marchers" submitted to General

MacArthur, August 4, 1932, World War Veterans-Bonus, Reports, Army, Appendix No. 4, Presidential Papers – Subject File, Herbert Hoover Presidential Library, West Branch, Iowa.

21. Maurice P. Sneller, "The Bonus March of 1932," *Essays in History* 3: 27–44. MacArthur's report to Hoover, reprinted in the main in Theodore Joslin, *Hoover Off the Record* (New York: Doubleday, Duran & Company, 1934), pp. 269-275.

22. "City of Hovels is Wiped Out by Fire and Swords of Troops," *The Evening Star*, July 29, 1932.

Chapter Fourteen

1. John L. Shover, "The Farmers' Holiday Strike, August 1932," *Agricultural History*, October 1965, Vol. 39, No. 4, p. 198.

2. "The Farmers Go On Strike," *The New Republic*, August 31, 1932. "Reno's Attorneys File Libel Suit," September 7, 1932, *Des Moines Tribune*.

3. John L. Shover, "The Farmers' Holiday Strike, August 1932," *Agricultural History*, October 1965, Vol. 39, No. 4, pp. 198-199. Shover also cites the Reno letter to Ben McCormack, November 8, 1933.

4. "500 Producers Back Move to Check Supply," *The Sioux City Journal*, August 11, 1932.

5. "Milk Delivered at Sioux City," *Des Moines Register*, August 12, 1932.

6. "Strikers Plan Bureau Here," The *Sioux City Journal*, August 12, 1932. "Sheriff's 'Army' Will Patrol Roads," The *Sioux City Journal*, August 16, 1932.

7. Reynold M. Wik, "The Radio in Rural America During the 1920s," *Agricultural History*, Vol. 55, No. 4 (October 1981), pp. 339-350. 1930 Census, "Families-United States Summary," Table 12.

8. John L. Shover, "The Farmers' Holiday Strike, August 1932," *Agricultural History*, October 1965, Vol. 39, No. 4, p. 199.

9. W.E. Christenson, "The Strike 'Just Happened,'" August 29, 1932, *Omaha World-Herald*.

10. "Stomach Strike," *Time*, August 29, 1932.

11. Details of these strike actions, unless otherwise noted, are drawn from daily coverage by *The Sioux City Journal*, *The Des Moines Register*, and wire service reports published around the country.

12. "Midwest Governors Submit Relief Plan," September 12, 1932, The *Sioux City Journal*.

13. John L. Shover, *Cornbelt Rebellion: The Farmer' Holiday Association* (Urbana: University of Illinois Press, 1965), pp. 51-54.

14. "Barney Von Bonn, Unable to Reach Shelter, Killed – Body Pierced by Splinters," May 7, 1930, *Nebraska State Journal* in Lincoln.

15. Details from an interview with Christenson by the Newspaper Enterprise Association wire service re-published in "Saving 'The Old Homestead,'" *Fremont Evening Tribune*, December 15, 1932.

Chapter Fifteen

1. Samuel I. Rosenman, *Working With Roosevelt* (New York: Harper and Brothers, 1952), p. 22.

2. Kenneth S. Davis, *FDR: The New York Years, 1928-1933* (New York: Random House, 1979), pp. 342-343. Details of the trip drawn from such articles as, "Roosevelt Ready for N.E. Cruise," *Boston Globe*, July 11, 1932.

3. Arthur M. Schlesinger Jr., *The Crisis of the Old Order: 1919-1933* (Boston: Houghton Mifflin Company, 1957), pp. 244-245.

4. Letter from H.A. White of the Railway Mail Service division of the Post Office Department, December 18, 1931, Herbert Hoover Papers, Misrepresentations, Citizenship, April 1, 1932, to October 19, 1932, Herbert Hoover Presidential Library, West Branch, Iowa.

5. Letter dated August 3, 1932, W.R. Castle, Jr., to secretary to the president, White House, Misrepresentations, Citizenship April 8, 1932 – October 18, 1932, Herbert Hoover Papers, Herbert Hoover Presidential Library, West Branch, Iowa.

6. For a thorough description, see Chapter 11, Donald J. Lisio, *The President and Protest: Hoover, Conspiracy, and the Bonus Riot* (Columbia: University of Missouri Press, 1974). For Hurley and MacArthur's refusal of Hoover's request, see notes from Hurley telephone call by Lawrence Richey, July 30, 1932, Box 412 Folder 8, World War Veterans - Bonus — Reports, Depositions and Statements, 1932 July 26-31, Presidential Subject File, Herbert Hoover Papers, Herbert Hoover Presidential Library, West Branch, Iowa.

7. Dozens of the letters are collected in multiple folders in Presidential Papers – Subject File, Herbert Hoover Papers, Herbert Hoover Presidential Library, West Branch, Iowa.

8. "Eviction by Executive order, *The Washington Star*, July 29, 1932. "Time to End It," *The New York Times*, July 29, 1932. "The 'Bonus Army' Riots," *Los Angeles Times*, July 30, 1932. Also see Louis Liebovich, "Press Reaction to the Bonus March of 1932: A Re-evaluation of the Impact of an American Tragedy," *Journalism & Communication Monographs*; Columbia, South Carolina, Vol. 122, August 1, 1990.

9. Hurley (August 3) and Joslin (August 10) statements are in World War Veterans-Bonus, Correspondence, 1932, July-August, Presidential Papers, Herbert Hoover Presidential Library, West Branch, Iowa.

10. Mitchell's report to Hoover, September 9, 1932, is included in entry 285, *Public Papers of The Presidents of The United States: Herbert Hoover, 1932-33,* (Washington, D.C.: United States Government Printing Office, 1977).

11. Floyd Gibbons address, Summary of Proceedings, Fourteenth Annual National Convention of the American Legion, September 12-15, Portland, Oregon, pp. 40-44.

12. Republican presidential nomination acceptance speech, August 11, 1932, reprinted in *Public Papers of the Presidents of the United States, Herbert Hoover, January 1, 1932, to March 4, 1933* (Washington, D.C.: U.S. Government Printing Office, 1977), pp. 357-376.

13. "Stand of Hoover gets Ford's O.K.," *The Evening Star*, Washington, D.C., August 13, 1932. "W.C.T.U. is Puzzled About How to Vote," *The New York Times*, August 13, 1932.

14. See *New York Times* and *Washington Star* coverage, among other, July 11-July 15, 1932.

15. Houser to Ray Lyman Wilbur, secretary of commerce, June 22, 1932, J. David Houser folder, Name and Subject File, Early Career, Lewis L. Strauss Papers, Herbert Hoover Presidential Library, West Branch, Iowa.

16. Strauss to Richey, March 7, 1932, J. David Houser folder, Name and Subject File, Early Career, Lewis L. Strauss Papers, Herbert Hoover Presidential Library, West Branch, Iowa.

17. Houser's March 12 meeting is recorded in the daily diaries of chief steward Ike Hoover, Irwin Hood Hoover papers, Manuscript Division, Library of Congress.

18. Hoover press conference, August 23, 1932, reprinted in *Public Papers of the Presidents of the United States, Herbert Hoover, January 1, 1932, to March 4, 1933* (Washington, D.C.: U.S. Government Printing Office, 1977), pp. 384-387.

Chapter Sixteen

1. James A. Farley, *Behind the Ballots* (New York: Harcourt, Brace and Company, 1938), pp. 165-166.

2. September 13 and 14, 1932, diary entries in Theodore G. Joslin Papers, Herbert Hoover Presidential Library, West Branch, Iowa. Hoover to Everett Sanders, September 13, 1932, reprinted in *Public Papers of the Presidents of the United States, Herbert Hoover, January 1, 1932, to March 4, 1933* (Washington, D.C.: U.S. Government Printing Office, 1977), pp. 425-426.

3. September 6 and September 11 diary entries in Theodore G. Joslin Papers, Herbert Hoover Presidential Library, West Branch, Iowa.

4. Itineraries and travelers' names are in Trips of the President, Campaign – 1932, Franklin D. Roosevelt Presidential Library and Museum, Hyde Park,

New York. "Roosevelt Greeted by Crowds in the Midwest," *New York Times*, September 13, 1932.

5. James A. Farley, *Behind the Ballots* (New York: Harcourt, Brace and Company, 1938), p. 164.

6. R.G. Tugwell, *The Brains Trust* (New York: The Viking Press, 1968), pp. 501-502.

7. R.G. Tugwell, *The Brains Trust* (New York: The Viking Press, 1968), pp. 503-504.

8. "10,000 Cheer the Nominee," *New York Times*, September 15, 1932. Text of speech included in *Public Papers of Franklin D. Roosevelt, 1932* (Albany: J.B. Lyon Company, 1939), pp. 643-653.

9. "President Decides to Take the Stump," *New York Times*, September 15, 1932.

10. "Roosevelt Outlines 6-Point Plan," *New York Times*, September 18, 1932. H. W. Brands, *A Traitor to his Class: The Privileged Life and Radical Presidency of Franklin Delano Roosevelt* (New York: Doubleday, 2008), p. 255. *46th Annual Report of the Interstate Commerce Commission* (Washington: United States Government Printing Office, 1932), p. 15.

11. "Merchants to Close for Roosevelt Train," *Record Searchlight*, Redding, California, September 21, 1932. "Roosevelt Hailed by 2,500 Redding Folk on Journey," *Sacramento Bee*, September 22, 1932.

12. "100,000 Hail Him at San Francisco," *New York Times*, September 23, 1932.

13. Roosevelt's speech has been widely reprinted and available from multiple online sources, including https://www.presidency.ucsb.edu/documents/campaign-address-progressive-government-the-commonwealth-club-san-francisco-california.

14. "Roosevelt Airs Business Views," *Los Angeles Times*, September 24, 1932.

15. September 19, 1932, diary entry in Theodore G. Joslin Papers, Herbert Hoover Presidential Library, West Branch, Iowa.

16. September 16, 1931, diary entry in Theodore G. Joslin Papers, Herbert Hoover Presidential Library, West Branch, Iowa. Transcript from recorded speech delivered October 18, 1932, in Indianapolis, collected in *Public Papers of the Presidents of the United States, Herbert Hoover, January 1, 1932, to March 4, 1933* (Washington, D.C.: U.S. Government Printing Office, 1977), entry 358. The phrase often is truncated to "a chameleon on plaid."

17. James A. Farley, *Behind the Ballots* (New York: Harcourt, Brace and Company, 1938), pp. 159-160.

18. September 25, 1932, diary entry in Theodore G. Joslin Papers, Herbert Hoover Presidential Library, West Branch, Iowa.

19. "Mills Challenges Roosevelt's Fitness," *New York Times*, October 4, 1932. "Hoover Radio Drive Will Start Tonight," *New York Times*, October 3, 1932.

20. October 3 diary entry in Theodore G. Joslin Papers, Herbert Hoover Pres-
    idential Library, West Branch, Iowa. "2,000 Parade for Farmers," *Des
    Moines Tribune*, October 4, 1932.

21. October 4 and October 5 diary entries in Theodore G. Joslin Papers, Her-
    bert Hoover Presidential Library, West Branch, Iowa. "Iowa Poll for
    President," *New York Times*, October 3, 1932.

Chapter Seventeen

1. "Scottsboro Cases Get Extra Guard," *Evening Star*, October 10, 1932. "Supreme Court Ready to Hear Negroes Appeal," Universal Press wire story,
   October 10, 1932. The Supreme Court met in the Old Senate Chamber
   until 1935, when the current Supreme Court building opened.

2. Estolv E. Ward, *The Gentle Dynamiter* (Palo Alto, California: Ramparts
   Press, 1983), pp. 181-183.

3. "Fate of Scottsboro Lads Rest with U.S. Supreme Court," *The Black Dispatch*, Oklahoma City, October 20, 1932.

4. Hoover's remarks during the campaign trips are collected in *Public Papers
   of The Presidents of The United States, Herbert Hoover, Containing the Public
   Messages, Speeches, and Statements of the President, January 1, 1932, To March
   4, 1933* (Washington, D.C.: U.S. Government Printing Office, 1977).

5. "Mr. Hoover at Cleveland," *New York Times*, October 17, 1932.

6. Edmund W. Starling with Thomas Sugrue, *Starling of the White House*
   (New York: Simon & Schuster, 1946), p. 299. Scott Martelle, *Detroit: A Biography* (Chicago: Chicago Review Press, 2012), pp. 114-115.

7. Donald A. Ritchie, *Electing FDR: The New Deal Campaign of 1932* (Lawrence: The University Press of Kansas, 2007), pp. 139-142.

8. Raymond Moley, *After Seven Years* (New York: Harper & Brothers, 1939),
   p. 52.

9. See, for instance, "National B.E.F. Now Tottering," *Newcastle (Pa.) News*,
   October 18, 1932, and "Three B.E.F. Staff Members Form New District,"
   The Daily Republican, Monongahela, Pennsylvania, October 21, 1932.

10. "Read the Editorial Again," *Miami Herald*, November 25, 1932.

11. Andrew Krupnick's travelogue is held by the Archives & Records Center
    of the Catholic Diocese of Pittsburgh, generously shared by archives direc-
    tor Dennis P. Wodzinski.

12. Richard Gazarik, *The Mayor of Shantytown: The Life of Father James Ren-
    shaw Cox* (Jefferson, North Carolina: McFarland and Co., 2019), pp. 131-133.

13. "Cox Quits Race, Aids Roosevelt," *Pittsburgh Press*, and "Roosevelt on Way
    to Pittsburgh; Cox Out of Race, Backs Cox," *Pittsburgh Sun-Telegraph*, Oc-
    tober 18, 1932.

14. The report can be found under Houser's name in Name and Subject File: Early Career, Campaign of 1932, H-general to Campaign of 1940, Box 33, Lewis L. Strauss Papers, Hoover Presidential Library, West Branch, Iowa.
15. "Corn Belt Ignores Dry Law as Issue," *New York Times*, October 16, 1932.
16. William Z. Foster, *From Bryan to Stalin* (New York: International Publishers, 1937), p. 156.
17. Edward P. Johanningsmeier, *Forging American Communism: The Life of William Z. Foster* (Princeton, New Jersey: Princeton University Press, 1994), pp. 266-267.
18. "Foster, Leader of Reds, Jailed," June 29, 1932, and "Foster Freed, Flies East," June 30, 1932, both *Los Angeles Times*.
19. "Tour Strain Forces Rest on Foster," *Daily Worker*, September 15, 1932.

Chapter Eighteen

1. Entries for October 18, November 5 and November 6, 1932, Theodore G. Joslin Papers, Box 10 (transcript provided), Herbert Hoover Presidential Library and Museum, West Branch, Iowa.
2. "Crowds Rush Gates, Battle 500 Police," *New York Times*, November 1, 1932.
3. In 2023, it takes more than four months for the nation's workers to have earned enough to meet their collective tax burden, more than twice Hoover's estimate. Hoover's speech is reprinted as entry 366, *Public Papers of the Presidents of the United States: Herbert Hoover; Containing the Public Messages, Speeches, and Statements of the President*, January 1, 1932, to March 4, 1933 (Washington, D.C.: United States Government Printing Office, 1977).
4. Interview with Vice Admiral Joel Thompson Boone, p. 219, Oral History Collection, Herbert Hoover Presidential Library, West Branch, Iowa.
5. Entry for November 5, 1932, Theodore G. Joslin Papers, Box 10 (transcript provided), Herbert Hoover Presidential Library and Museum, West Branch, Iowa.
6. Entry for November 5, 1932, Edgar Rickard diary, Edgar Rickard Papers, Herbert Hoover Presidential Library, West Branch, Iowa. President's News Conference, November 6, 1932, Entry 382, Presidents of the United States: Herbert Hoover; Containing the Public Messages, Speeches, and Statements of the President, January 1, 1932, to March 4, 1933 (Washington, D.C.: United States Government Printing Office, 1977). Interview with Vice Admiral Joel Thompson Boone, p. 223, Oral History Collection, Herbert Hoover Presidential Library, West Branch, Iowa. "Extemporaneous Remarks in St. Paul," *New York Times*, November 7, 1932.
7. The Hoover quote is not in his prepared remarks but apparently was either ad libbed or added at the last minute by the president. It is included in the

"stenographers report" copy found in Importance of Economic Recovery with Administration Measures Adopted to Meet Emergency, November 5, 1932, Public Statements, Herbert Hoover Papers, Herbert Hoover Presidential Library and Museum, West Branch, Iowa. Edmund W. Starling with Thomas Sugrue, *Starling of the White House* (New York: Simon & Schuster, 1946), p. 300. Entry for November 5, 1932, Theodore G. Joslin Papers, Box 10 (transcript provided), Herbert Hoover Presidential Library and Museum, West Branch, Iowa.

8. "Roosevelt in Maine Pleads for Change," *New York Times*, November 1, 1932.

9. "Roosevelt Asks Maine's Vote," *Portland Evening Express*, October 31, 1932.

10. "7 Negroes Facing Death Saved by U.S. High Court," *Chicago Tribune*, November 8, 1932. "Scottsboro Ruling Reversed as 100 Reds are Routed at Capitol Plaza," *Evening Star*, November 7, 1932.

11. See *Powell v. Alabama*, 1932. The miscarriage of justice against the Scottsboro would continue for decades. See James Goodman, *Stories of Scottsboro* (New York: Random House, 1994).

12. "The Scottsboro Boys," *Chattanooga News*, November 8, 1932.

13. "The Scottsboro Case," *New York Times*, November 8, 1932.

14. "The Scottsboro Verdict," *Daily Worker*, November 8, 1932.

15. Trips 1932 folder, Box 347, Presidential Subject Files, Herbert Hoover Papers, Herbert Hoover Presidential Library and Museum, West Branch, Iowa.

16. Entry for November 8, 1932, Theodore G. Joslin Papers, Box 10 (transcript provided), Herbert Hoover Presidential Library and Museum.

17. Interview with Vice Admiral Joel Thompson Boone, pp. 230-231, Oral History Collection, Herbert Hoover Presidential Library, West Branch, Iowa.

18. "Roosevelt, Buoyant, Gets Returns Here," *New York Times*, November 9, 1932.

19. Lela Stiles, *The Man Behind Roosevelt: The Story of Louis McHenry Howe* (Cleveland: The World Publishing Company, 1954), p. 215. James A. Farley, *Behind the Ballots* (New York: Harcourt, Brace and Company, 1938), p. 187.

20. "President Offers 'Every Possible Effort' to Aid his Successor," *Oakland Tribune*, November 9, 1932.

21. "Wets Clinch Margin for Repeal in the House," *New York Times*, November 10, 1932.

22. Eleanor Roosevelt, *The Autobiography of Eleanor Roosevelt* (New York: Harper and Brothers Publishers, 1961), p. 163.

Diaries V

1. James Ball and his family operated a sheep farm about 30 miles west of Helena, Montana. James Ball Diaries, Archives and Special Collections,

Maureen and Mike Mansfield Library, University of Montana-Missoula. Nellie Suydam Cowley papers (MS 158), Special Collections & University Archives, University of California, Riverside. Emily Almira C. Rich Diary, Special Collections Department, Stewart Library, Weber State University.

Chapter Nineteen

1. Henry L. Stimson and McGeorge Bundy, *On Active Service in Peace and War* (New York: Harper & Brothers, 1947), p. 201.
2. Kenneth Whyte, *Hoover: An Extraordinary Life in Extraordinary Times* (New York: Random House, 2017), p. 439.
3. "Debt Holiday is Now Law," *New York Times*, December 23, 1931.
4. Entry for November 22, 1932, Theodore G. Joslin Diaries, National Archives, Herbert Hoover Presidential Library and Museum, West Branch, Iowa. Raymond Moley, *After Seven Years* (New York: Harper & Brothers Publishers, 1939), p. 73.
5. "Governor Gives His Views," *New York Times*, November 24, 1932.
6. "Hunger Parade Held After Petitions Put Before Congress," *Evening Star*, December 6, 1932. Dorothy Day, "Hunger Marchers in Washington," *The American Magazine*, December 24, 1932.
7. John L. Shover, *Cornbelt Rebellion: The Farmers' Holiday Association* (Urbana: The University of Illinois Press, 1965), pp. 73-75.
8. Reno to Hoover, January 20, 1933, Correspondence, Milo Reno Papers, The University of Iowa Libraries, Iowa City, Iowa.
9. Letters are in Correspondence, Milo Reno Papers, The University of Iowa Libraries, Iowa City, Iowa.
10. "Hoover Will Spend Christmas Eve Fishing; Leaves Tonight to Board Boat at Savannah," *New York Times*, December 23, 1932.
11. Near-daily updates on Hoover's trip were published in newspapers around the country.
12. "The Astor Yacht Nourmahal Also a Floating Laboratory," *New York Times*, February 12, 1933. Jean Edward Smith, *FDR* (New York: Random House, 2007), p. 296.
13. "President-elect Smiles as Bullets Whistle Past Him," *The Miami News*, February 16, 1933. Raymond Moley, *After Seven Years* (New York: Harper & Brothers Publishers, 1939), pp. 138-139.
14. "Eyewitnesses Tell Graphic Story of Shooting," *The Miami News*, February 15, 1933.
15. "How Roosevelt Saw It," *New York Times*, February 17, 1933.
16. Entry for February 16, 1932, Theodore G. Joslin Diaries, National Archives, Herbert Hoover Presidential Library and Museum, West Branch, Iowa.

"Hoover Guard at Palisade Tells Details of Attack," *Nevada State Journal*, November 8, 1932. Telegram to Roosevelt February 15, 1933, entry 466 in Public Papers of the Presidents of The United States: Herbert Hoover, Containing the Public Messages, Speeches, and Statements of the President January 1, 1932 to March 4, 1933.

17. Benjamin J. Davis, *Communist Councilman from Harlem* (New York: International Publishers, 1969), pp. 65-68.

18. A transcript of Herndon's testimony is included in Angelo Herndon, *Let Me Live* (New York: Random House, 1937, reprinted by University of Michigan Press, 2007), pp. 342-348.

19. A transcript of Davis's closing statement is reprinted in Angelo Herndon, *Let Me Live* (New York: Random House, 1937, reprinted by University of Michigan Press, 2007), pp. 351-354.

20. Benjamin J. Davis, *Communist Councilman from Harlem* (New York: International Publishers, 1969), pp. 75-76. Davis went on to become the first open member of the Communist Party to win election to the New York City Council, and was one of the defendants in the first of the Cold War-era Smith Act trials in 1949.

21. David E. Kyvig, *Repealing National Prohibition* (Chicago: University of Chicago Press, 1979), p. 169.

22. "States Pressing Repeal Action," *The Detroit Free Press*, March 13, 1933.

23. Francis Gloyd Awalt, "Recollections of the Banking Crisis in 1933," *Business History Review*, Vol. XLIII, No. 3, Autumn 1969. Awalt was Hoover's acting controller of the currency at the time of the banking crisis.

24. Entry for February 6, 1933, Theodore G. Joslin Diaries, National Archives, Herbert Hoover Presidential Library and Museum, West Branch, Iowa.

25. Barry Eichengreen, *Hall of Mirrors: The Great Depression, the Great Recession, and the Uses – and Misuses – of History* (New York: Oxford University Press, 2015), pp. 164-166.

Chapter Twenty

1. Hoover to Roosevelt, February 18, 1933, and John S. West to W.H. Moran, chief, Secret Service Division, February 27, 1933, *Papers of the Presidents of the United States: Herbert Hoover, Containing the Public Messages, Speeches, and Statements of the President of the United States, 1932-33* (Washington: Government Printing Office, 1977), 1030-1033.

2. Kenneth Whyte, *Hoover: An Extraordinary Life in Extraordinary Times* (New York: Alfred A. Knopf, 2017), 521-523.

3. Raymond Mosley, *After Seven Years* (New York: Harper & Row, 1939), 143-144.

4. For Hoover's view of these events, see *The Memoirs of Herbert Hoover: The Great Depression, 1929-1941* (New York: The MacMillan Company, 1952), 205-216.

5. Kenneth Whyte, *Hoover: An Extraordinary Life in Extraordinary Times* (New York: Alfred A. Knopf, 2017), p. 523. "Sightseers Jam Capital Centers," *The Evening Star*, Washington, D.C., March 4, 1933.

6. James Roosevelt and Sidney Shalett, *Affectionately, F.D.R.: A Son's Memoir of a Lonely Man* (New York: Harcourt, Brace & Company, 1959), pp. 251-252.

7. "Hoover Kept Busy in Final Hours," *The Evening Star*, Washington, D.C., March 4, 1933.

8. Jean Edward Smith, *FDR* (New York: Random House, 2007), 301.

9. "Cabinet Sworn In at White House," *New York Times*, March 5, 1933.

INDEX